# THE IDEA OF PUB

# THE IDEA OF PUBLIC LAW

MARTIN LOUGHLIN

*Professor of Public Law*
*London School of Economics & Political Science*

OXFORD
UNIVERSITY PRESS

# OXFORD
**UNIVERSITY PRESS**

Great Clarendon Street, Oxford OX2 6DP

Oxford University Press is a department of the University of Oxford.
It furthers the University's objective of excellence in research, scholarship,
and education by publishing worldwide in

Oxford New York

Auckland Bangkok Buenos Aires Cape Town Chennai
Dar es Salaam Delhi Hong Kong Istanbul Karachi Kolkata
Kuala Lumpur Madrid Melbourne Mexico City Mumbai Nairobi
São Paulo Shanghai Taipei Tokyo Toronto

Oxford is a registered trade mark of Oxford University Press
in the UK and in certain other countries

Published in the United States
by Oxford University Press Inc., New York

© M. Loughlin, 2003

The moral rights of the author have been asserted
Database right Oxford University Press (maker)

First published 2003
Published in paperback 2004

Crown copyright material is reproduced under Class Licence
Number C01P0000148 with the permission of the Controller of
HMSO and the Queen's Printer for Scotland

All rights reserved. No part of this publication may be reproduced,
stored in a retrieval system, or transmitted, in any form or by any means,
without the prior permission in writing of Oxford University Press,
or as expressly permitted by law, or under terms agreed with the appropriate
reprographics rights organization. Enquiries concerning reproduction
outside the scope of the above should be sent to the Rights Department,
Oxford University Press, at the address above

You must not circulate this book in any other binding or cover
and you must impose this same condition on any acquirer

British Library Cataloguing in Publication Data
Data available

Library of Congress Cataloging in Publication Data
Data available

ISBN 0–19–926723–5 (hbk.)
ISBN 0–19–927472–X (pbk.)

3 5 7 9 10 8 6 4

Typeset by Hope Services (Abingdon) Ltd.
Printed in Great Britain
on acid-free paper by
Biddles Ltd., King's Lynn

For Chris

# *Preface*

This book is the product of an extended period of research and reflection on the foundations of a subject I am employed to profess. For this opportunity I am greatly indebted to two institutions: the Leverhulme Trust, which generously awarded me a Major Research Fellowship enabling me to devote two years (2000–02) entirely to the study; and the London School of Economics & Political Science, which, when appointing me to the chair of public law from September 2000, willingly granted me leave for the purpose of taking up the Leverhulme Fellowship.

My main objective has been to uncover the foundations of public law, especially as the subject has evolved in Britain. In carrying through what is largely a historical investigation, I concluded that since much of what passes for received wisdom in the field was unfounded, I needed to develop a clearer account of the nature of the discipline than I had previously been able to offer. I tried to resolve this by sketching the conceptual foundations of public law as part of the larger, more historically orientated, study, but this proved unwieldy. I have therefore effected a partial separation between the conceptual and historical, and in this book present an outline of the conceptual aspects of the subject.

This division has not been without its difficulties, not least because of this exercise of theorizing—of moving towards the unconditional engagement of understanding. To move from the practical (what is the time?) to the philosophical (what is time?) is a journey that most of us trained as lawyers are singularly unsuited to travel. Why might we be encouraged to go beyond the practical world of decision and judgment and treat such judgments as contingent verdicts that invite further interrogation? The best answer I can offer is that in doing so we arrive at a more satisfactory account of much of what is merely implicit in our experience of government. And I am therefore mindful of the fact that a large part of that question remains to be answered. At best, this account of the idea of public law can be considered only to be a contingently acceptable formulation. But here I gather reassurance from Oakeshott's observation that the irony of all theorizing lies in 'its propensity to generate, not an understanding, but a not-yet-understood'.

In addition to the two institutions mentioned above, I have greatly benefited from invitations to talk about many of the issues in the book at the Universities of Aberdeen, Cambridge, Glasgow, Nottingham, Southampton and Victoria (British Columbia); the Queen's University, Kingston, Ontario and the European University Institute in Florence; and at seminars on 'Constitutionalism and Governance in Transition' in Belfast, on 'America and the Enlightenment: Constitutionalism in the 21st Century' in London, and 'Theory and International Law' in Oxford. In relation to these occasions I should like to thank all the participants, and especially John McLaren, Stephen Tierney, James Tully, Mark Walters, and Neil Walker. I must also thank Jean Lee, who did a fine job locating and retrieving texts for me, and the following for reading and commenting on various drafts: Margit Cohn, Neil Duxbury, Elizabeth Frazer, Nicola Lacey, James Penner, Thomas Poole, and Adam Tomkins. Finally, I am again much indebted to Chris Foley for her editorial work in helping to make it all a little more readable.

ML
*Dobcross*
*May 2003*

# *Acknowledgements*

Chapters 3, 4 and 5 draw on the following previously published papers:

'Constitutional Law: The Third Order of the Political' in Nicholas Bamforth and Peter Leyland (eds), *Law in a Multi-layered Constitution* (Oxford: Hart, 2003), 1–25.

'Representation and Constitutional Theory' in Paul Craig and Richard Rawlings (eds), *Law and Administration in Europe* (Oxford: Oxford University Press, 2003), 47–66.

'Ten Tenets of Sovereignty' in Neil Walker (ed.), *Sovereignty in Transition* (Oxford: Hart, 2003), 55–86.

# *Contents*

1. Introduction — 1
2. Governing — 5
3. Politics — 32
4. Representation — 53
5. Sovereignty — 72
6. Constituent Power — 99
7. Rights — 114
8. Method — 131
9. The Pure Theory of Public Law — 153

*Bibliography* — 165
*Index* — 185

# 1

# *Introduction*

The question is this: what is public law? This book argues that the question can only be answered on the premiss that public law is an autonomous discipline. Public law has a distinctive character that is formed from the unique nature of the tasks it undertakes. My method will therefore be to inquire into *what* public law does for the purpose of indicating *how* it does it. By adopting this approach, I try to uncover the most basic elements of the subject. And by laying bare the foundations of public law, I offer an account of the idea of public law as a singular entity.

The claim that public law constitutes an autonomous discipline has become obscured in modern times. This is mainly due to the predominant influence within jurisprudence of legal positivism. The general, and laudable, objective of positivism has been to place the study of law on a scientific foundation. But legal positivists were able to establish law as a separate subject of investigation only by drawing a distinction between law and the state or, in the case of Hans Kelsen's more refined treatment, between the legal and the political.[1] In order to be scientifically understood, positivists claimed, law must be severed from its social and political origins: positive law rests only on some postulated fact (a 'rule of recognition' whose existence is 'an empirical, though complex, question of fact'[2]) or on a hypothesis (a basic norm that validates other norms but which is simply a presupposition that expresses the autonomy of legal order[3]). Such strategies might be adequate for the purpose of presenting the idea of law as a system of civil obligation.[4] But with respect to public law, they are entirely inappropriate.

The reasons why this is the case are evident the moment we reflect on the basic tasks of public law, which can briefly be defined as those concerning the constitution, maintenance and regulation of governmental authority. Tasks of this nature cannot be understood without undertaking a detailed inquiry into the relationship between law and the state, and into the affinities between the legal and the political. The divisions on which legal positivism is founded—between law and state, between positive law and natural law, between positive law and political philosophy—are precisely

---

[1] See Hans Kelsen, *Introduction to the Problems of Legal Theory*, Bonnie L. Paulson and Stanley L. Paulson trans. of first edn. [1934] of *Reine Rechtslehre* (Oxford: Clarendon Press, 1992).
[2] H. L. A. Hart, *The Concept of Law* (Oxford: Clarendon Press, 1961), 245.
[3] Hans Kelsen, 'God and the State' in his *Essays in Legal and Moral Philosophy*, Ota Weinberger intro. (Dordrecht: Reidel, 1973), ch. 3. See Stanley Paulson, 'The Neo-Kantian Dimension of Kelsen's Legal Theory' (1992) 12 *Oxford Journal of Legal Studies* 311–332.
[4] See, e.g., Ernest J. Weinrib, 'Legal Formalism: On the Immanent Rationality of Law' (1988) 97 *Yale Law Journal* 949–1016; Ernest J. Weinrib, *The Idea of Private Law* (Cambridge, Mass.: Harvard University Press, 1995).

those that for public law must remain central issues of investigation. It makes no sense to commence an inquiry into the idea of public law on assumptions—that state and law are distinct entities, that the political and the legal are contrasting modes of discourse, or that government operating in the world of fact and law occupying the normative realm belong to different worlds—that dispose of the question.

What remains hidden from juristic knowledge within legal positivism is that it is only because of the operation of public law that a system of private law with its own inner coherence is able to function.[5] Kelsen accepted as much when acknowledging that the maintenance of the duality of the legal and the political 'performs an ideological function of extraordinary significance'.[6] If this is the case, then this inquiry must be concerned with elaborating the conditions under which this 'ideological function' continues to be effectively performed.

For the purpose of doing so, we might try to capture some sense of the role that law has played in maintaining a governing order.[7] The historical claim I make is of a general nature. In mainstream European thought, for example, the idea of public law evolved in the early modern period, flourished during the late nineteenth and early twentieth centuries, but has since waned.[8] The situation with respect to the British case is different. In Britain, the modern conception of the subject is founded on a negative proposition. Modern British history is based on a rejection of the idea of public law.

Given the peculiarities of English (and, later, British) constitutional history, this is a curious position. Having been effected without any fundamental, irrevocable breakdown of institutional forms, constitutional modernization in Britain has been a political achievement. This is a considerable feat, one that during the nineteenth century spawned eulogies on the matchless character of Britain's unique constitutional arrangements.[9] The achievement has generated a great deal of celebratory rhetoric about the innate genius of the English in handling the practical affairs of government. But it has left us with a massive gulf between the legal form and the actual practices of government.

---

[5] The consequence of the failure of legal positivists and other formalists to distinguish between public law and private law is highlighted by explanations of the legal significance of a revolutionary break in governmental authority. Kelsen, for example, assumes that it must result in a break in the continuity of validity of the entire legal order. But although it will undoubtedly result in a rupture in the system of public law, it seems more realistic to treat the continuing validity of private law arrangements as a contingent matter. Governments come and go, by lawful and other means. But a legal theory that assumes that these changes automatically have an impact on the validity of contractual relations or property transactions entered into by private parties seems lacking. The deficiency flows from an unwillingness to acknowledge public law's separate existence.

[6] Kelsen, above n. 1, 96–97.

[7] For an overview see R. C. van Caenegem, *An Historical Introduction to Western Constitutional Law* (Cambridge: Cambridge University Press, 1995).

[8] Although focusing on public international law, the best recent presentation of this thesis is: Martti Koskenniemi, *The Gentle Civilizer of Nations: The Rise and Fall of International Law 1870–1960* (Cambridge: Cambridge University Press, 2002). See also Peter Wagner, *A History and Theory of the Social Sciences* (London: Sage, 2001), ch. 2.

[9] See, e.g., J. W. Burrow, *A Liberal Descent: Victorian Historians and the English Past* (Cambridge: Cambridge University Press, 1981).

It does not seem unreasonable to expect that the existence of such a gulf between law and practice would stimulate lawyers to try to uncover the juristic foundations of this distinctive political constitution. It could conceivably have led to a rejuvenation of interest in what Roman law called the *lex regia*,[10] or what early modern political theorists termed *droit politique*.[11] But this has not happened. Lawyers have ducked the challenge of developing a conception of public law that addresses the juristic issues concerning the establishment and maintenance of governmental authority.

The resulting confusion is thrown into relief by relaying the tale Charles Taylor tells about a passer-by coming to the assistance of a drunk who is stumbling around late at night looking for his key under a street lamp. After searching unsuccessfully for some time, the passer-by asks the drunk if he can remember precisely where he dropped it. 'Over there', answers the drunk, pointing to a dark corner. 'Then why are we searching for it here?' 'Because', the drunk replies, 'there's much more light here'.[12] So it is with public law in Britain. Rather than trying to reveal the shadowy practices of government for the purpose of explaining the role of law in establishing and regulating this activity, lawyers have shifted their ground. They have repositioned themselves so as to reveal the legal framework of government in a sharper focus, but only at the cost of considerably narrowing the boundaries of the subject. Having withdrawn from any serious attempt to explain the foundations of the authority structure of the British state, constitutional lawyers—in a manifest display of superficial thinking—have concluded that public law does not exist.[13]

This claim has caused continental European observers of British government to express exasperation about these arrangements. Giovanni Sartori was not alone amongst European scholars when complaining that 'many English scholars understate their constitution, seem to make a particular point of not being helpful, and leave the alien reader with the feeling that the British constitution really amounts to the fact that, in the final analysis, the British people are clever and fine people who

---

[10] *Lex regia* refers to that body of jurisprudence concerned with working through the terms and conditions under which the Senate and People of Rome had made the grant of *imperium* to the Emperor. Its study was reinvigorated during the middle ages by Bartolus of Saxoferrato, who made the radical methodological innovation of suggesting that when the law and the facts collide, it is the law (rather than the facts) that must be adjusted. See Quentin Skinner, *The Foundations of Modern Political Thought* (Cambridge: Cambridge University Press, 1978), i, 8–12.

[11] See, e.g., Jean-Jacques Burlamaqui, *Principes du droit politique* [1754], *The Principles of Natural and Politic Law*, Thomas Nugent trans. (London: Nourse, 2nd edn. 1763); Jean-Jacques Rousseau, *Le Contrat Social, ou Principes du Droit Politique* [1762]. Maurice Cranston, translator of Rousseau's work, notes: 'This *droit politique*, which I have been obliged for lack of a better alternative (there is no English equivalent of *le droit*) to translate as "political right", Burlamaqui employed as a semi-technical expression to designate the general abstract study of law and government, and Rousseau uses the word in the same sense'. See Jean-Jacques Rousseau, *The Social Contract*, Maurice Cranston ed. (Harmondsworth: Penguin, 1968), 26. Cf. Thomas Hobbes, *The Elements of Law Natural and Politic* [1640], Ferdinand Tönnies ed., M. M. Goldsmith intro. (London: Cass, 1969), in which 'politic' law is defined as civil law and therefore as the will of the sovereign.

[12] Charles Taylor, 'The Diversity of Goods' in his *Philosophical Papers, vol. 2: Philosophy and the Human Sciences* (Cambridge: Cambridge University Press, 1985), 230–247, 241.

[13] The classic work in this vein is A. V. Dicey, *Introduction to the Study of the Law of the Constitution* (London: Macmillan, 8th edn. 1915).

know how to go about in politics'.[14] Since the 1960s, however, this veneer of effortless superiority has worn thin.[15] And today, in the face of structural developments affecting government that have all but destroyed what remains of the historic constitution, British scholars are engaged in the exercise of assembling imaginary foundations or, like alchemists, devising 'fundamental' precepts from a jumble of customary arrangements of whose practical significance they have only a dim appreciation.

Like the drunk in our tale, many lawyers—and especially those attempting to insert the precepts of modern liberal constitutionalism into the arrangements of British government—are starting from the wrong place. Rather than devising some ideal of modern liberal democracy and then re-interpreting governmental practices in compliance with this model, we should begin by paying closer attention to the particular circumstances of their evolution. As part of that general exercise, we need to reassess the way in which public law has been treated in modern thought.

Since the main objective of this book is not historical but conceptual, I do not propose to rehearse the particular intellectual arguments relating to the British case.[16] Whilst the specific circumstances of particular regimes can be instructive, the book's aim is to analyse the foundations of the concept of public law. I argue that these foundations are those of governing, politics, representation, sovereignty, constituent power, and rights. Each is examined in the chapters that follow and, building on these, I then present an account of the method of public law. Finally, by pulling these conceptual building blocks into a classificatory frame, I sketch an outline of the idea of public law. Those that prefer to read conclusions first may therefore wish to turn immediately to the last chapter. Here, I draw the argument together by portraying public law as an autonomous discipline, one that being stripped of political ideology might be called the pure theory of public law.

[14] Giovanni Sartori, 'Constitutionalism: A Preliminary Discussion' (1962) 56 *American Political Science Review* 853–864, 854.

[15] See, e.g., Nevil Johnson, *In Search of the Constitution: Reflections of State and Society in Britain* (Oxford: Pergamon Press, 1977); David Marquand, *The Unprincipled Society: New Demands and Old Politics* (London: Fontana, 1988), esp. ch. 7; Ferdinand Mount, *The British Constitution Now* (London: Heinemann, 1992).

[16] These are addressed in my *Public Law and Political Theory* (Oxford: Clarendon Press, 1992) and 'Pathways of Public Law Scholarship' in G. P. Wilson (ed.), *Frontiers of Legal Scholarship* (Chichester: Wiley, 1995), 163–188.

# 2

# *Governing*

Public law maintains its distinctive character because of the singularity of its object. That object is the activity of governing. With respect to this activity, law has a range of tasks to perform. It is only once the nature of these tasks is appreciated that we are able to identify public law as a special body of knowledge. But the nature of these tasks cannot be understood without first reflecting on the activity of governing itself.

As a general phenomenon, the activity of governing exists whenever people are drawn into association with one another, whether in families, firms, schools, or clubs. In order to maintain themselves, and certainly to be able to develop and flourish, such groups must establish some set of governing arrangements, however rudimentary. The formation of governing arrangements is a ubiquitous feature of group life. Whatever the type of governing arrangement established, an iron law of necessity holds sway. Since it simply is not possible for associations of any significant scale and degree of permanence to be capable of governing themselves, the business of governing invariably requires the drawing of a distinction that has become fundamental to the activity: the division between rulers and ruled, between a governing authority and its subjects.[1]

Although the general activity of governing is a feature of all human associations, a certain type of association commands our special attention, and over which the struggle to establish authority has been intense. That body has been given a variety of names. In ancient Greece it was referred to as a *polis*,[2] and the Romans thought of it as *res publica*.[3] Throughout medieval Europe, the body was commonly called a *regnum* or a principality.[4] When, during the seventeenth century, Thomas Hobbes sought to explicate its character, he made use of the expression 'commonwealth'.[5] In modern terminology, however, the body is invariably referred to as 'the state'.[6]

---

[1] See Michael Oakeshott, *Morality and Politics in Modern Europe: The Harvard Lectures* [1958], Shirley Robin Letwin ed. (New Haven: Yale University Press, 1993), 7–8.

[2] Aristotle, *The Politics* [c.335–323 BC], T. A. Sinclair trans., Trevor J. Saunders ed. (Harmondsworth: Penguin, 1981).

[3] Marcus Tullius Cicero, *De Respublica* [c.52 BC], Clinton Walker Keyes trans. (London: Heinemann, 1928).

[4] Ptolemy of Lucca, *On the Government of Rulers. De Regimine Principum* [c.1300], James M. Blythe trans. (Philadelphia: University of Pennsylvania Press, 1997); Sir John Fortescue, *De Laudibus Legum Anglie* [1468–71], S. B. Chrimes trans. (Cambridge: Cambridge University Press, 1942).

[5] Thomas Hobbes, *Leviathan* [1651], Richard Tuck ed. (Cambridge: Cambridge University Press, 1996). Note especially the division of this book into four parts: 'Of Man', 'Of Commonwealth', 'Of A Christian Commonwealth' and 'Of the Kingdome of Darkness'.

[6] See Quentin Skinner, 'The State' in Terence Ball, James Farr, and Russell L. Hanson (eds), *Political Innovation and Conceptual Change* (Cambridge: Cambridge University Press, 1989), 90–131; Raymond Geuss, *History and Illusion in Politics* (Cambridge: Cambridge University Press, 2001), ch. 2.

Whatever the complexities of the modern notion of the state, we are able to recognize its basic identity as that institution which claims the ultimate allegiance of its citizens and which maintains 'the monopoly of the legitimate use of physical force within a given territory'.[7] Some scholars have argued that the state is not qualitatively different from other group-units.[8] But, especially given our juristic objectives,[9] it seems more appropriate to maintain that the state has a unique, if ambiguous, identity. Because of its characteristic forms, distinctive ways and special tasks, the state should be regarded as an association *sui generis*.

The idea of the state emerged in recognition of the differentiation that was capable of being drawn between the personality of the ruler and the impersonal character of the arrangements through which his rule was exercised. The ancients were familiar with the distinction between private and public—between *oikos* and *polis*—and hence between the concepts of ownership and rulership.[10] But in referring to the collectivity they had a sense only of 'the public' or 'the people'; hence we find Cicero defining *res publica* as 'an assembly of men living according to law'.[11] It was not until the beginnings of the modern period that the idea of the state as an entity distinct both from its members and from its officers was articulated. This notion of the state as an institution that mediated between governed and governors arose out of attempts to make sense of a set of elaborate and bureaucratic governing arrangements: not only were the ruler's public and private capacities to be separated but these public capacities could be exercised only through a variety of impersonal forms. From this perspective, the state represents 'the second most important invention in [political] history after the Greek separation between ownership and government'.[12]

Although the modern idea of the state is of central importance to our task, the main focus of inquiry at this stage will not be on the state as such, but on the activity of governing through the institution of the state. Three basic and related issues concerning the nature of this activity need to be addressed. The first is the question of the engagement of government: what are the main tasks that have been allocated to

---

[7] Max Weber, 'Politics as a Vocation' [1919] in H. H. Gerth and C. Wright Mills (eds), *From Max Weber* (London: Routledge & Kegan Paul, 1948), 77–128, 78.

[8] This view was most strongly associated with the political pluralists (Figgis, Barker, Laski, and Cole) who explored these questions in the early decades of the twentieth century: see Paul Q. Hirst, *The Pluralist Theory of the State: Selected Writings* (London: Routledge, 1989); David Nicholls, *The Pluralist State: The Social and Political Ideas of J. N. Figgis and his Contemporaries* (London: Macmillan, 2nd edn. 1994); Julia Stapleton, *Englishness and the Study of Politics: The Social and Political Thought of Ernest Barker* (Cambridge: Cambridge University Press, 1994); David Runciman, *Pluralism and the Personality of the State* (Cambridge: Cambridge University Press, 1997).

[9] See, e.g., J. D. B. Mitchell, 'The Anatomy and Pathology of the Constitution' (1955) 67 *Juridical Review* 1–22, 21: 'Governments cannot be treated as larger and more interfering Lever Bros. or ICI. They are different in purpose, different in kind, and should often be subject to different rules of law'.

[10] See, e.g., Aristotle, above n. 2, i.2: 'It is an error to suppose, as some do, that the roles of the statesman, of a king, and of a household-manager and of a master of slaves are the same on the ground that they differ not in kind but only in point of numbers of persons . . .'.

[11] Cicero, above n. 3, i.39.

[12] Martin van Creveld, *The Rise and Decline of the State* (Cambridge: Cambridge University Press, 1999), 58.

government? The second issue concerns modes of governing: how is the character of the activity of governing to be conceptualized? The third involves an inquiry into the nature of the office of government.

I have presented the issues in this sequence for a particular reason. Whenever the relationship between law and government is considered within legal thought, it is the third issue that provides the focus of inquiry and absorbs the greatest degree of attention. Legal commentary usually begins with the construction of a model of the office of government and the manner of its authorization. Only after this do lawyers generally consider questions relating to engagement and modes. By this stage, however, the stage is already set both for moralizing about the range of engagements of government and for resolving ambiguities concerning the mode of governance. Since such models are invariably based on the acceptance of liberal democratic precepts, this type of approach throws into relief the tendency of legal conceptualization to become used as an ideological device. If modern government operates at some distance from its ideal liberal democratic form and yet also seems to be a fixed feature of the contemporary world, then the scholarly postulation of a normative frame that bears little relation to the reality as experienced is unhelpful. By examining the activity of governing in this sequence, then, my intention is to address the issues from a positive perspective.

THE ENGAGEMENT OF GOVERNMENT

It might be argued that the task of governing has throughout history remained relatively constant. In general, the basic engagement of government has been one of maintaining and enhancing the well-being of the state and its people. When, for example, Hobbes suggested that the responsibilities of the state are all implicit in one phrase, *salus populi suprema lex esto*,[13] he was simply reiterating a famous Ciceronian maxim.[14] Ancient and modern writers, it would appear, have maintained a common appreciation of the basic nature of the task. But the claim has a deceptive simplicity. Although the ancient formulation has been regularly invoked in modern times, its popularity is largely the consequence of its equivocal meaning.

Even in classical Latin, the meaning of *salus* ranges widely. As Michael Oakeshott has explained, the meaning of the term has varied 'from mere *safety* (relief from threatened extinction), through *health* (which is normal), and *abundance* (which is excessive), and *welfare* (which is comprehensive), and on *salvation* (which leaves nothing to be desired)'.[15] The phrase, Oakeshott suggests, is nothing less than 'the

---

[13] Thomas Hobbes, *On the Citizen* [1647], Richard Tuck and Michael Silverthorne eds (Cambridge: Cambridge University Press, 1998), xiii.2.

[14] Marcus Tullius Cicero, *De Legibus* [c.51 BC], Clinton Walker Keyes trans. (London: Heinemann, 1928), iii.6. See also Samuel Pufendorf, *On the Duty of Man and Citizen According to Natural Law* [1673], James Tully ed. (Cambridge: Cambridge University Press, 1991), ii.11.3.

[15] Michael Oakeshott, *The Politics of Faith and the Politics of Scepticism* [c.1952], Timothy Fuller ed. (New Haven: Yale University Press, 1996), 39.

emblem of all the ambiguity of our political vocabulary'.[16] If we want to identify the basic tasks of government with any degree of precision, we cannot rest on such generalities.

Unpacking the classical formulation, Hobbes concluded that the tasks of government fell into four main categories: to maintain defence from external enemies; to preserve internal peace; to enable the citizen to acquire wealth, so far as that is consistent with public security; and to promote the full enjoyment of the citizen's liberty.[17] This package presents itself as a relatively limited range of activities. What government does within these categories, however, can vary considerably. The engagement of government is greatly affected by the knowledge-based and material resources at its disposal. Before the modern period, such resources were highly limited, and the tasks of government were correspondingly constrained. The scale and power of modern government has therefore grown in tandem with the development of techniques that have strengthened the capacity of governments to appropriate and deploy available resources in furtherance of these basic tasks. In the name of promoting security, liberty, and prosperity, modern governments have greatly expanded the range of their activities, and have now assumed responsibility for furthering economic and social development, managing the economy, and providing for the welfare of their citizens.

The modern state is the institution through which such innovation was harnessed. With the transmutation of the king's servants into officers of the state, a decisive step was taken in establishing an impersonal, specialized administrative apparatus that could exploit developments in printing, record-keeping, indexing, and such like.[18] Consequently, although the enforcement of justice and peace continued to be exercised in the king's name, these activities increasingly had little to do with the monarch.[19] With the establishment of a specialized administration, statistical information—'political arithmetic' as it was called[20]—about the territory of the state and society was acquired: borders were marked, maps of the country were drawn, and the population, property, and productive capacities of society were measured.

This improved technical competence enabled the state to increase its efficiency in extracting revenues by way of taxation.[21] But as the ancient maxim of Tacitus states,

---

[16] Michael Oakeshott, *The Politics of Faith and the Politics of Scepticism* [c.1952], Timothy Fuller ed. (New Haven: Yale University Press, 1996), 39. See also John Selden, *Table Talk* [1689] (London: Dent, 1898), ciii: 'there is not anything in the World more abased than this Sentence, *salus populi suprema lex esto*'.

[17] Hobbes, above n. 13, xiii.6.

[18] G. R. Elton, *The Tudor Revolution in Government: Administrative Changes in the Reign of Henry VIII* (Cambridge: Cambridge University Press, 1953), esp. 415–427.

[19] Sir Frederick Pollock, 'The King's Peace' in his *Oxford Lectures and Other Discourses* (London: Macmillan, 1890); F. W. Maitland, *Justice and Police* (London: Macmillan, 1885).

[20] Karin Johannisson, 'Society in Numbers: The Debate over Quantification in Eighteenth-Century Political Economy' in Tore Frängsmyr, J. L. Heilbron, and Robin E. Rider (eds), *The Quantifying Spirit in the Eighteenth Century* (Berkeley, Calif.: University of California Press, 1990), 343–361, 348–350.

[21] D. V. Glass, *Numbering the People: The Eighteenth-Century Population Controversy and the Development of Census and Vital Statistics in Britain* (Farnborough, Hants: D. C. Heath, 1973), ch. 2.

you need armies to maintain peace and 'you cannot have troops without pay; and you cannot raise pay without taxation'.[22] So it was that alongside the growth in revenue-generating capacity, and in a reversal of the thrust of the maxim, a transformation in the nature and scale of warfare occurred. From being a series of essentially private squabbles amongst members of the governing classes who drew on feudal obligations to form their armies, warfare became a large-scale, disciplined, and highly technical activity.[23] This was made possible only because of the establishment of regular, hierarchically organized, and bureaucratically managed armed forces of the state.[24]

But perhaps the most significant changes in the tasks of government during the modern era have been those that concern the management of the economy and the promotion of the welfare of society. Government today is involved in these activities to an extent unimaginable even in the nineteenth century. Consider, for example, the changing role of government with respect to the currency. The function of pre-modern rulers in relation to the currency was not essentially to *create* value in money. By impressing his seal on such valuable commodities as gold and silver, the king's function was mainly that of confirming an existing value.[25] By the twentieth century, however, government had become centrally involved in the business of creating and destroying the value of money. The key stages in this transformation might briefly be noted.[26]

The starting point of this modern development is the recognition that the regal underwriting of the value of the currency bolstered the people's confidence in its stability, and this meant that tokens such as tallies were able to enter into circulation. Building on this growing confidence, it became possible, after the establishment of the Bank of England in 1694, to issue paper notes. The subsequent expansion of paper currency permitted a rapid expansion of credit which paved the way for the industrial revolution. The success of paper currency, van Creveld argues, was made possible only by 'the separation between the monarch's person and the state', since after 1694 'it was no longer the former but the latter, operating by means of the Bank and resting on an alliance between the government and the city, which guaranteed the notes'.[27] Until the end of the nineteenth century, people, in theory at least, were able to exchange their paper notes for gold. But this changed with the coming of the First World War, with the result that government expenditure, which had stood at approximately 15 per cent of GNP before the war, was able to increase to 85 per cent

---

[22] Cornelius Tacitus, *The Histories* [c.109], W. H. Fyfe trans., D. S. Levene ed. (Oxford: Oxford University Press, 1977), iv.74.
[23] Michael Howard, *War in European History* (Oxford: Oxford University Press, 1976), chs 2–5.
[24] John Brewer, *The Sinews of Power: War, Money and the English State, 1688–1783* (London: Hutchinson, 1989); Thomas Ertman, 'The Sinews of Power and European State-building Theory' in Lawrence Stone (ed.), *An Imperial State at War* (London: Routledge, 1993), 33–51.
[25] See, e.g., William Blackstone, *Commentaries on the Laws of England* (Oxford: Clarendon Press, 1765), i. 266–268.
[26] For details see Glyn Davies, *A History of Money: From Ancient Times to the Present Day* (Cardiff: University of Wales Press, 1994).
[27] van Creveld, above n. 12, 229.

of GNP by 1916–17. This remarkable shift in the scale of government expenditure was achieved by increased taxation, the issuance of government bonds, and, significantly, by the government's printing of money.[28] Although the rate of government expenditure after the war decreased, it still remained at around double the pre-war rate, and after the fiasco of the attempt to return to the gold standard, all means of payment were to be made in a paper currency produced and controlled by the state. This transformation thus provided government with the tools by which—in the particular circumstances which materialized as a result of the outbreak of the Second World War—it was able to dominate the economy.

The growing involvement of government in the business of money is instructive. Once the state was in a position to determine what counted as money, the financial restraints on governmental action—restrictions that had caused rulers immense difficulties[29]—more or less evaporated. The fiscal levers acquired by government effected a vast increase in governmental power.[30] This power was applied mainly for the purpose of strengthening the state's control over society. The changes wrought by modernization and industrialization had eroded feudal ties and weakened the authority of the church. The displacement of these traditional sources of social authority led to the emergence of property ownership as the cement of modern social order. And after the possessing classes had acquired control of the state—the singular achievement of the Glorious Revolution of 1688—the task of government turned more explicitly to the protection of private property.

It is at this stage in the evolution of government that 'the people'—that is, the great majority of the population who previously had been beneath the horizon of consciousness of the governing classes—first began to emerge as a political presence. The French revolution of 1789 had provided a graphic demonstration of the potential of the masses to overthrow the most well-established of governing regimes. Its general impact on the governing classes of European states was to impress on them the need to extend the range of their controls over society. From the early nineteenth century, we see in Britain—in parallel with other European states—a series of measures which result in the formation of modern police forces, prison systems, and security services.[31]

---

[28] van Creveld, above n. 12, 235.

[29] Such difficulties had, for example, provided a major source of the English constitutional conflicts of the seventeenth century. See Johan P. Sommerville, *Politics and Ideology in England, 1603–1642* (London: Longman, 1986).

[30] The recent reversal of this power, whereby states become increasingly susceptible to the fluctuations of international financial markets, should, however, be noted. See: Susan Strange, *The Retreat of the State: The Diffusion of Power in the World Economy* (Cambridge: Cambridge University Press, 1996). For a particular illustration—when the pound was forcibly withdrawn from the exchange rate mechanism of the European Monetary System—see Philip Stephens, *Politics and the Pound: The Tories, the Economy and Europe* (London: Macmillan, 1996), ch. 10. And the contemporary trend has been to remove this power of the state from the control of politicians. See, e.g., Art. 107 EC: 'When exercising the powers and carrying out the tasks and duties conferred upon them by this Treaty . . . neither the European Central Bank, nor a national central bank, nor any member of their decision-making bodies shall seek or take instructions from Community institutions or bodies from any government of a Member State or from any other body'.

[31] From a voluminous literature see: Geoffrey Marshall, *Police and Government* (London: Methuen, 1965); Michael Ignatieff, *A Just Measure of Pain: The Penitentiary in the Industrial Revolution 1750–1850*

Being part of an attempt to extend its grip over society, this growth in the state's powers for maintaining public order was paralleled by an unprecedented degree of inquiry into the conditions of the working population. The appalling conditions revealed by the blue books[32] led to ameliorative legislation relating to industrial working conditions, the relief of poverty, and the promotion of public health, sanitary, and housing arrangements. This function of the state in the promotion of the welfare of the people was considerably expanded with the growth of state education and (though not until the beginning of the twentieth century) the establishment of a system of social security.[33]

The impact of this extension of governmental tasks has been profound. At the beginning of the nineteenth century, government was mainly concerned with law and order, external affairs and defence, and raising revenue to finance these activities. By the end of the twentieth century, there were few areas not only of public but also of personal life in which government performed no role. The extent of the shift in the scope of government was summarized by the Report of the Royal Commission on the Constitution in 1973 in these terms:

The individual a hundred years ago hardly needed to know that the central government existed. His birth, marriage and death would be registered, and he might be conscious of the safeguards for his security provided by the forces of law and order and of imperial defence; but, except for the very limited provisions of the poor law and factory legislation, his welfare and progress were matters for which he alone bore the responsibility. By the turn of the century the position was not much changed. Today, however, the individual citizen submits himself to the guidance of the state at all times. His schooling is enforced; his physical well-being can be looked after in a comprehensive health service; he may be helped by government agencies to find and train for a job; he is obliged while in employment to insure against sickness, accident and unemployment; his house may be let to him by a public authority or he may be assisted in its purchase or improvement; he can avail himself of a wide range of government welfare allowances and services; and he draws a state pension on his retirement. In these and many other ways unknown to his counterpart a century ago, he is brought into close and regular contact with government and its agencies.[34]

---

(London: Macmillan, 1978); Bernard Porter, *The Origins of the Vigilant State: The London Metropolitan Special Branch Before the First World War* (London: Weidenfeld and Nicolson, 1987); Laurence Lustgarten and Ian Leigh, *In From the Cold: National Security and Parliamentary Democracy* (Oxford: Clarendon Press, 1994).

[32] S. E. Finer, *The Life and Times of Sir Edwin Chadwick* (London: Methuen, 1952), 39: 'The Royal Commission of Enquiry is a legislative device barely met with before 1832. By 1849 more than 100 had been set up, and every major piece of social legislation between 1832 and 1871 was ushered in by this type of legislation'.

[33] See Oliver MacDonagh, *Early Victorian Government, 1830–1870* (London: Weidenfeld and Nicolson, 1977); David Roberts, *Victorian Origins of the British Welfare State* (New Haven: Yale University Press, 1960); Jose Harris, *Unemployment and Politics: A Study of English Social Policy, 1886–1914* (Oxford: Clarendon Press, 1972).

[34] *Report of the Royal Commission on the Constitution, 1969–1973* Cmnd. 5460 (London: HMSO, 1973), para. 232.

But in moving beyond safety to embrace health and welfare, the powers of government impact not only on the individual citizen but also on business organizations of every type. The concern of government extends not only to the welfare of the individual but also to the performance of the economy and prosperity of the nation. The Royal Commission identified some of the consequences:

> Industrialists, too, are much more involved with government. An industrialist in the nineteenth century, if he wished to build a factory, could do so by entirely private arrangement, and government hardly need know about the project. In these days, however, a prospective factory developer is faced with a host of Acts and regulations—to do, for instance, with environmental planning, industrial development certificates, government grants, allowances and inducements, the welfare and training of employees, employee insurance and taxation, industrial relations, licences, waste disposal, air pollution and the collection of trade statistics—any aspect of which his nineteenth century forbear might well have regarded as an unwarranted intrusion.[35]

My general point is that the range of governmental tasks has increased dramatically. Modern government has had to acquire a large and sophisticated administrative apparatus as it has increased taxes, acquired statistical data about society, established police and security forces, formed agencies to promote health, education and welfare, and assumed responsibility for the regulation of money, trade, and the economy.[36] The interests of government today extend to a concern both for the welfare of the individual citizen and for the corporate well-being of the nation, and while the causes of this may be complicated, they are inextricably bound up with the 'rise of the masses' as a political presence. This leads to two final points. The first is that the political role of the masses has emerged in tandem with the harnessing of the forces of nationalism to the pursuit of governmental objectives.[37] And the second is that this growth in governmental power has had a major impact on government's manner of authorization: today, for example, it is almost universally accepted that since it disposes of such an immense power, government must be democratically constituted.

---

[35] *Report of the Royal Commission on the Constitution, 1969–1973* Cmnd. 5460 (London: HMSO, 1973), para. 233.

[36] From the extensive literature that now exists on the growth of the modern state see: Charles Tilly (ed.), *The Formation of National States in Western Europe* (Princeton, NJ: Princeton University Press, 1975); Michael Mann, *The Sources of Social Power, vol. II: The Rise of Classes and Nation-States, 1760–1914* (Cambridge: Cambridge University Press, 1993); Thomas Ertman, *Birth of the Leviathan: Building States and Regimes in Medieval and Early Modern Europe* (Cambridge: Cambridge University Press, 1997); van Creveld, above n. 12, esp. ch. 4.

[37] See Ernest Gellner, *Nations and Nationalism* (Oxford: Blackwell, 1983); John Breuilly, *Nationalism and the State* (Manchester: Manchester University Press, 2nd edn. 1993); Michael Hechter, *Containing Nationalism* (Oxford: Oxford University Press, 2000).

## MODES OF GOVERNANCE

In the light of this sketch of the modern development of the tasks of government, we can now address a critical issue: how are we to characterize the activity of governing the state? The answer to this question offers a key to understanding the nature of the activity of governing. It also takes us a considerable way towards appreciating the ambiguities that pervade any inquiry into the subject of public law.

The early modern period is one in which, as a result of social, economic, and technological changes, inherited beliefs concerning divine authorization of rulers and the natural justification of a hierarchical organization of governmental authority were losing much of their authority. Jurists were thus motivated to devise more rational explanations of the nature of political association. Writing in the late sixteenth century, Jean Bodin was perhaps the first of the early modern theorists to retrieve the Aristotelian distinction between *polis* and *oikos*, between government and the household, thereby differentiating between a natural hierarchy based on master and slave (or, more generally, superior and inferior) operating in the private sphere, and an arrangement of government constituted by freely consenting individuals (in Latin, *cives*) functioning in the public sphere.[38] Bodin's work was built upon by Thomas Hobbes, who produced a systematic account of the state as an 'artificial man' which, by virtue of the idea of representation, could be distinguished both from society and from the personality of the ruler.[39] At this relatively early stage, then, jurists were exploring the idea of the modern state as a singular form of human association.

A central theme running through their attempts to specify the principles which legitimate the engagement of government is that of consent. This theme is rooted in the idea of some founding compact through which individuals agree to entrust certain of their natural rights to the governing authority in order that the common good might be realized.[40] From this body of work we derive many of the concepts that have been highly influential in shaping modern theories of government, including the public/private distinction, the idea of the representative character of governmental authority, the notion that political association is established as a result of covenanting between freely consenting individuals, and the idea of sovereignty as the form

---

[38] Jean Bodin, *The Six Bookes of a Commonweale* [1576], Richard Knolles trans., Kenneth Douglas McRae ed. (Cambridge, Mass: Harvard University Press, 1962), i.2. See also John Locke, *Two Treatises of Government* [1680], Peter Laslett ed. (Cambridge: Cambridge University Press, 1988). Locke's first treatise, which took the form of a critical analysis of Robert Filmer's *Patriacha*, was designed to show that paternal power and political power must be differentiated.

[39] Thomas Hobbes, *Leviathan* [1651], Richard Tuck ed. (Cambridge: Cambridge University Press, 1995), Introduction. The importance of the theme of representation in Hobbes's scheme is examined below in Ch. 4, 55–61.

[40] See John Dunn, 'Contractualism' in his *History of Political Theory and Other Essays* (Cambridge: Cambridge University Press, 1996), 39–65; Jody S. Kraus, *The Limits of Hobbesian Contractarianism* (Cambridge: Cambridge University Press, 1993); Russell Hardin, *Liberalism, Constitutionalism, and Democracy* (Oxford: Oxford University Press, 1999), ch. 3.

through which governmental power is given expression. Work of this nature also tends to elaborate the idea of the governing relationship as constituting a particular mode of association.

Important though such juristic writing may be, we should remember that it was crafted primarily with a view to providing an answer to a relatively specific question: how is the authorization of government to be explained and justified? That is, the body of work represented by, amongst others, Bodin, Hobbes, and Locke, does not provide an answer to the question of how the tasks actually undertaken by government can best be understood or conceptualized. It is this limitation of early modern political theory that Michel Foucault, in his project on governmentality, confronts.

Sixteenth century writing, Foucault explains, tended to treat the activity of governing as a common undertaking. Three basic types of governing provide recurrent themes of the period: self-government (morality), family government (economy), and the science of running a state (politics). In contrast with the work of early modern political theorists such as Bodin and Hobbes, who sought to draw a line between a juridical conception of authority and other forms of power, Foucault argues that these types operate on a spectrum. A common strand, he suggests, was that 'a person who wishes to govern the state must first learn how to govern himself, his goods and his patrimony, after which he will be successful in governing the state'.[41] The generic skills acquired in these activities, such as those of economy and efficiency, are also instilled into the practices of governing the state. The precepts derived from experience in such practices came to be known as the science of police[42] or political economy.[43]

Foucault argues that with the emergence of 'the social question' or what he calls 'the problem of population'—the extension of the consideration of government to those parts of the population that had previously been beneath its notice—the art of government moved beyond the juridical frame of sovereignty. This resulted from a revaluation of the idea of economy, together with the formation of a science of statistics. With the consequent realization 'that population has its own regularities, its own rate of deaths and diseases, its cycles of scarcity'[44] the family or household was displaced as a model of government and the art of government emerged as a distinctive mode of association. But this notion of the art of government 'has as its purpose not the act of government itself, but the welfare of the population, the improvement of its condition, the increase of its wealth, longevity, health'.[45] And while the population is the subject of needs, 'it is also the object in the hands of the government'.[46]

---

[41] Michel Foucault, 'Governmentality' in Graham Burchell, Colin Gordon, and Peter Miller (eds), *The Foucault Effect: Studies in Governmentality* (Hemel Hempstead: Harvester Wheatsheaf, 1991), 87–104, 91.

[42] See Albion Woodbury Small, *The Cameralists: The Pioneers of German Social Polity* (Chicago: University of Chicago Press, 1909); Adam Smith, *Lectures on Jurisprudence* [1766], R. L. Meek, D. D. Raphael, and P. G. Stein eds (Oxford: Clarendon Press, 1978), 331–339.

[43] Blackstone, above n. 25, iv.162: 'By the public police and oeconomy I mean the due regulation and domestic order of the kingdom: whereby the individuals of the state, like members of a well-governed family, are bound to conform their general behaviour to the rules of propriety, good neighbourhood, and good manners; and to be decent, industrious, and inoffensive in their respective stations'.

[44] Foucault, above n. 41, 99.   [45] Ibid. 100.   [46] Ibid.

Foucault highlights the character of this distinctive mode of association by invoking the idea of pastorship, government understood in terms of the metaphor of the shepherd and his flock. The shepherd 'gathers together, guides, and leads his flock', he wields power over a flock rather than over the land, and his role is that of ensuring its 'salvation'.[47] In the Christian tradition of pastorship, knowledge of the general state of the flock is not sufficient; the pastor must possess an individualized knowledge, to be acquired through the techniques of self-examination and guidance of conscience. Foucault argues that, as a result of the growth of political technology, the type of individualized power implicit in the notion of pastorship can be combined with the growing centralization of political power that is a characteristic of the modern idea of the state. Through this conjunction, a transition takes place 'from the art of government to a political science, from a regime dominated by structures of sovereignty to one ruled by techniques of government'.[48] He calls this process 'the governmentalization of the state'.[49]

This development is not to be seen 'in terms of the replacement of a society of sovereignty by a disciplinary society and the subsequent replacement of a disciplinary society by a society of government'.[50] Foucault suggests that 'in reality one has a triangle, sovereignty-discipline-government, which has as its primary target the population and as its essential mechanism the apparatuses of security'.[51] That is, the two modes of governance—rulership (sovereignty) and pastorship—are each bound up in a modern process of governmentalization.

Foucault's argument has a particular significance for the idea of public law. Although law performs a pivotal role within the idea of rulership, it tends to be displaced within pastorship, where the art of government becomes essentially one of 'disposing of things'. By this, he means that government becomes a method 'of employing tactics rather than laws, and even using laws themselves as tactics—to arrange things in such a way that, through a certain number of means, such and such ends may be achieved'.[52] Within the idea of rulership, the objective of government is internal to itself. By contrast, the end of government understood as pastorship resides in the things it manages. Here Foucault claims, 'law is not what is important' since 'it is not through law that the aims of government are to be reached'.[53]

Foucault's analysis of modes of governance can usefully be compared with Michael Oakeshott's earlier account of the character of the modern European state. Like Foucault's, Oakeshott's analysis is historical rather than philosophical. The formation of the modern state, he explains, has its origins in a ceaseless process of conquest, rebellion, secession, murder, treaties, intermarriage of ruling families, hereditary succession to estates, and such like. The states of Europe were forged from a variety of ancient communities or their fragments, often by yoking together communities

---

[47] Michel Foucault, '*Omnes et singulatim*: Towards a Criticism of "Political Reason"' in Sterling M. McMurrin (ed.), *The Tanner Lectures on Human Values II* (Salt Lake City: University of Utah Press, 1981), 225–254, 228–229.
[48] Foucault, above n. 41, 101.
[49] Ibid. 103.
[50] Ibid. 102.
[51] Ibid.
[52] Ibid. 95.
[53] Ibid. 95–96.

without a common history, a common language, or a common tradition of law. They began as 'mixed and miscellaneous collections of human beings precariously held together, disturbed by what they had swallowed and were unable to digest, and distracted by plausible or fancied *irredèntà*.[54] No European state, he emphasizes, 'has ever come within measurable distance of being a "nation state" '.[55]

The point Oakeshott impresses upon us is that the modern state is a 'somewhat ramshackle construction', being 'constructed, for the most part, by second-hand materials . . . by artisans who were their own designers following conventions they made for themselves'.[56] Consequently, 'the claims of governments to authority have been supported, for the most part, by the most implausible and gimcrack beliefs which few can find convincing for more than five minutes together and which bear little or no relation to the governments concerned: "the sovereignty of the people" or of "the nation", "democracy", "majority rule", "participation" etc.'.[57] As Oakeshott puts it, governments 'have become inclined to commend themselves to their subjects merely in terms of their power and their incidental achievements, and their subjects have become inclined to look only for this recommendation'.[58]

Given the circumstances of its formation, the modern state can hardly be conceived as some pristine model. In this respect Oakeshott is only echoing Maitland's observation that 'the more we study our constitution whether in the present or the past, the less do we find it conform[s] to any such plan as a philosopher might invent in his study'.[59] But although Oakeshott rejects easy analogies, such as the state as being analogous to the family or an organism, he does suggest that two ideas encapsulate the kind of thinking around which notions of the modern state have revolved. These two ideas, deriving from Roman law, represent two different modes of association: the idea of the state as *societas* and that of the state as *universitas*. Oakeshott argues that the modern state is to be understood as an unresolved tension between these two irreconcilable dispositions.[60]

The mode of association understood as *societas* suggests that agents comprise an association that is *not* an engagement in pursuit of a common substantive purpose or some common interest; the only tie that joins them is that 'of loyalty to one another, the conditions of which may achieve the formality denoted by the kindred word "legality" '.[61] *Societas* is simply the product of a pact to acknowledge the authority of certain arrangements: it is 'a formal association in terms of rules, not a substantive relationship in terms of common action'.[62] Oakeshott specifies these terms of association as follows:

[T]he ruler of a state when it is understood as a *societas* is the custodian of the loyalties of the association and the guardian and administrator of its conditions which constitute the relation-

---

[54] Michael Oakeshott, 'On the Character of a Modern European State' in his *On Human Conduct* (Oxford: Clarendon Press, 1975), 185–326, 188.
[55] Ibid.   [56] Ibid. 198.   [57] Ibid. 191.   [58] Ibid. 192.
[59] F. W. Maitland, *The Constitutional History of England* (Cambridge: Cambridge University Press, 1908), 197.
[60] Oakeshott, above n. 54, 201.   [61] Ibid.   [62] Ibid.

ship of *socii*. He cannot, for example, be the owner or trustee of its property, because there is none; and he is not the manager or director of its activities, because there are no such activities to be managed. This ruler is a master of ceremonies, not an arbiter of fashion. His concern is with the 'manners' of convives, and his office is to keep the conversation going, not to determine what is said. . . . [I]ts government (whatever its constitution) is a nomocracy whose laws are understood as conditions of conduct, not devices instrumental to the satisfaction of preferred wants.[63]

Oakeshott here expresses *societas* as an ideal form, a conception abstracted from the contingencies and ambiguities of its actual manifestations.[64] By doing so, he is able to capture with greater precision what Foucault meant by the condition of sovereignty (what I have termed rulership), when the latter stated that:

What characterizes the end of sovereignty, this common and general good, is in sum nothing other than submission to sovereignty. This means that the end of sovereignty is circular: the end of sovereignty is the exercise of sovereignty. The good is obedience to the law, hence the good for sovereignty is that people should obey it.[65]

This mode of governance is clearly recognizable in the idea that the king occupies an office of authority. This office incorporates certain expectations about the conduct of the ruler as the supreme dispenser of justice and defender of the realm, and it claims the allegiance of those he rules. Even if medieval kings were over-zealous in seeking to protect the rights—and especially the income—of the crown, the 'emergent realm was neither a landed estate, nor a commercial enterprise (customs dues were not items in a design to direct traders into more profitable undertakings), nor a military organization but an association in terms of legal relationships'.[66]

This image of the office of ruler was not, however, without a rival. This is the state as *universitas*, the state conceived not as a partnership but as a corporate association. Medieval jurists were familiar with the idea of the corporation aggregate, exemplified in such group units as churches, boroughs, and universities. Corporate bodies of this type united 'persons associated in respect of such identified common purpose, in the pursuit of some acknowledged substantive end, or in the promotion of some specified enduring interest'.[67] When the idea of the state emerged in early modern Europe, this corporate form—the *persona ficta*—offered a ready analogy.

In terms of *universitas*, the state is recognized as a form of joint undertaking in pursuit of a common substantive objective. Consequently, its responsibility for maintaining the *salus populi*—a purely formal requirement of *societas*—acquires a more precise teleocratic meaning. The land and resources of its territory—even, ultimately, the talents of the people—may be treated as corporate property. The activity of governing becomes a managerial undertaking, with the ruler being 'related to this enterprise in some such manner as that of its custodian, guardian, director, or manager'.[68] This

[63] Ibid. 202–203.
[64] This ideal character of the state understood as *societas* can be equated with what Oakeshott elsewhere calls a *civitas*: see Oakeshott, 'On the Civil Condition' in his *On Human Conduct*, above n. 54, 108–184.
[65] Foucault, above n. 41, 95.   [66] Oakeshott, above n. 54, 212.   [67] Ibid. 203.
[68] Ibid. 218.

conception of the state as *universitas* parallels, and in many respects enhances, Foucault's account of the mode of governing that emerges as a science of police.

Oakeshott recognizes that the ideas of *universitas* and *societas* were intermingled in the formation of the modern state mainly because in medieval practice the distinction between rulership and lordship—'between ruling a realm and managing a *seigneurie* or a manor, between a subject and a tenant, a retainer or an *homme*, between a "public" and a "private" relationship, between the exchequer of a realm and the fisc of a ruler's household, between a custodian of law and a custodian of a common interest'[69]—had never fully been separated. But there is a further reason, which connects with Foucault's idea of pastorship, and this is the influence of the jurisprudence of the Christian church.

Oakeshott argues that although the Pope's claims to possess a *plenitudo potestatis* over the *universitas humana* never even came close to being accepted by medieval rulers, when the modern state emerged, secular rulers absorbed aspects of this papal mission as part of their sovereign authority. This had particular significance because, by virtue of his office, the Pope claimed not only to be custodian of the law and property of the corporation (his *potestas jurisdictionis*), but also to be guardian of the Faith (his *potestas ordinis*) and to be director of education, guardian of learning, and arbiter of knowledge (his *potestas docendi*).[70] Rulers thus became 'the residuary legatees of a notionally all-embracing ecclesiastical authority'[71] and acquired, in particular, aspects of the Pope's *potestas docendi* relating to the moral and spiritual welfare of the community.

The existence of these two competing modes of governance, especially when placed alongside Foucault's triangle of 'sovereignty-discipline-government', offers an illuminating insight into the character of the modern state. The tensions between these modes that were present at the birth of the state have become much more intense as a result of the growth and extension of the apparatus of central government. This, as Oakeshott emphasizes, has nothing to do with the concept of sovereignty as some mistakenly believe, but has its source in our understanding of the state as a particular mode of association. This administrative engagement of government is distinctive 'because its procedures were not those of a court of law and its agents were not themselves judicial officers: constables, comptrollers, surveyors, prefects, commissioners, proctors, wardens, superintendents, inspectors, overseers, collectors of information, and officials of all kinds, together with their assistants, their Bureaux, Boards, Commissions, Committees, Conferences etc., and the regulations they enforce and administer'.[72] This extensive administrative apparatus, common to all modern states, does not necessarily mean that the conception of the state as *universitas* predominates. But what is evident is that the pursuit of a common substantive purpose could hardly be undertaken without the existence of such an administrative apparatus.

---

[69] Oakeshott, above n. 54, 218–219.
[70] Ibid. 220, 279–295. See further Michael J. Wilks, *The Problem of Sovereignty in the Later Middle Ages* (Cambridge: Cambridge University Press, 1963), esp. Pt. I.
[71] Ibid. 224.   [72] Ibid. 267.

In a passage that has strong affinities to Foucault's analysis, Oakeshott highlights a particular aspect of the state understood as *universitas* that recently has come to prominence: that of the state as 'an association of invalids, all victims of the same disease and incorporated in seeking relief from their common ailment'.[73] In this mode, the office of government becomes a form of remedial engagement in which rulers 'are *therapeutae*, the directors of a sanatorium from which no patient may discharge himself by a choice of his own'.[74] Just as Saint-Simon identified the industrial enterprise as the predominant form of modern society and concluded that the state should itself be an industrial enterprise,[75] Oakeshott surmises that here 'the outstanding "fact" of modern times is understood to be universal neurosis and it is concluded that a state should be understood as an association of human beings undergoing treatment'.[76] Remote as this might seem from the character of the modern state,[77] Oakeshott argues that 'numerous writers have guided European thought along this path', a path leading to a place in which 'everything is understood in relation to "sanity"; that is, a uniform so-called normality' and where subjects are 'understood to be "disturbed" patients in need of "treatment"'.[78] And, in a comment echoed in Foucault's theme on the displacement of law, Oakeshott quips that while utopia has no lawyers, 'it bristles with inspectors and overseers'.[79]

Although *societas* and *universitas* each stand for an independent self-sustaining mode of association, Oakeshott's argument is that they have become 'contingently joined' in the character of a modern European state. Since these two modes of association yield somewhat divergent understandings about the activity of governing, they add significantly to the complexity of our task. But if this is the situation, then rather than suppressing one or other modes, it is essential that this condition of modernity be recognized.[80] The only way forward in developing a positive account of public law is to incorporate these competing modes of governing within a framework that permits us to acknowledge these complexities of governing within the modern state.

---

[73] Ibid. 308.  [74] Ibid.
[75] On the thought of Henri, Comte de Saint-Simon, see Geoffrey Hawthorn, *Enlightenment and Despair: A History of Social Theory* (Cambridge: Cambridge University Press, 2nd edn. 1987), ch. 4.
[76] Oakeshott, above n. 54, 309.
[77] See, however, Alasdair MacIntyre, *After Virtue: A Study in Moral Theory* (London: Duckworth, 2nd edn. 1985), ch. 3.
[78] Oakeshott, above n. 54, 309–310. Cf. Foucault on the issue of 'normalization': see Michel Foucault, *Discipline and Punish: The Birth of the Prison*, Alan Sheridan trans. (Harmondsworth: Penguin, 1991), 177–184; François Ewald, 'Norms, Discipline and the Law' in Robert Post (ed.), *Law and the Order of Culture* (Berkeley: University of California Press, 1991), 138–161.
[79] Oakeshott, above n. 54, 268.
[80] For a sociological analysis of this aspect of ambivalence of the modern condition, see Peter Wagner, *A Sociology of Modernity: Liberty and Discipline* (London: Routledge, 1994).

## THE OFFICE OF GOVERNMENT

Government is an office of authority. When, in *Leviathan,* Hobbes offered an explanation of how the modern state is instituted, at the core of his account lay the formation of the 'office of the sovereign representative'.[81] This office of government is charged with the making and enforcing of those rules of conduct that sustain the association.[82] Government and the state are not identical: the government is the person or group that discharges the tasks of government, whereas the state is an expression of a particular historical form that government has taken. But modern government and the state are closely connected. The way in which states have been formed has invariably had a profound influence on the constitution of authority of government. But our understanding of the activity of governing has exerted an influence on the way in which the modern state is configured. The modern state rests on an unresolved tension between the two irreconcilable modes of governance represented in *societas* and *universitas* and this tension might help us not only to understand the character of the modern British state but also certain ambiguities concerning the office of its government.

Our starting point must be that of the office of the crown. The origins of the distinction between king and crown lie buried in the medieval juristic thought of the twelfth century, when a distinction needed to be drawn between the personality of the king and the office he occupied.[83] This distinction was well understood by the fourteenth century, when the coronation oath of the period required kings to swear to maintain unimpaired the rights of the crown.[84] The crown represented the entire body politic or the community of the realm. In the reports of Plowden, the body politic is defined by the judiciary as 'a body . . . consisting of policy and government, and constituted for the direction of the people, and the management of the public-weal'.[85] Although the history is messy, with no consistent differentiation being effected in law between the king and the crown,[86] it is from this idea of the crown that our understanding of the office of government has evolved.

---

[81] Hobbes, above n. 5, ch. 30.

[82] Cf. Oakeshott, *Rationalism in Politics and other essays* (London: Methuen, 1962), 187–189: 'the office of government is merely to rule [and] the only appropriate manner of ruling is by making and enforcing rules of conduct'. Foucault defined government as 'the conduct of conduct': see Colin Gordon, 'The Soul of the Citizen: Max Weber and Michel Foucault on Rationality and Government' in Sam Whimster and Scott Lash (eds), *Max Weber, Rationality and Modernity* (London: Allen & Unwin, 1987), 293–316, 296.

[83] George Garnett, 'The Origins of the Crown' in John Hudson (ed.), *The History of English Law: Centenary Essays on 'Pollock and Maitland'* (Oxford: Oxford University Press, 1996), 171–214.

[84] R. S. Hoyt, 'The Coronation Oath of 1308' (1955) 11 *Traditio* 235–257; H. G. Richardson, 'The Coronation Oath in Medieval England: The Evolution of the Office and the Oath' (1960) 16 *Traditio* 111–202; Gaines Post, 'Roman Law and the "Inalienability Clause" in the English Coronation Oath' in his *Studies in Medieval Legal Thought: Public Law and the State, 1100–1322* (Princeton, NJ: Princeton University Press, 1964), 415–433.

[85] *Case of the Duchy of Lancaster* (1561) 1 Plowden 212, 213.

[86] I examine this issue in 'The State, the Crown, and the Law' in Maurice Sunkin and Sebastian Payne (eds), *The Nature of the Crown: A Legal and Political Analysis* (Oxford: Oxford University Press, 1999), 33–76.

The concept of the crown provides the basis for differentiating between private and public, and between lordship and office. These are the key terms by which, for example, the historic importance of Magna Carta of 1215 is to be assessed. In Finer's summation, the overriding significance of the charter was that it 'limits the Crown as *dominus* but upholds it as *rex*'; its thrust 'was to accept the strengthened Crown and its expanded jurisdiction, yet to try to eliminate the caprices of the individual monarch'.[87] The king's authority to govern was not questioned. What the charter emphasizes is that this authority must be exercised through his council. Stubbs may have both exaggerated and misconstrued its significance in his famous comment that 'the whole of the constitutional history of England is little more than a commentary on Magna Carta',[88] but in the recognition that acts of the king have an official character that must be exercised through certain forms, the charter marks a milestone in the emergence of English governing arrangements.

This work of the crown in council was gradually amplified through the formation of a parliament that came into existence as an act of royal will and as an instrument of royal government. Although in modern thought parliament is often presented as an institution that operates as a counterbalance to government,[89] parliament's origins lie entirely in its perceived value to the king in assisting him in the activity of governing. In order to appreciate its strength, it is essential to recognize that the king's council was centrally embedded within his parliament. When we talk of the establishment of sovereign authority, then, we should in strictness refer to the work undertaken by the 'crown in council in parliament'. The great service which the English parliament rendered in the later middle ages, A. F. Pollard notes, 'was not . . . to make England a constitutional state, but to foster its growth into a national state based on something broader and deeper than monarchical centralization'.[90]

The role of parliament in forging a national state is seen most clearly in relation to the innovative work of the Reformation parliament which, using the authority of the crown in parliament to the full, sought to eliminate those medieval liberties or privileges which had acted as encumbrances on the complete exercise of sovereign authority. The greatest of these medieval privileges belonged, of course, to the church. The revolutionary act of breaking with the church in Rome was one in which Henry VIII made full use of the instrumentality of parliament; crown and parliament united to challenge any rival jurisdictions. Consequently, while making full use of his regal

---

[87] S. E. Finer, *The History of Government from the Earliest Times* (Oxford: Oxford University Press, 1997), ii. 904–905.

[88] William Stubbs, *The Constitutional History of England in its Origins and Development* (Oxford: Clarendon Press, 1880), i.597–598. Cf. J. C. Holt, *Magna Carta* (Cambridge: Cambridge University Press, 2nd edn. 1992).

[89] This tradition—based on a division between the function of governing and that of 'checking of government'—can be traced to James Mill, *An Essay on Government* [1820], Ernest Barker intro. (Cambridge: Cambridge University Press, 1937). The theme is developed by John Stuart Mill, *Considerations on Representative Government* [1861] in his *Three Essays* (Oxford: Oxford University Press, 1975), 145–423, esp. 211–228.

[90] A. F. Pollard, *The Evolution of Parliament* (London: Longmans, 1920), 133.

powers of kingship, Henry also accepted that 'we at no time stand so highly in our estate royal as in the time of Parliament; wherein we as head and you as members are conjoined and knit together into one body politic'.[91]

The process by which an absolute legislative power was established marks a critical stage both in the formation of the modern state and in the extension in the apparatus of government. In the early medieval period, legislation was regarded as a declaratory process, and therefore as an aspect of judicial procedure. In juristic terms, all governmental action was understood to involve the interpretation and application of the law. The activity of legislation, and hence its differentiation from adjudication, comes about only as the result of the growing acceptance of law as an expression of the command of the sovereign rather than as a reflection of an unchanging pattern of custom. But of equal importance is the recognition that this power of command is impersonal and institutional. Authority resides not in the personal power of the king but in the institutional power of the crown in council in parliament.

Of similar importance is the acknowledgement that executive government itself is a public office. The Henrician age saw great strides being made towards the realization of this condition. In addition to establishing a modern conception of legislative sovereignty, Henry's reign saw the creation of a 'revised machinery of government whose principle was bureaucratic organization in place of the personal control of the king, and national management rather than management of the king's estate'.[92] Notwithstanding the transformation in central government from household to bureaucratic methods and instruments, it remained the case that throughout the sixteenth century, appointments to governmental offices were invariably obtained through patronage. But the basis had been provided for the challenge to patrimonial government and the eventual establishment of a more impersonal public administration.[93]

The growing recognition that the jurisdictional authority of government was absolute thus coincided with an acknowledgement that the exercise of such power was circumscribed in form. Competence was unlimited; as Blackstone explained, the crown in parliament 'hath sovereign and uncontrollable authority in making, confirming, enlarging, restraining, abrogating, repealing, reviving, and expounding of laws, concerning matters of all possible denominations, ecclesiastical, or temporal, civil, military, maritime, or criminal'.[94] But this 'omnipotent' power could be exercised only through established forms and defined procedures, and generally only in accordance with some basic understanding of the 'proper' uses of such power. The establishment of such formalities indicates the formation of a constitutional regime.

---

[91] *Ferrers' case* (1543); excerpted in G. R. Elton, *The Tudor Constitution: Documents and Commentary* (Cambridge: Cambridge University Press, 1960), 267–270, 270.

[92] G. R. Elton, above n. 18, 4. Cf. Christopher Coleman and David Starkey (eds), *Revolution Reassessed: Revisions in the History of Tudor Government and Administration* (Oxford: Clarendon Press, 1986).

[93] See Ertman, above n. 36, ch. 4; Sir Norman Chester, *The English Administrative System, 1780–1870* (Oxford: Clarendon Press, 1981); Richard A. Chapman and J. R. Greenaway, *The Dynamics of Administrative Reform* (London: Croom Helm, 1980).

[94] Blackstone, above n. 25, i.156.

Some form of constitutional ordering is, of course, implicit in the medieval notion of the 'body politic'.[95] This became more explicit in the idea of 'mixed government', whereby the king (as head) and peers and people (as members) exercised a co-ordinated power, the object being to ensure that one estate was unable unilaterally to impose its will on the others.[96] In the late seventeenth century, the ancient organic language of the mixed constitution tended to be replaced by the mechanical metaphor of the 'balanced constitution', in which the king, lords, and commons were presented as operating a complex system of checks and balances.[97] This shift in metaphor contained the seeds of innovation, especially since the idea of balance presupposed a separation of functions that was almost entirely novel in conception.

In the early modern period, writers such as Bodin and Hobbes had deliberated over the principal 'marks of sovereignty', being such basic activities of government as law-making, declaring war and making peace, appointing magistrates, and coining money.[98] But such discussion focused on the engagement of government: it could be transformed into a discourse on the office of government only by re-ordering these 'tasks' into an appropriate institutional allocation of certain basic 'functions'. Since the strength of parliamentary institutions throughout the medieval period resided in the fact that the king's court, council, and parliament constituted an elaborate system of multi-layered government, this was no simple exercise. It was the intimacy of these connections rather than a separation of institutional functions that accounted for the peculiar strength of English medieval government.

There was one precedent to work from: England's first and only written constitution—the Instrument of Government of 1653—had provided for a formal separation of legislative and governmental power.[99] Although at the Restoration this idea of separation—since it would have removed the crown from a role in legislation—could not be countenanced, the theme became a significant one in contemporary political thought. The necessity of separating legislative and executive power underpinned Locke's *Second Treatise*[100] and during the eighteenth century Montesquieu developed the theme in his chapter in *The Spirit of the Laws* on the nature of the English constitution. Montesquieu claimed that the key to England's political liberty lay in

---

[95] For the most elaborate presentation of the imagery of the body politic—one based on the necessity of the king to exercise power in a moderate manner—see John of Salisbury, *Policraticus* [c.1154–1156], Cary J. Nederman trans. (Cambridge: Cambridge University Press, 1990).

[96] See Francis D. Wormuth, *The Origins of Modern Constitutionalism* (New York: Harper & Brothers, 1949), 50–58; James M. Blythe, *Ideal Government and the Mixed Constitution in the Middle Ages* (Princeton, NJ: Princeton University Press, 1992), esp. 260–277.

[97] The transition is most clearly marked in Hobbes's *Leviathan* (above n. 5). At the outset, Hobbes uses the metaphor of the sovereign as the 'artificial soul' that gives 'life and motion to the body' (ibid. 9, 18). But mechanical metaphors tend to take over as Hobbes, who likens the state to those 'engines that move by themselves by springs and wheels as doth a watch' (ibid. 9), elaborates on its nature.

[98] See Bodin, above n. 38, i.10; Hobbes, above n. 5, ch. 18.

[99] Wormuth, above n. 96, 59–72; M. J. C. Vile, *Constitutionalism and the Separation of Powers* (Indianapolis: Liberty Fund, 2nd edn. 1998), 52–57.

[100] John Locke, above n. 38, ii. § 159: 'Where the Legislative and Executive Power are in distinct hands (as they are in all moderated Monarchies, and well-framed Governments) . . .'.

the separation of legislative, executive and judicial power, noting that 'as they are constrained to move by the necessary motion of things, they will be forced to move in concert'.[101]

Montesquieu was quite wrong about the eighteenth century English constitution: what made the peculiar arrangements of British government work in a relatively harmonious fashion was not 'the necessary motion of things' but the fact that the entire apparatus of government was in the hands of the landed class. Since Montesquieu's basic objective had been to indicate how arrangements to preserve English political liberty are 'established by their laws'[102] this may perhaps be pardonable. But Blackstone, in copying Montesquieu's error, had no such excuse.[103] The mistake has ever since been a source of confusion about the nature of the office of government within the British system. After the Restoration and the Revolution of 1688, the course taken was not that of dividing and separating power but of maintaining the formal unity of the office of government. This was achieved by ensuring that the crown remained an essential element in parliament and that, far from separating executive and legislature, ministers of the crown were obliged to maintain their positions within the legislature. The idea that 'the king can do no wrong' thus flourished as a maxim during the eighteenth century precisely because it was recognized that the king could only act officially through a set of arrangements which ensured that governmental action commanded the confidence of parliament.[104] And the vital link in these arrangements—what Bagehot was later to call the 'efficient secret' of the constitution[105]—was the emergence of the cabinet as the collective decision-making institution of the government.

This essential unity must be acknowledged, and those who present the crown and parliament as distinct and competing entities generally fail so to do. Textbook writers often state that the legislature controls the executive, leading critics to retort that it is the other way round—the executive in fact controls the legislature. Both are in danger of missing the basic point. It is the extensive and intricate character of the connections between legislative and executive (and, notwithstanding formal independence, also judicial[106]) functions that is the defining feature of the British system.

---

[101] Montesquieu, *The Spirit of the Laws* [1748], Anne M. Cohler, Basia Carolyn Miller, and Harold Samuel Stone trans. (Cambridge: Cambridge University Press, 1988), xi.6.

[102] Montesquieu, ibid: 'It is not for me to examine whether at present the English enjoy this liberty or not. It suffices for me to say that it is established by their laws, and I seek no further'. This point is reinforced by Oakeshott's (above n. 54, 246) observation that in reality Montesquieu was concerned primarily with 'modes of association and with the offices of government' rather than with the constitutions of states.

[103] See Blackstone, above n. 25, i.157. See further, Vile, above n. 99, 110–116.

[104] Blackstone, ibid, i. 239; Janelle Greenberg, 'Our Grand Maxim of State, "The King can do no Wrong"' (1991) 12 *History of Political Thought* 209–228.

[105] Walter Bagehot, *The English Constitution* [1867], Miles Taylor ed. (Oxford: Oxford University Press, 2001).

[106] Although since the Act of Settlement 1700 the judiciary has maintained its formal independence, there has been no clear separation of functions. Having begun life as a court, parliament retains many of the features of a court through its writs, petitions, and such like and, with respect to private bill procedure, it fulfils the equivalent of a judicial function. Judges are lords of parliament appointed by the crown and

This juristic unity of the office of government, symbolized by the crown, expresses the basic difference between the British system of government and modern constitutional arrangements that provide the framework of the governing regimes of other European systems. Modernization in the British system has been an evolutionary rather than a revolutionary achievement. Rather than a fundamental reconstitution of the structure of the office of government taking place, there has been a rearrangement in predominance of the partners in authority. Modernization is the product of political adaptation, not juristic reconstruction.

### THE TASKS OF LAW

This peculiar history has bequeathed an ambiguous legacy. The emergence of the modern state within the frame of a formal unity of the office of government has left us confused about the subject of public law. The fundamental legal doctrine of the British constitution—that of the omnicompetence of the crown in council in parliament—has meant that, especially in the hands of the analytical positivists, lawyers have had little of significance to contribute to an understanding of modern governmental arrangements. One law lord summarized the orthodox position in these terms:

> It is often said that it would be unconstitutional for the United Kingdom Parliament to do certain things, meaning that the moral, political and other reasons against doing them are so strong that most people would regard it as highly improper if Parliament did these things. But that does not mean that it is beyond the power of Parliament to do such things. If Parliament chose to do any of them the courts would not hold the Act of Parliament invalid.[107]

If the basic duty of the judge is to give effect to the will of the state as expressed through Acts of Parliament, then the judiciary is unable to perform any significant role in specifying and elaborating the constitutional framework of government. The failure of modern scholars of public law is (in a juristic sense) to have defined their discipline within the frame of the positive law that is enforced in the courts. But even in such terms, the nature of the modern tasks of law has unsettled many traditional assumptions.

One of the defining features of modern government has been the dramatic expansion, over the last 150 years, in the range of its tasks as a consequence of the extension in its administrative responsibilities. This has resulted in an unprecedented degree of interaction between government, economy, and society. We live in a highly regulated society. Since this growth in the range of government has been achieved

---

are removable on an address from both houses, and the most senior—the law lords and lords justices of appeal—are sworn privy counsellors. And presently we have two supreme courts of appeal (the House of Lords and the Judicial Committee of the Privy Council), one of which is a branch of the legislature and the other a committee of the executive. But see Department for Constitutional Affairs Consultation Paper, *Constitutional Reform: A Supreme Court for the United Kingdom* (London: Department for Constitutional Affairs, July 2003).

[107] *Madzimbamuto* v. *Lardner-Burke* [1969] 1 AC 645, 723 *per* Lord Reid.

through the instrument of legislation, the emergence of this administrative state has had a significant impact on the character of modern positive law.

The formation of the administrative state has resulted in an explosion of legislative activity, as duties are laid down by law and new agencies of government are formed to carry out new tasks or to oversee the implementation of new responsibilities. Since the late nineteenth century, the statute books have been growing in length, changing in form, and increasing in technical complexity. The volume of executive legislation now greatly outstrips the amount of primary legislation, and the great bulk of legislation is more likely to be directed to the specific, often highly technical concerns of particular bodies rather than laying down general rules of conduct. The rise of the administrative state has therefore resulted in the emergence of an extensive body of administrative law, as agencies are equipped with jurisdictional competence, allocated powers and duties, and subjected to elaborate statutory codes of procedure.

This growth in the volume of administrative law has also had a major impact on the workload of the judiciary. Even in the 1880s, Maitland was able to note that if you 'take up a modern volume of the reports of the Queen's Bench division, you will find that about half the cases reported have to do with the rules of administrative law'.[108] This growing body of administrative law has posed major problems for the judiciary. Because England had been able so early in its history to establish the authority of its centralized institutions of government, it had never found it necessary, unlike most European systems, to establish a special jurisdiction to deal with legal disputes concerning government.[109] This factor, alongside the unusual degree of continuity in the form of its governing institutions, has had important juristic consequences. It has meant, for example, that the state has never been accorded a formal status in English law. And the fact that all officials have, since the reign of Henry II, been made subject to the jurisdiction of the High Court has given the concept of the rule of law a special meaning.[110] In Ernest Barker's words, 'not our Parliament, or our Cabinet, but the rule of our judicature constitutes our form of State a different species'.[111] But this common law tradition of 'the rule of law', with its avoidance of any formal jurisdictional division between public law and private law, has come under strain during the twentieth century.

The evolutionary character of the British constitution has meant that the administrative functions of the modern state have grown in an unsystematic manner. A plethora of boards, agencies, commissions, and inspectors have been brought into existence without any institutional pattern of design being readily discernible.[112]

---

[108] F. W. Maitland, above n. 59, 505.

[109] See J. W. F. Allison, *A Continental Distinction in the Common Law: A Historical and Comparative Perspective on English Public Law* (Oxford: Clarendon Press, 1996).

[110] The *locus classicus* is A. V. Dicey, *Introduction to the Study of the Law of the Constitution* (London: Macmillan, 8th edn. 1915), 198–199: the rule of law means 'the equal subjection of all classes to the ordinary law of the land administered by the ordinary Law Courts'.

[111] Ernest Barker, 'The Rule of Law' (1914) 1 (o.s.) *Political Quarterly* 117–140, 118. Although Barker is right about the judiciary, he seems on less sound ground about the impact of our traditions of parliamentary and cabinet government.

[112] See W. H. Greenleaf, *The British Political Tradition*, iii: *A Much Governed Nation* (London: Methuen, 1987), chs 1–6, 10.

This has generated a certain juristic confusion. The inherited problem has been that since the courts were, in Dicey's words, obliged to act in accordance with 'the strict rules of law', they were unsuited to 'manage a mass of public business'.[113] Consequently, when administrative bodies were vested by statute with a broad range of decision-making powers which could significantly affect the rights and interests of citizens, the courts were ill-equipped, both procedurally and temperamentally, for the task of maintaining adequate judicial supervision.[114] After various faltering starts, it was only from the late 1960s that the judiciary was able to begin to develop more efficient procedures and more rationalistic principles for reviewing such administrative action.[115]

The basic concepts that have since been developed—legality, rationality, fairness, and proportionality—appear to provide the basis of a more coherent framework of public law. But this edifice rests on uncertain foundations. This is because modern government generally employs 'tactics' rather than 'laws', and thus has a tendency to use law tactically[116] or as 'instruments of managerial policy'.[117] This in turn has meant that positive law often forms part only—and not necessarily the constitutive part—of an administrative scheme, and this presents obvious problems of legal interpretation. Underlying this difficulty—one that the legacy of the juristic unity of the office of government has masked—is that of identifying modern government as an expression of a particular mode of association. Is modern government a formal engagement concerned with maintaining order through the establishment of general rules of conduct? Or is it a purposive engagement in which the rules of conduct are to be interpreted as being incidental to the pursuit of some common good? This basic tension cannot be resolved through the judiciary's project of modernizing the machinery and the conceptual framework of judicial review. Shifting the language of judicial review from jurisdiction to legality, from reasonableness to rationality, or from natural justice to fairness might enable the judiciary to grapple in a more intellectually satisfying manner with the question of whether governmental decision-making has taken account of the interests of others. But this type of exercise inevitably falls prey to fundamental ambiguities concerning the legitimate aims and purposes of the modern state.

In the face of such complexities, many lawyers have simply withdrawn from the attempt to understand the character of the modern state and have retreated to a

---

[113] Dicey, above n. 110, xxxix.

[114] See Judith Shklar, 'Political Theory and the Rule of Law' in Allan C. Hutchinson and Patrick Monahan (eds), *The Rule of Law: Ideal or Ideology?* (Toronto: Carswell, 1987), 1–16, 6: 'The Rule of Law [as interpreted by Dicey] was . . . both trivialized as the peculiar patrimony of one and only one national order, and formalized, by the insistence that only one set of inherited procedures and court practices could sustain it. Not the structure or purposes of juridical rigour, but only its forms became significant for freedom. No wonder that Dicey thought England's law and freedoms were already gravely threatened. If its liberty hung on so slender a thread as the avoidance of new courts to deal with new kinds of cases, the end was indeed at hand'.

[115] See Martin Loughlin, 'Courts and Governance' in P. B. H. Birks (ed.), *Frontiers of Liability* (Oxford: Oxford University Press, 1994), i.91–112.

[116] Foucault, above n. 52. [117] Oakeshott, above n. 54, 312.

simplistic interpretation rooted in classical liberalism.[118] It may be tempting to portray law solely in the image of *societas*—as a set of general, non-purposive rules of conduct—but this ideal bears little relation to the tasks that law now performs in relation to the activity of governing. Modern government in the image of *universitas* may indeed be the product of what Oakeshott calls an 'unpurged relic of "lordship" hidden in the office of modern monarchs and which the successors to kings inherited', but it is an aspect of governing that modern rulers 'have shown no inclination to relinquish'.[119] In the late nineteenth century, Maitland warned that if the administrative role of government, and the tasks of law with respect to it, were left out of the picture, one would be left with 'a partial one-sided obsolete sketch'.[120] If administrative law were omitted from the 'general conception of what English law is', he elaborated, 'you will frame a false and antiquated notion of our constitution'.[121] This is a warning that few contemporary public lawyers have heeded.

The fact is that public law is a highly polarized discourse. The polarities, which elsewhere I have characterized as being between the normativist and functionalist styles of thought,[122] are replications in legal consciousness of unresolved tensions between *societas* and *universitas*. We are unlikely to make progress in understanding the idea of public law by devising some ideal construct of law—whether as a model of rules[123] or a model of rights[124]—and then seeking to re-interpret the world in accordance with its precepts. From a positive perspective, it is essential that we keep these competing rationalities open to investigation and accommodation. Such tensions have generally been placed within a bounded framework whenever states have adopted a modern formal constitution. Within the British system, however, these ambiguities can and do permeate all facets of legal discourse. Henry Maine expressed this point well when, writing in 1885, he suggested that there is 'no country in which the newer view of government [*sc.* the state as *societas*] is more thoroughly applied to practice, but almost all the language of the law and constitution is still accommodated to the older ideas concerning the relation of ruler and subject'.[125] The significance of

---

[118] See, e.g., T. R. S. Allan, *Law, Liberty, and Justice: The Legal Foundations of British Constitutionalism* (Oxford: Clarendon Press, 1993); Allan, *Constitutional Justice: A Liberal Theory of the Rule of Law* (Oxford: Oxford University Press, 2001).

[119] Oakeshott, above n. 54, 268.      [120] Maitland, above n. 108, 506.      [121] Ibid.

[122] See Martin Loughlin, *Public Law and Political Theory* (Oxford: Clarendon Press, 1992), esp. ch. 4.

[123] See H. L. A. Hart, *The Concept of Law* (Oxford: Clarendon Press, 1961). Oakeshott (above n. 64, 151) presents a more sophisticated conception of law, even under the conditions of *societas*, when he explains that civil association is a practice in which 'all civil rules are conditions to be subscribed to in conduct, and there is none . . . which is exclusively a rule for the recognition of the authority of other rules. There is no place in civil association for any but a conditional distinction between so-called "private" and "public" law. Nor can there be a single rule of recognition, an unconditional and unquestionable norm from which all others derive their authority: a "constitution" not subject to interpretation and immune from inquiry. . . . In short, the validity of *lex* is a matter to be decided in terms of the resources for decision which *lex* itself provides'.

[124] See Ronald Dworkin, *Taking Rights Seriously* (Cambridge, Mass: Harvard University Press, 1977); Dworkin, *Law's Empire* (London: Fontana, 1986).

[125] Sir Henry Sumner Maine, *Popular Government* [1885] (Indianapolis: Liberty Classics, 1976), 35.

the tensions between positive law and governmental practice inherent in the British system now seem lost to contemporary lawyers. If some understanding of this matter is to be retrieved, we need to adopt a broader and more inclusive conception of the subject: public law as practice.

### PUBLIC LAW AS PRACTICE

The argument of this chapter has been that the activity of governing must be understood as a complex practice that has emerged as a living tradition within European thought. This notion of practice requires some elaboration, especially since practices can vary in their complexity from simple conventions (such as queuing) to embrace an entire way of life. Alasdair MacIntyre defines a practice as 'any coherent and complex form of socially established co-operative human activity through which goods internal to that form of activity are realized in the course of trying to achieve those standards of excellence which are appropriate to, and partially definitive of, that form of activity'.[126] This is a broad conception of practice, that can include games like chess as well as a variety of activities that sustain human societies. But it provides an appropriate starting point for recognizing the activity of governing as a practice.

The critical point about government understood as a practice is that it is an activity that is neither fixed nor finished, since in Oakeshott's words 'no practice can be so definitively contrived or so securely insulated from circumstance as to become immune to modifications incidentally imposed on it by the performance it qualifies'.[127] The practice of governing is thus 'composed of conventions and rules of speech, a vocabulary and a syntax, and it is continuously invented by those who speak it'.[128] A practitioner is always a performer, one who is not commanded to undertake specific actions but who, when acting, must have regard to certain adverbial considerations. The customs, rules, canons, and conventions that comprise a practice are not commands but considerations to be taken into account. A practice, Oakeshott pithily observes, 'is an instrument to be played upon, not a tune to be played'.[129]

In European thought, the activity of governing incorporates implicit standards of correctness. Just as a language generates norms of grammar and pronunciation, so too does the practice of governing contain criteria of right conduct. Adherence to these conventions, whether of language or of governing, remains an essential aspect of effective performance. But there is no ultimate standard of correctness: the way that it is generally done within the practice supplies its own justification. Just as the standard of correctness about the way we pronounce words is just the way we do, so too in relation to the activity of governing the appropriate mode of conduct is that of

---

[126] MacIntyre, above n. 77, 187.
[127] Michael Oakeshott, 'On the Theoretical Understanding of Human Conduct' in his *On Human Conduct*, above n. 54, 1–107, 56.
[128] Ibid. 58.   [129] Ibid.

adherence to the ways it is conventionally carried on.[130] Standards of conduct are internal to the practice and have nothing to do with morality in the sense of 'strong evaluation', that is, of making discriminations between right and wrong that are independent of the ways of the practice.[131]

Once the activity of governing is understood to be a practice—albeit a highly complex practice replete with ambiguities and tensions[132]—the idea of public law can be grasped. What I want to argue is that public law—the law relating to the activity of governing—must be conceived as an assemblage of rules, principles, canons, maxims, customs, usages, and manners that condition and sustain the activity of governing. More specifically, public law is neither a system of general principles nor a code of rules. Rather, it is a vernacular language.[133] Although general principles and specific rules certainly provide part of the corpus of public law, these should be treated as cribs, or guides to conduct; they do not in themselves yield the source of knowledge of the subject. Public law is generated through usage (by a variety of governmental actors); it is not simply the creation of grammarians (i.e., judges and jurists). In this sense, the law relating to the activity of governing is not solely a mechanism for determining judgments about conduct but is a practice within which criteria about right conduct are elicited.[134] And while the language of public law often presents itself as a language of propriety, this language is governed by precepts of prudence.

The subject of public law cannot be grasped without having regard to a myriad of informal practices concerning the manner in which the activity of governing is

[130] Cf. Hegel's notion of *Sittlichkeit*: G. W. F. Hegel, *Philosophy of Right* [1821], T. M. Knox trans. (Oxford: Clarendon Press, 1952), § 153; Hegel, *Natural Law* [1802–3], T. M. Knox trans. (Philadelphia: University of Pennsylvania Press, 1975), 115: 'As regards ethical life, the saying of the wisest men of antiquity is alone true, that "to be ethical is to live in accordance with the ethics of one's own country"'.

[131] See Charles Taylor, 'The Diversity of Goods' in his *Philosophical Papers*, ii: *Philosophy and the Human Sciences* (Cambridge: Cambridge University Press, 1985), 230–247.

[132] Oakeshott (above n. 54, 201) specifically recognizes that the tension between the dispositions represented as *societas* and *universitas* 'has imposed a particular ambivalence upon all the institutions of a modern state and a specific ambiguity upon its vocabulary of discourse'. See further, Michael Oakeshott, 'The Vocabulary of a Modern European State' (1975) 23 *Political Studies* 319–341; 409–414.

[133] Cf. Oakeshott, above n. 127, 78.

[134] This notion of public law as practice has certain similarities with Pierre Bourdieu's theory of practice, rooted in the key concepts of *habitus* and field. Bourdieu argues that just as grammar organizes speech, so the structures of *habitus* organize a range of possible practices: see his *The Logic of Practice*, Richard Nice trans. (Stanford, Calif.: Stanford University Press, 1990), chs 1, 3. For Bourdieu, the idea of field denotes the social setting within which *habitus* operates. Hence, *habitus* + field = practice. See Bourdieu, *Distinction: A Social Critique of the Judgement of Taste*, Richard Nice trans. (London: Routledge, 1984), 101. For an application of Bourdieu's theory to law see his 'The Force of Law: Toward a Sociology of the Juridical Field' (1986–87) 38 *Hastings Law Journal* 814–853, esp. 818–819: '[T]he juridical field tends to operate like an "apparatus" to the extent that the cohesion of the freely orchestrated *habitus* of legal interpreters is strengthened by the discipline of a hierarchized body of professionals who employ a set of established procedures for the resolution of any conflicts between those whose profession is to resolve conflicts. Legal scholars thus have an easy time convincing themselves that the law provides its own foundation, that it is based on a fundamental norm, a "norm of norms" such as the Constitution, from which all lower ranked norms are in turn deduced. The *communis opinio doctorum* (the general opinion of professionals), rooted in the social cohesion of the body of legal interpreters, thus tends to confer the appearance of a transcendental basis on the historical forms of legal reason and on the belief in the ordered vision of the social whole that they produce'.

conducted. David Easton has used the term 'regime' as an expression meaning the 'regularized method for ordering political relationships'. By this, he means 'much more than a mere "constitution", for the term implies also the notions of the goals and limits of tolerance, the norms and accepted procedures and the formal and informal structure of authority, all rolled up together'.[135] Easton's use of regime to incorporate the temper and manner as much as the formal arrangements of rule comes close to identifying the sense in which public law must be understood. Positive law acquires its meaning only within a context of conventional understandings, and conventions 'cannot be understood "with the politics left out" '.[136] Although this feature of the British system is often expressed, its juristic significance has rarely been recognized. In this book, I explore this idea of public law by examining a number of practices which have evolved within the European tradition of governing—including politics, representation, sovereignty, democracy, and rights—and which both have shaped our understanding of the discipline and established conditions for effective utterance within it.

[135] David Easton, *The Political System: An Inquiry into the State of Political Science* (New York: Knopf, 1953), 193.
[136] G. H. L. Le May, *The Victorian Constitution* (London: Duckworth, 1979), 21.

# 3

## Politics

In an influential essay on the vocation of politics, Max Weber defined politics as an activity through which 'the leadership, or the influencing of the leadership of a *political* association, hence today, of a *state*' is acquired.[1] Weber's definition highlights critical aspects of the conduct of politics. It suggests that politics is a practice operating within an institutional setting and is primarily concerned with the guidance of public decision-making—with governing—the state.

This type of definition is common. But although it provides an explanation of political practice within an institutional framework, it does not reach to the core of the engagement of politics. It suggests that politics influences the leadership of a political association, thereby laying itself open to the criticism of being self-referential. If the phenomenon is to be grasped, we cannot start by assuming any particular form through which the activity of politics is conducted within the state. Rather than deriving an understanding of the political from a theory of the state, the concept of the state presupposes the concept of the political.

Although the main objective of this chapter is to identify the characteristic features of the practice of politics, we should begin with the concept of the political.[2] The value of this phenomenological approach is that it highlights the achievement that is realized whenever an elaborate set of political practices of the type with which Weber was concerned is institutionalized. By adopting this approach, I also hope to demonstrate how public law forms a distinctive aspect of political practice.

---

[1] Max Weber, 'Politics as a Vocation' [1919] in H. H. Gerth and C. Wright Mills (eds), *From Max Weber: Essays in Sociology* (London: Routledge & Kegan Paul, 1948), 77–128, 77. See also Max Weber, *Economy and Society: An Outline of Interpretive Sociology*, Guenther Roth and Claus Wittich eds. (Berkeley: University of California Press, 1978), 55: politics is public activity aimed at 'exerting influence on the government of a political organization; especially at the appropriation, redistribution or allocation of the powers of government'.

[2] See David Ames Curtis, 'Translator's foreword' to Jean-Marc Coicaud, *Legitimacy and Politics: A Contribution to the Study of Political Right and Political Responsibility* (Cambridge: Cambridge University Press, 2002), ix–xxvii, xiii: 'In French, the well-known feminine noun *la politique*, derived from the Greek via the Latin, translates as "politics" (or "policy"). *Le politique*, as a masculine noun of relatively recent origin . . . is usually rendered in English by the less familiar phrase "the political", which derives from the conservative Nazi-era jurist Carl Schmitt's usage (coinage?) of *das politische* in German. This unusual noun, *the political*, has been employed and reflected upon in various ways by a number of German-born twentieth-century authors, including Schmitt's former student Leo Strauss, and it has been associated with Martin Heidegger's anti-totalitarian student Hannah Arendt. Some anti-totalitarian French-language political thinkers, Cornelius Castoriadis and Claude Lefort, explicitly distinguish *politics* from *the political*, treating the former as historical in character and the latter as a basic attribute of any society'.

## THE CONCEPT OF THE POLITICAL

Locating the concept of the political as an autonomous activity has been closely associated with the work of Carl Schmitt. Schmitt suggested that the concept of the political must rest on its own distinctions. Just as 'in the realm of morality the final distinction is between good and evil, in aesthetics beautiful and ugly, in economics profitable and unprofitable', the question Schmitt asks is 'whether there is a special distinction which can serve as a simple criterion of the political'.[3] The answer he provides is that political action is founded on the distinction between friend and enemy.

Schmitt's provocative answer stems from a conviction that conflict is a primordial condition. It is this basic fact which gives rise to politics. But his position is liable to be misunderstood. He is not suggesting that the contest between opposing political factions within the state arises from the distinction between friend and enemy. Nor does he maintain that this distinction yields the substance of politics.[4] Schmitt here is not concerned with the practices of politics—what I will be calling the second order of the political—but with a first order phenomenon: the concept of the political itself.

Schmitt's contention is that at the core of the concept of the political lies 'the most intense and extreme antagonism', in other words, 'the ever present possibility of conflict' and even of 'armed combat'.[5] And it is the persistence of this threat 'which determines in a characteristic way human action and thinking and thereby creates a specifically political behaviour'.[6] Only through this most basic understanding, Schmitt contends, are we able to render meaningful that which otherwise must remain obscure and incoherent. His claim is that the political is an inescapable aspect of the human condition.[7]

By pursuing an understanding of the political to its very foundations, Schmitt seeks to reveal its essential character. That this continues to be a pressing question is illustrated by John Dunn's recent declaration to the effect that:

Here we all are, loose in history and dubiously at ease within ourselves and with each other. What are we going to do about it? This is certainly the political question: and an eminently practical and exceedingly insistent one too.[8]

---

[3] Carl Schmitt, *The Concept of the Political* [1932], George Schwab trans. (Chicago: University of Chicago Press, 1996), 26.

[4] This is the error that Agnes Heller appears to make in her assessment of Schmitt: see Agnes Heller, 'The Concept of the Political Revisited' in David Held (ed.), *Political Theory Today* (Cambridge: Polity Press, 1991), 330–343, 332–333.

[5] Schmitt, above n. 3, 29, 32. Cf. Heraclitus (535–475 BC): 'War is the father of all and king of all, and some he shows as gods, others as men; some he makes slaves, others free'. See G. S. Kirk, J. E. Raven, and M. Schofield, *The Presocratic Philosophers: A Critical History with a Selection of Texts* (Cambridge: Cambridge University Press, 2nd edn. 1983), 193 [frag. 53, Hippolytus, ix.9.4.].

[6] Schmitt, above n. 3, 34.

[7] Cf. Leo Strauss, 'Notes on Carl Schmitt, *The Concept of the Political*' in Schmitt, above n. 3, 81–107, 94: 'The political [for Schmitt] is a basic characteristic of human life; politics in this sense *is* destiny; therefore man cannot escape politics'.

[8] John Dunn, 'What is Living and What is Dead in the Political Theory of John Locke?' in his *Interpreting Political Responsibility* (Cambridge: Polity Press, 1990), 9–25, 21–22.

*The Concept of the Political* is a systematic attempt by Schmitt to isolate the essence of the phenomenon. But the work goes further. The book also offers an answer to the most critical question posed in classical political thought: how should I live? In *Euthyphro*, Plato asks about the nature of those disagreements that we cannot settle and which cause enmity. The answer offered in the dialogue is not so dissimilar to Schmitt's:

> I suggest you consider whether it would not be the just and the unjust, beautiful and ugly, good and evil. Are not these the things, when we disagree about them and cannot reach a satisfactory decision, concerning which we on occasion become enemies—you and I, and all other men?[9]

Moral values are certainly not irrelevant in politics. The point that Schmitt impresses upon us is that they are not authoritative. Although humans are norm-loving animals, they live in a world comprising a multiplicity of moral maps, and it is the inevitability of clashes between these that determines the political. There is, after all, scarcely a war that has been fought in which all of the combatants did not believe that they had right on their side. The political can thus 'derive its energy from the most varied human endeavours, from the religious, economic, moral and other antitheses'.[10] But whatever its cause, the 'political entity is by its very nature the decisive entity, regardless of the sources from which it derives its last psychic motives'.[11] The enemy according to Schmitt is not an evil person to be reviled: that would be too moralistic. Nor is he a criminal to be punished: that is too legalistic. The enemy is simply a foe to be defeated.[12]

Schmitt reinforces the essentially political nature of this 'enemy' by highlighting its public aspect. The enemy is 'not the private adversary whom one hates' but 'is solely the public enemy'; the enemy is *hostis*, not *inimicus*.[13] 'The enemy exists', he elaborates, 'only when, at least potentially, one fighting collectivity of people confronts a similar collectivity'.[14] Echoing Hobbes, whose work he much admired, Schmitt argues that it is this potential which underpins the political:

> The political does not reside in the battle itself, which possesses its own technical, psychological, and military laws, but in the mode of behaviour which is determined by this possibility, by

---

[9] Plato, *Euthypro*, 7c–d in *The Dialogues of Plato* [c.399–387 BC], R. E. Allen trans. (New Haven: Yale University Press, 1984), i.47. See also Plato, *The Laws* [c.335–323 BC], R. G. Bury trans. (London: Heinemann, 1926), Bk. 1, where Clinias explains why the original Cretan legislator had devised such a warlike polity: 'And herein . . . he condemned the stupidity of the mass of men in failing to perceive that all are involved ceaselessly in a lifelong war against all States . . . every State is, by a law of nature, engaged perpetually in an informal war with every other State'.
[10] Schmitt, above n. 3, 38.        [11] Ibid. 43–44.
[12] In this respect, Schmitt is following Weber: see Weber, 'Politics as a Vocation', above n. 1, 117–118.
[13] Schmitt, above n. 3, 28.
[14] Ibid. This distinction also has parallels in classical political thought. See, e.g., Cicero, *De Officiis* [c.43 BC], Cyrus R. Edmonds trans. (London: Bell & Daldy, 1865), iii.29: 'There are also rights of war, and the faith of an oath is often to be kept with an enemy . . . [But] if you should not pay a price for your life, agreed on with robbers, it is no fraud if you should not perform it, though bound by an oath. For a pirate is not comprehended in the number of lawful enemies, but is the common foe of all men'.

clearly evaluating the concrete situation and thereby being able to distinguish correctly the real friend and the real enemy.[15]

Schmitt's work is not without its ambiguities and difficulties.[16] But by focusing on what I have called the first order of the political, he impresses on us a message which anthropologists have also affirmed, namely that cultures are formed only once a group is able to define itself in contrast to some other which they are not.[17] Working with a friend/enemy—or inclusionary/exclusionary[18]—dynamic offers acute insights into the role of the state, the conduct of politics within a system of governance, and also— especially as Schmitt himself claimed that his studies were of a juristic nature[19]—into the idea of public law.

POLITICS AND THE STATE

Schmitt's work is less clear on the relationship between the state and the political. Since politics orders everything, he argues that it does not function within a particular domain; rather, it is an aspect of intensity of conflict. But because Schmitt also highlights the role of politics in managing conflict, he sometimes conveys the converse impression, implying that the essence of the political comes from the limitation rather than the intensification of conflict. So although he starts by asserting that the political must be defined apart from a definition of the state, there is, as Gopal

---

[15] Schmitt, above n. 3, 37. Cf. Thomas Hobbes, *Leviathan* [1651], Richard Tuck ed. (Cambridge: Cambridge University Press, 1996), ch. 13: 'the nature of War, consisteth not in actuall fighting; but in the known disposition thereto, during all the time there is no assurance to the contrary. All other time is Peace'.

[16] Schmitt's work has recently attracted a great deal of attention from Anglo-American scholars. For valuable critical appraisals see especially: Gopal Balakrishnan, *The Enemy: An Intellectual Portrait of Carl Schmitt* (London: Verso, 2000); David Dyzenhaus, *Legality and Legitimacy: Carl Schmitt, Hans Kelsen and Herman Heller in Weimar* (Oxford: Oxford University Press, 1997), ch. 2; David Dyzenhaus (ed.), *Law as Politics: Carl Schmitt's Critique of Liberalism* (Durham: Duke University Press, 1998); John P. McCormick, *Carl Schmitt's Critique of Liberalism: Against Politics as Technology* (Cambridge: Cambridge University Press, 1997); Chantal Mouffe (ed.), *The Challenge of Carl Schmitt* (London: Verso, 1999); William E. Scheuerman, *Carl Schmitt: The End of Law* (Lanham: Rowan & Littlefield, 1999).

[17] See Peter Wagner, *A Sociology of Modernity: Liberty and Discipline* (London: Routledge, 1994), 38. See further, Hayden White, *Tropics of Discourse: Essays in Cultural Criticism* (Baltimore: Johns Hopkins University Press, 1978), 151: 'The notion of savagery belongs to a set of culturally self-authenticating devices which includes, among many others, the ideas of "madness" and "heresy" . . . They . . . dictate a particular attitude governing a relationship between a lived reality and some area of problematical existence'.

[18] See William E. Connolly, *Identity/Difference: Democratic Negotiations of Political Paradox* (Ithaca, NY: Cornell University Press, 1991).

[19] Of *The Concept of the Political*, Schmitt later wrote that: 'The challenge that issues from the text itself is aimed primarily at experts on the constitution and jurists of international law'. See Carl Schmitt, *Der Begriff des Politischen. Text von 1932 mit einem Vorwort und drei Corollarien* (Berlin: Duncker & Humblot, 1963), Preface: cited in Heinrich Meier, *Carl Schmitt and Leo Strauss: The Hidden Dialogue*, J. Harvey Lomax trans. (Chicago: University of Chicago Press, 1995), 3. See also Carl Schmitt, *Political Theology: Four Chapters on the Concept of Sovereignty* [1922], George Schwab trans. (Cambridge, Mass: MIT Press, 1988), 29–31.

Balakrishnan has noted, a tendency surreptitiously to reintroduce the state, as a vehicle for conflict management, 'as the natural subject of political life'.[20] This ambiguity notwithstanding, Schmitt's objective in isolating the concept of the political yields a powerful insight into the question of what the intricate exercise of forming a state might involve.

From Schmitt's perspective, it is only through the establishment of the state that a group of people within a certain territory becomes 'a pacified unity encompassing the political'.[21] Once it becomes possible to define a group that can be differentiated from other political units, what emerges is a sense of 'national consciousness', by which is meant a minimal degree of cohesion and distinctiveness forged amongst a people.[22] With the recognition of a 'we' that can be set against the 'they' of the rest of mankind, the friend-enemy distinction is externalized. Michael Howard has observed how, from the very beginning, 'the principle of nationalism was almost indissolubly linked, both in theory and practice, with the idea of war'.[23] But it is also a consequence of this process that domestic antagonisms become capable of being managed effectively, therefore remaining below the level of intensity of friend *versus* enemy.

By acquiring a monopoly of coercive power, the state is able to impose peaceable order and forge some notion of the unity of a people. This perspective on state formation helps us to recognize the significance of the distinction (one which is often drawn in international relations) between external and internal conceptions of sovereignty.[24] It also signals the importance of the ideology of nationalism as a source of state-building energy.[25] Since the state can institutionalize domestic political antagonism at a lower level of intensity than that of friend *versus* enemy, one of its most basic achievements is that of being able to keep conflict inside a framework of order. For these conditions to be realized, the tensions that exist within the state must be actively managed. And once this positive role of the state is acknowledged, we can see the state as an artefact or, in Jacob Burckhardt's expression, as 'a work of art'.[26]

---

[20] Balakrishnan, above n. 16, 110. This ambivalence is also reflected in Schmitt's treatment of Hobbes who, in the first edition of *The Concept of the Political*, he described as 'by far the greatest and perhaps the sole truly systematic political thinker', a position from which he resiled in the light of Leo Strauss's observation (above n. 7, 89–93) that Hobbes's individualistic principles are constructed precisely for the purpose of negating, in Schmitt's sense, the political. See Meier, above n. 19, esp. 32–38.

[21] Ernst-Wolfgang Böckenförde, 'The Concept of the Political: A Key to Understanding Carl Schmitt's Constitutional Theory' in Dyzenhaus (ed.), above n. 16, 37–55, 39.

[22] See Karl W. Deutsch, *Nationalism and Social Communication: An Inquiry into the Foundations of Nationality* (Cambridge, Mass.: MIT Press, 2nd edn. 1966), 173.

[23] Michael Howard, 'Empires, Nations and Wars' in his *The Lessons of History* (Oxford: Clarendon Press, 1991), 21–48, 39.

[24] See, e.g., R. B. J. Walker, *Inside/Outside: International Relations as Political Theory* (Cambridge: Cambridge University Press, 1993).

[25] See Benedict Anderson, *Imagined Communities: Reflections on the Origin and Spread of Nationalism* (London: Verso, rev. edn. 1991). Gellner captures something of this spirit when he observes that states are 'groups which *will* themselves to persist as communities': Ernest Gellner, *Nations and Nationalism* (Oxford: Blackwell, 1983), 53.

[26] Jacob Burckhardt, *The Civilization of the Renaissance in Italy* (Oxford: Phaidon Press, 1945), Pt. I.

Within a stable political regime, such as that of the United Kingdom today, this achievement is in danger of being overlooked.[27] Nevertheless, 'today virtually everywhere in the world, groups of human beings need with the utmost urgency to decide whom to fear and whom to trust, whom to identify with and whom to identify against, with whom and against whom to seek to cooperate or to struggle, even, *in extremis*, whom to seek to kill'.[28] State formation is a complex process through which many of these fears and tensions are controlled, regulated, and manipulated. It is at this second-order level of the political, politics within a viable system of government, that the practices of politics emerge. Here, the political system operates through a range of second-order distinctions, such as those between governors and governed, or government and opposition.[29]

### POLITICS AS STATECRAFT

Schmitt believed that conflict was not only endemic but also existential: group life without conflict—society without politics—constituted a denial of the human condition which, if ever realized, would amount to a moral loss.[30] This is a view that Schmitt shared with Machiavelli. But whereas Schmitt concentrated on the existential character of the phenomenon, Machiavelli's aim had been to offer advice to rulers on the most effective way to govern. Furthermore, although both Schmitt and Machiavelli accepted the intrinsically political nature of society and embraced the political reality of conflict, important differences exist between them. The nature of these differences is revealing.

Although Schmitt explicated the concept of the political in a systematic manner, he had the unsound tendency to raise the inevitability of conflict into a foundational principle. Machiavelli, by contrast, wanted to demonstrate how, through the cultivation of sound political practice, enmities could not only be handled but positively harnessed. For Machiavelli, a sound politics required *virtù*, by which he meant courage, vigour, vitality, and strength of purpose. By acting with *virtù* and in accordance with the requirements of necessity, *fortuna*—the unpredictable or fortuitous—could be tamed and glory secured.[31] Machiavelli provided guidance on how to handle

---

[27] Nevertheless, the situation in Northern Ireland is instructive. Here, ever since its founding in 1920, and especially over the last 30 years, the integrative function of the state in forging a unity of the people has been placed in question. In this type of situation, the danger exists that the friend-enemy distinction does indeed become determinative of all significant issues within domestic politics.

[28] John Dunn, 'Specifying and Understanding Racism' in his *The History of Political Theory and Other Essays* (Cambridge: Cambridge University Press, 1996), 148–159, 151.

[29] See Niklas Luhmann, *Political Theory in the Welfare State*, John Bednarz trans. (Berlin: de Gruyter, 1990), esp. chs 3 and 5.

[30] This explains why Schmitt opposed the forces of technology which he believed to be threatening the political: see McCormick, above n. 16. We might also note Joseph Cropsey's comment that, in his attack on modern liberalism, Schmitt believed that liberalism was 'complicitous with communism in standing for the withering away of the political and replacing it with the technological—the reduction of humanity to the last man'. See Cropsey, 'Foreword' to Meier, above n. 19, x.

[31] Niccolò Machiavelli, *The Prince* [1513], Stephen J. Milner trans. (London: Dent, 1995), chs 25, 26.

this contest between freedom and necessity whereas Schmitt, having constructed a political reality based on conflict, appeared simply to celebrate this condition and to 'transform enmity and brokenness into metaphysical principles'.[32] As F. R. Ankersmit comments, this is 'as if marital quarrels were seen not as an unavoidable aspect of living together, but as its very basis'.[33] As an account of politics within a system of governance, Machiavelli's approach is to be preferred.

Machiavelli was the first writer to argue that politics, understood as a set of practices relating to the art of the state, rests on its own rules and principles. Emphasizing the point that politics is concerned with the pursuit of power, Machiavelli rejected the classical view that it is the art of maintaining 'the good community'. But in order to appreciate his argument, we should first consider how he derived this notion of the autonomy of the political from his views about human nature. For Machiavelli, the inner life of man (*animo*) is not a sphere of repose, harmony, or self-control, but one of continual motion. Man is ruled not by reason but by appetite and ambition, characteristics which lead to competition and conflict. This analysis of the human condition causes Machiavelli to take a novel approach to the issue of scarcity. For the ancients, the problem of scarcity in the world was resolved by self-discipline and education. But Machiavelli argues that 'since the scarcity of objects is the result of the nature of appetite and passion, and not the other way around, competition and conflict between men is natural and inevitable'.[34] Machiavelli's innovation was to suggest that man is a political animal precisely because people are required to engage with one another as a means to their own satisfaction. Because people strive not only to achieve material success but also to attain fame and glory—qualities which require public acknowledgement—politics must be a natural condition.

Although Machiavelli breaks with classical assumptions, his writing remains part of the republican tradition of treating politics as a set of practices that promote the common good.[35] Machiavelli employs the term 'politics' to denote those practices operating within a regime constrained by laws, and he contrasts such a regime with the unrestrained exercise of power, generally called tyranny.[36] Consequently, although Machiavelli displaces the rule of reason both within the individual and the collectivity, he does not suggest that politics can be reduced to the pursuit of appetite and desire. While there is no room in Machiavelli's world for an objective natural law that yields authoritative precepts of right conduct, this does not mean that politics is reducible to the pursuit of material self-interest.

---

[32] F. R. Ankersmit, *Aesthetic Politics: Political Philosophy Beyond Fact and Value* (Stanford: Stanford University Press, 1996), 127.

[33] Ibid.

[34] Martin Fleisher, 'A Passion for Politics: The Vital Core of the World of Machiavelli' in Fleisher (ed.), *Machiavelli and the Nature of Political Thought* (New York: Atheneum, 1972), 114–147, 130.

[35] See Maurizio Viroli, 'Machiavelli and the Republican Idea of Politics' in Gisela Bock, Quentin Skinner, and Maurizio Viroli (eds), *Machiavelli and Republicanism* (Cambridge: Cambridge University Press, 1990), 143–171.

[36] See Niccolò Machiavelli, *The Discourses* [1531], Leslie J. Walker trans., Bernard Crick ed. (Harmondsworth: Penguin, 193), i. 25 (contrasting a 'political regime' with 'despotism' or 'tyranny').

This last point is central to the understanding of politics as an autonomous sphere of activity. Machiavelli's work emphasizes the gulf between the private and public spheres, between what Hannah Arendt, echoing the classical division, called 'the sheltered life in the household' and 'the merciless exposure of the *polis*'.[37] Attending to the arrangements of the public sphere, Machiavelli argues, requires special skills that go beyond those of household management. It is for this reason that Arendt suggested that Machiavelli is the 'only postclassical political theorist who, in an extraordinary effort to restore its old dignity to politics, perceived the gulf and understood something of the courage needed to cross it'.[38]

Those that seek to rule for the common good, Machiavelli argued, have to act with vigour and courage. But they must also cultivate the virtue of prudence. Prudence in politics requires rulers to possess skills of practical reason, including those of being able to speak fluently, to act persuasively, and to deliberate wisely. In chapter 15 of *The Prince*, he lists eleven pairs of qualities that bring a ruler praise or blame: generosity or miserliness; beneficence or greed; mercy or cruelty; trustworthiness or faithlessness; strength or weakness; humanity or pride; chastity or lasciviousness; uprightness or guile; flexibility or severity; seriousness or light-heartedness; religiosity or scepticism. Although it would be laudable to find all the good qualities combined in a ruler, he recognizes that 'since it is not possible either to possess or wholly to observe them, because human nature does not allow it, it is necessary for him to be sufficiently prudent that he knows how to avoid the infamy of those vices that will deprive him of his state'.[39] But he also goes on to comment that the ruler 'should not worry about the infamy incurred by those vices which are indispensable in maintaining his state, because if he examines everything carefully, he will find that something which seems virtue [*virtù*] can, if put into practice, cause his ruin, while another thing which seems a vice can, when put into practice, result in his security and well-being'.[40]

Machiavelli here is forthrightly asserting the autonomy (and amorality) of the political. Within the sphere of politics, he suggests, there can be no power of reason superior to that of prudence. Since this idea of prudence is critical to our understanding of politics, we must be clear about its meaning. Martin Fleisher provides a useful explanation of Machiavelli's conception of prudence:

Prudence is not to be measured principally by the existing standards of right and wrong but by the assessment of the best means to achieve one's ends. Prudence is not synonymous with caution, nor is it the dominance of reason over the appetites and passions. It is, instead, the cool calculation of what must be done in a given situation to accomplish one's purposes without judgment of the situation being unduly affected by passions or the contemporary conventions and ideals of right and wrong.[41]

---

[37] Hannah Arendt, *The Human Condition* (Chicago: University of Chicago Press, 1958), 35. Cf. Aristotle, *The Politics* [c.335–323 BC], T. A. Sinclair trans., Trevor J. Saunders ed. (Harmondsworth: Penguin, 1981), i.2.
[38] Ibid.     [39] Machiavelli, *The Prince*, above n. 31, ch. 15.     [40] Ibid.
[41] Fleisher, above n. 34, 139–140.

Prudence is an ability to assess the situation and adopt the most appropriate course of action. It is to be distinguished from rule-governed action or from following the precepts of conventional morality. It must also be distinguished from following the dictates of appetite, since the function of prudence is properly to serve the appetites (such as ambition) through an ability dispassionately to assess the requirements of the situation.

It might be noted that missing from the qualities listed above is that of justice. Machiavelli believed that to govern well rulers must be able to cultivate a reputation for being good.[42] But he suggests that at base the measure of justice is prudence. Cities and empires that are ruled well increase in glory, reputation, and power. Such regimes will be law-governed. But the limits of laws should also be acknowledged and rulers might find it necessary, for the promotion of the common good, to break promises, to proceed deceptively, or act belligerently.[43]

In common with Schmitt, then, Machiavelli's conception of politics is built on the belief that there can be no single over-arching normative criterion for resolving existential conflicts.[44] His genius was to have recognized so early that there is no one true answer to the classical question: how should I live? Moral and political values are irreducibly plural and conflicts are inevitable: politics arises from the necessity of having to make choices between rival, sometimes incommensurable, goods in circumstances where there can be no authoritative principle or standard for resolving the dispute.[45]

This *agonal* conception of politics is not one that Schmitt shared. Heinrich Meier has convincingly argued that although he located politics in the necessity of action in the face of conflict, Schmitt ultimately answers the critical question—how should I live?—by appealing to a political theology built on the necessity of faith and the truth of divine revelation. Drawing on the authority of biblical teaching,[46] Schmitt affirms the centrality of original sin, believes that these existential questions cannot be solved by reason alone and places his faith in 'the certainty of the God who demands obedience, rules absolutely, and judges in accordance with his own law'.[47]

---

[42] Machiavelli, *The Prince*, above n. 31, ch. 18. In this chapter Machiavelli indicates that political power depends primarily on what the people believe. The distinction between appearance and reality is thus irrelevant to the pursuit of politics: appearances—what the people believe—is the reality of politics.

[43] See, e.g., Machiavelli, *The Discourses*, above n. 36, iii. 9: 'Piero Soderini [Florence's *Gonfaloniere a vita*, 1502–12] conducted all his affairs in his good-natured and patient way. So long as circumstances suited the way in which he carried on, both he and his country prospered. But when afterwards there came a time which required him to drop his patience and his humility, he could not bring himself to do it; so that both he and his country were ruined'. On Soderini see: Felix Gilbert, *Machiavelli and Gucciardini: Politics and History in Sixteenth Century Florence* (Princeton: Princeton University Press, 1965), ch. 2.

[44] See Isaiah Berlin, 'The Originality of Machiavelli' in his *Against the Current: Essays in the History of Ideas* (Oxford: Clarendon Press, 1989), 25–79.

[45] Following Machiavelli, Weber observes that one 'who seeks the salvation of the soul, of his own and of others, should not seek it along the avenue of politics, for the quite different tasks of politics can only be solved by violence': Weber, 'Politics as a Vocation', above n. 1, 126.

[46] Genesis 3:15: 'I will put enmity between thy seed and her seed'. In tracing matters back to the doctrine of original sin, Schmitt's thought displays similarities with the work of de Maistre: see Joseph de Maistre, 'The Saint Petersburg Dialogues' [c.1802–17] in Jack Lively (ed.), *The Works of Joseph de Maistre* (London: Allen & Unwin, 1965), 183–290, 196.

[47] Heinrich Meier, *The Lesson of Carl Schmitt: Four Chapters on the Distinction between Political Theology and Political Philosophy* (Chicago: University of Chicago Press, 1998), 11.

Schmitt's political theology is not content to leave matters of politics to deliberation and contest; he recognizes that the battle between faith and errant faith admits of no neutral and must be waged in favour of the truth of divine revelation. Schmitt's path is one that few can—and none should—follow.

The overriding significance of Schmitt's analysis of the concept of the political is that it helps us to appreciate the true originality of Machiavelli's thought. Although Schmitt explains how the political may have its source in enmity, the conduct of politics—what has been called the second order of the political—is not built on the celebration of conflict: it is generated by the need to ensure its effective management. Politics is, as Michael Oakeshott expresses it, often an 'unpleasing spectacle':

The obscurity, the muddle, the excess, the compromise, the indelible appearance of dishonesty, the counterfeit piety, the moralism and the immorality, the corruption, the intrigue, the negligence, the meddlesomeness, the vanity, the self-deception and finally the futility . . . offend most of our rational and all of our artistic susceptibilities.[48]

But in so far as it succeeds in 'modifying the reign of arbitrary violence in human affairs, there is clearly something to be said for it, and it may even be thought to be worth the cost'.[49]

Politics enables the activity of governing to be effectively conducted. Through the development of political practices, especially when harnessed to the forces of nationalism, bonds of allegiance are strengthened and a unity of a people is forged. And this forging of a sense of common identity, which may be based on ethnicity, culture, language, or common history, provides the key to explaining why the political antecedes the state. As Ulrich Preuss expresses it, 'the common feeling of a group's oneness is the determining state-building social energy'.[50] Politics is thus a significant achievement, the nature of which was eloquently voiced by Lord Balfour when he remarked of the British system that the 'whole political machinery pre-supposes a people so fundamentally at one that they can safely afford to bicker; and so sure of their moderation that they are not dangerously disturbed by the never-ending din of political conflict'.[51]

This is a conception of politics that has its roots in Machiavelli's realistic portrayal of the human condition. His starting point has been concisely summarized in these terms: 'God did not give us a perfect beginning, as the Bible says, and nature did not provide us with a potentiality for politics, as Aristotle says. We began bare,

---

[48] Michael Oakeshott, *The Politics of Faith and the Politics of Scepticism* [c.1952], Timothy Fuller ed. (New Haven: Yale University Press, 1996), 19.
[49] Ibid. 19–20.
[50] Ulrich K. Preuss, 'Political Order and Democracy: Carl Schmitt and His Influence' in Chantal Mouffe (ed.), above n. 16, 155–179, 157.
[51] Earl of Balfour, 'Introduction' to Walter Bagehot, *The English Constitution* (Oxford: Oxford University Press, 1928), v–xxvi, xxiv; cited in Schmitt, *Political Theology*, above n. 19, xxiii. See also Ernest Barker, 'The Discredited State: Thoughts on Politics before the War' (1915) 2 (o.s.) *Political Quarterly* 101–121, which emphasizes the vital condition of unstable equilibrium in state-society relations as being necessary for the continuation of progress.

unprotected, insecure, and justly fearful'.[52] Politics, according to Machiavelli, springs from what is necessary to ensure human survival and flourishing and it has evolved to ensure that conflict is constructively handled.[53]

But this does not mean that politics seeks the elimination of conflict. Machiavelli argued that, far from being a destructive condition, conflict and dissension are vital ingredients of cohesion. Reflecting on the Roman republic, he noted that 'those who condemn the quarrels between the nobles and the plebs, seem to be cavilling at the very things that were the primary cause of Rome's retaining her freedom'.[54] In every republic, he concludes, 'there are two different dispositions, that of the populace and that of the upper class and that all legislation favourable to liberty is brought about by the clash between them'.[55] Machiavelli here impresses on us two important messages: that politics is concerned with handling conflict, not its elimination, and that the source of liberty is not to be found in ideas or texts but in political struggle.

### THE THIRD ORDER: CONSTITUTIONAL LAW

Although conflict remains an important element of politics, the cultivation of a sense of even-handedness constitutes a vital aspect of the project of state-building. For conflict to be positively harnessed, a less partisan framework of rule needs to be devised. This brings us directly to the question of constitutional law. Many of the ideals associated with law, especially those of the rule of law and the assimilation of law to justice, help to create intimacy, shape identity, generate trust, and strengthen allegiance. Institutions of government that aspire to operate at one remove from direct manipulation by power-wielders remove certain disputes from partisan political processes and this too bolsters faith in the system. Belief in the law-governed nature of the state can be a means of generating political power and a powerful aspect of state-building. But does this mean that law transcends the political?

We should begin by treating constitutional law as a third order of the political. The establishment of a legal system that operates in accordance with its own conceptual logic while remaining free from gross manipulation by power-wielders is an achievement of considerable importance. But whenever this modern idea of the rule of law is invoked, the predominant image is that of a legal system that serves the purpose of adjudicating between citizens[56] or ensures that rigorous procedures governing the

---

[52] Harvey C. Mansfield, *Machiavelli's Virtue* (Chicago: University of Chicago Press, 1996), 55.
[53] Cf. Michael Oakeshott, *Rationalism in Politics and Other Essays* (London: Methuen, 1962), 127: 'In political activity, then, men sail a boundless and bottomless sea; there is neither harbour for shelter nor floor for anchorage, neither starting place nor appointed destination. The enterprise is to keep afloat on an even keel; the sea is both friend and enemy; and the seamanship consists in using the resources of a traditional manner of behaviour in order to make a friend of every hostile occasion'.
[54] Machiavelli, *The Discourses*, above n. 36, i.4.     [55] Ibid.
[56] See Ernest J. Weinrib, 'The Intelligibility of the Rule of Law' in Allan C. Hutchinson and Patrick Monahan (eds), *The Rule of Law: Ideal or Ideology?* (Toronto: Carswell, 1987), 59–84, 62: 'I wish to argue that in private law the non-instrumental aspect of law shines forth with particular brilliance, so that through reflection on private law we can grasp the Rule of Law as a coherent conceptual possibility'.

imposition of criminal penalties are maintained.[57] This image derives primarily from Montesquieu who, in Judith Shklar's words, advocated the establishment of 'a properly equilibrated political system in which power was checked by power in such a way that neither the violent urges of kings, nor the arbitrariness of legislatures could impinge directly upon the individual in such a way as to frighten her and make her feel insecure in her daily life'.[58]

In a legal system that exists for the purpose of handling civil claims between citizens or for enforcing the norms of criminal conduct, it can be assumed that judges perform the important but mundane task of resolving disputes in accordance with the rule system that has been laid down.[59] Concerning matters of constitutional law, however, things are much more complicated. Here law presents itself not as the expression of the sovereign authority of the state, but as a means by which the sovereign authority of the state can be recognized.[60] The image of law as command must, in this context, be jettisoned: law now presents itself as a species of 'political right'.[61]

I do not propose to elaborate here on the idea of political right.[62] In this context, law is best understood as a set of practices embedded within, and acquiring its identity from, a wider body of political practices. Whilst it is possible to formulate constitutional law as a discrete set of rules (that is, as positive law),[63] the meaning, function and mode of application of such rules is in reality governed by the practices of politics.[64] This is not meant in the trite sense that constitutional law is rooted in the political because it regulates political institutions, processes, and decisions. Following Machiavelli and (to a lesser extent) Schmitt,[65] the claim is founded on three convictions. The first is that of the autonomy of the political. The second is the promotion

---

[57] See Douglas Hay, 'Property, Authority and the Criminal Law' in Hay *et al* (eds), *Albion's Fatal Tree* (Harmondsworth: Penguin, 1975), 17–63; E. P. Thompson, *Whigs and Hunters: The Origin of the Black Act* (Harmondsworth: Penguin, 1975), 258–269.

[58] Judith Shklar, 'Political Theory and the Rule of Law' in Hutchinson and Monahan (eds), above n. 56, 1–16, 4.

[59] See, however, Martin Loughlin, *Sword and Scales: An Examination of the Relationship between Law and Politics* (Oxford: Hart, 2000), ch. 6.

[60] Cf. Justinian, *Digest* [534], Alan Watson trans. (Philadelphia: University of Pennsylvania Press, 1998), i.1.1: '*Publicum ius est quod ad statum rei Romanae spectat*' ('Public law is that which pertains to the constitution of the Roman state') (Ulpian).

[61] Our attempts to analyse this conception of law, it might be noted, are handicapped by the fact that, while other European languages are able to draw a distinction between *jus*, *droit*, *diritto*, and *Recht* on the one hand, and *lex*, *loi*, *legge*, and *Gesetz* on the other, there exists no corresponding differentiation in English of the word 'law'.

[62] See below, Ch. 8, 134–148. For a values-based analysis of political right/ *droit politique* as 'the right to govern', see Coicaud, above n. 2.

[63] In the British context, this was Dicey's outstanding achievement: A. V. Dicey, *Introduction to the Study of the Law of the Constitution* (London: Macmillan, 8th edn. 1915), esp. ch. 1.

[64] This has been the major failure of Dicey and his followers. See, e.g., Dicey, ibid. 199: 'the principles of private law have ... been by the action of the Courts and Parliament so extended as to determine the position of the Crown and its servants'.

[65] Cf. Robert Howse, 'From Legitimacy to Dictatorship—and Back Again: Leo Strauss's Critique of the Anti-Liberalism of Carl Schmitt' in David Dyzenhaus (ed.), above n. 16, 56–91, 69: 'Schmitt puts Machiavelli's teaching in the form of legal scholarship, which at times appears to be a learned internal critique of an "autonomous discipline", i.e., juridical science'.

of a conception of constitutional law as law that is not handed down from above but which exists as part of the self-regulatory processes of an autonomous political realm, and which may therefore be conceptualized as principles or maxims of political prudence. And the third is the precept that the political cannot be subsumed into the rule-based logic of legal decision-making since the primacy of the political is a precondition of human well-being.

Since many contemporary misunderstandings flow from the mischaracterization of constitutions, it may be helpful to assess conventional approaches to modern constitutional arrangements in the light of this understanding.

CONSTITUTIONS

The term 'constitution' is itself a source of ambiguity. Its most consistent usage in ancient times was as an expression of formally declared legislation.[66] However, *constitutio* was also used as a translation of the Greek *politeia*, and therefore stood as a descriptive term for the entire body politic.[67] This latter formulation of the idea of constitution as an expression of the laws, institutions, and practices which make up a tradition of governing has been of particular influence in English thought. It is in this sense that we might refer to Britain's distinctive political constitution. This formulation helps us to identify the constitution as 'an entailed inheritance'[68] and to recognize the intrinsically political character of the governing relationship.

Positive laws are vital ingredients of a political constitution: they regulate many of the basic rules of political conduct and, because they are interpreted by a judiciary insulated from direct political influence, they provide a source of stability in governing arrangements. This latter aspect is of particular importance because a belief in the law-bounded nature of the system helps maintain the system's legitimacy, and hence also its capacity. But all constitutions invariably leave space for what might be called extra-legal governmental action. The constitution here reflects a basic law of political necessity: the necessity of rulers being able to take action to ensure that conflict and dissension is handled effectively.

---

[66] Justinian, *Institutes* [534], Peter Birks and Grant McLeod trans. (London: Duckworth, 1987), i.2.6: 'whatever the emperor has determined (*constituit*) by rescript or decided as a judge or directed by edict is established to be law: it is these that are called constitutions'. That this formulation influenced the work of English jurists is evident in the work of Sir John Fortescue, *De Laudibus Legum Anglie* [1468–71], S. B. Chrimes trans. (Cambridge: Cambridge University Press, 1942), 36–37: 'But customs and the rules of the law of nature, after they have been reduced to writing, and promulgated by the sufficient authority of the prince, and commanded to be kept, are changed into a constitution or something of the nature of statutes'.

[67] See Graham Maddox, 'Constitution' in Terence Ball, James Farr, and Russell L. Hanson (eds), *Political Innovation and Conceptual Change* (Cambridge: Cambridge University Press, 1989), 50–57, 50–55; Howell A. Lloyd, 'Constitutionalism' in J. H. Burns (ed.), *The Cambridge History of Political Thought* (Cambridge: Cambridge University Press, 1991), 254–297, 254–255.

[68] Edmund Burke, *Reflections on the Revolution in France* [1790], Conor Cruise O'Brien ed. (London: Penguin, 1986), 119.

The form, breadth, and conditional nature of this extra-legal governmental power have varied throughout history. An early version of this power can be seen in the ancient Roman practices of constitutional dictatorship.[69] It appears in medieval literature in the form of the doctrine of necessity.[70] A more regularized variation appears in the distinction between *gubernaculum*, the inherent power of the king to govern his realm, and *jurisdictio*, a sphere of right in which the king is bound by the law.[71] And many of the English constitutional disputes of the seventeenth century were concerned with the boundaries between the 'absolute' and 'ordinary' prerogatives of the crown.[72] Since the seventeenth century, however, constitutional thought has been underpinned by the necessity of ensuring the accountability of governors to the people. One outcome of this development has been a tendency to formulate the concept of sovereign authority by reference to some institution that has the final word over the course of action that promotes the *salus populi*.

---

[69] See Clinton L. Rossiter, *Constitutional Dictatorship: Crisis Government in the Modern Democracies* (Princeton, NJ: Princeton University Press, 1948), ch. 2. We might note Machiavelli's assessment (*The Discourses*, i.34) of the Roman practice: 'It is clear that the dictatorship, so long as it was bestowed in accordance with public institutions, and not assumed by the dictator on his own authority, was always of benefit to the state'.

[70] See, e.g., F. M. Powicke, 'Reflections on the Medieval State' in his *Ways of Medieval Life and Thought: Essays and Addresses* (London: Odhams Press, 1949), 130–148, 135–136: '[T]he lords and knights about Philip the Fair were familiar with a conception of *utilitas* which carries us very far in the theory of statecraft. They could express or at least appreciate the expression of public utility in terms of *necessitas*, and by necessity they meant more than the public need. They meant the right and duty of the king and his agents ... to override positive law in the common interests for which they were responsible. The word "necessity" had had a long history in ecclesiastical literature. Pope Gregory VII [in the eleventh century] had asserted that the pope in case of necessity could make new laws. A century later we find, applied to policy, the phrase "necessity knows no law".... St. Thomas Aquinas developed a theory of necessity. He argued that, in certain circumstances, necessity knows no law; also that a tyrant can be removed on the ground of necessity ... The legists of Philip the Fair gave a more positive direction to the argument. Necessity, in their mind, was more than a sanction of self-protection; it was a call to assert the power of the king, over and above the limits set by custom and tradition, in the interests of his kingdom and of the Christian community of which his kingdom was a responsible part'.

[71] See Charles Howard McIlwain, *Constitutionalism: Ancient and Modern* (Ithaca, NY: Cornell University Press, rev. edn. 1947), ch. 4; S. B. Chrimes, *English Constitutional Ideas in the Fifteenth Century* (Cambridge: Cambridge University Press, 1936), 40–62; Francis D. Wormuth, *The Royal Prerogative 1603–1649: A Study in English Political and Constitutional Ideas* (Ithaca, NY: Cornell University Press, 1939), 55–60.

[72] See *Bate's Case* (1606) *State Trials*, II, 389 *per* Fleming C.B.: 'The Kings power is double, ordinary and absolute, and they have several laws and ends. That of the ordinary is for the profit of particular subjects, for the execution of civil justice, the determining of meum; and this is exercised by equitie and justice in ordinary courts, and by the civilians is nominated *jus privatum* and with us common law: and these laws cannot be changed, without parliament ... The absolute power of the King is not that which is converted or executed to private use, to the benefit of any particular person, but is only that which is applied to the general benefit of the people and is *salus populi*; as the people is the body, and the King the head; and this power is guided by the rules, which direct only at the common law, and is most properly named Pollicy and Government; and as the constitution of this body varieth with the time, so varieth this absolute law, according to the wisdom of the King, for the common good'. See Francis Oakley, 'Jacobean Political Theology: The Absolute and Ordinary Powers of the King' (1968) *Journal of the History of Ideas* 323–346. The Bill of Rights 1689, art. 1 abolished this absolute prerogative: 'The pretended power of suspending of laws, or the execution of laws by regal authority, without the consent of parliament, is illegal'.

The British solution—that sovereignty rests in the crown in parliament—is sufficiently abstract and general to provide a plausible response whilst fudging a variety of practical political questions, including that of the nature of any governmental power beyond law. Such ambiguities are challenged by Schmitt's provocative opening words to *Political Theology*: 'Sovereign is he who decides on the exception'.[73] The essence of his argument is that: 'The rule proves nothing; the exception proves everything: It confirms not only the rule but also its existence, which derives only from the exception'.[74] Once again, Schmitt pushes an astute insight to its extreme, thereby overstating its force. So although he seems correct both in his contention that the exception cannot be banished from the world and also in the observation that the exceptional situation has juristic significance,[75] he goes too far in asserting that the exceptional reveals the essence of the concept of sovereignty.

In modern constitutional thought, this question of the exception has been obscured by the precepts of constitutionalism.[76] Constitutionalism rests on the principle that constituent power resides in the people, who delegate a limited authority to government to promote the public good. Governors are presented as servants of the people, who are required to account for the powers entrusted to them. Governments, in Locke's words, are vested with 'only a fiduciary power to act for certain ends'.[77] From here it requires but a short step to embrace the idea of an original compact, the belief that the workings of the state are driven by the principle of self-government, and the acceptance of the claim that governmental action is based on enumerated powers. These beliefs acquired great impetus from the American and French revolutions, which not only introduced a radical shift in ideas about the source of governmental authority, but also led to a relatively novel understanding of the term 'constitution'. This was concisely expressed by Thomas Paine, when he argued that a constitution 'is a thing *antecedent* to a government' and that 'a government is only the creature of a constitution'.[78]

The constitution here assumes the form of a document that receives its authorization from the people. This constitution establishes and delimits the powers of government, lays down the principles of political engagement, and determines the relationship between the citizen and the state. By defining the rules of political conduct, the document becomes a powerful instrument for controlling the practices of politics and providing a measure of stability to what otherwise might be a volatile

---

[73] Schmitt, *Political Theology*, above n. 19, 5.

[74] Ibid. 15. Schmitt's continuing interest in this question is indicated by the fact that he also published a work specifically on the history of commissarial dictatorship: Schmitt, *Die Diktatur* (Leipzig: Duncker & Humblot, 1921). For analysis, see Balakrishnan, above n. 16, ch. 2.

[75] Schmitt, above n. 19, 7, 13.

[76] On this matter, Schmitt seems essentially correct: 'All tendencies of modern constitutional development point toward eliminating the sovereign in this sense' (*Political Theology*, above n. 19, 7). But see Rossiter, above n. 69.

[77] John Locke, *Two Treatises of Government* [1680], Peter Laslett ed. (Cambridge: Cambridge University Press, 1988), ii. § 149.

[78] Thomas Paine, *Rights of Man* [1791–92] in his *Rights of Man, Common Sense and Other Writings*, Mark Philp ed. (Oxford: Oxford University Press, 1995), 122.

contest. Provided this type of constitutional document is recognized to be the product of a political bargain—an attempt to devise a framework for the principal forms and working arrangements of the political constitution—it can be a useful aid to the activity of statecraft. But once 'the constitution' is assumed to establish the foundation for all political engagement and is viewed as a legal text to be interpreted and enforced by lawyers, we enter a new phase. Once the modern constitutional text is treated as positive law, the idea of the constitution undergoes an important shift.

CONSTITUTIONAL LEGALISM

A constitution has traditionally been seen as a set of institutions and practices that give identity to a political regime. In accordance with this political sense of a constitution, only some—not necessarily the most important—of these arrangements are reflected in positive law. The modern constitution, by contrast, presents itself as a body of 'fundamental law'. And when the precepts of this fundamental law are enforced by the judiciary,[79] positive law is treated as laying the foundations of political order.

This type of constitutional legalism obfuscates the issue of governmental authority. Operating on the fictions of original grant, self-government, and enumerated powers, constitutional legalism radically suppresses the issue of rulership. As a representative institution deriving its power from the people and encompassing law-making power, the authority of the legislature is readily acknowledged. As faithful servants of the legislature (and the people), charged with the responsibility of ensuring the will of the people is given precise effect, the status of the judiciary is assured. But the office of government occupies an ambivalent position. In effect, 'government' is replaced with the notion of 'the executive'. But the question remains: executive of what? Modern constitutions invariably present the executive as an agent. But the fact that everywhere and without exception this 'executive' exercises a greater power than any reading of constitutional texts would suggest presents a conundrum. Constitutional legalists see this phenomenon as an abuse that must be curtailed by a more assertive use of law to curb executive action. But is it possible that their analyses are mistaken? Rather than using the document to draw conclusions about the activity, should we not start with the character of the activity and then derive conclusions about the nature and function of the document?

If constitutionalist reasoning is rooted in error, what is its source? We gain some insight by returning to those early modern political theorists whose work helped to shape constitutionalism. Hobbes had little to contribute on this subject. By focusing on the power-conferring moment, that moment when sovereign power is brought

[79] The breakthrough with respect to the American constitution is achieved in *Marbury* v. *Madison* 1 Cranch 137 (1803). See Rogers Smith, *Liberalism and American Constitutional Law* (Cambridge, Mass.: Harvard University Press, 1985); Robert Lowry Clinton, Marbury v. Madison *and Judicial Review* (Lawrence, Kansas: University Press of Kansas, 1989).

into existence through the voluntary action of rights-bearing individuals, he radically modernized our understanding of government. But he had little to say about the forms through which governmental power is exercised. Hobbes in effect simplified political power by reducing it almost entirely to the legislative form—the power of command. For analysis of the constitutional forms of rule, we must turn to Locke and Montesquieu. And with regard to their work, we might note that although Locke and Montesquieu are rightly regarded as founders of the modern liberal doctrines of the separation of powers and the rule of law, both recognized the pivotal role of governmental power.

Locke was probably the first modern theorist to take seriously the issue of executive power. Recognizing three functions of government, the legislative, the executive, and the federative,[80] he argued that, since there are many things that the law cannot provide for, 'the good of Society requires, that several things should be left to the discretion of him, that has the Executive Power'.[81] Executive power is not simply the power of putting law into effect; it includes the 'Power to act according to discretion, for the publick good, without the prescription of the Law, and sometimes even against it'.[82] Locke recognized that governmental power could not be reduced to law and that, of necessity, constitutions must allow for extra-legal governmental action. This is essentially a sphere of prudential action. In Pasquale Pasquino's interpretation of Locke on this subject, 'the branch that exercises the executive function is not reducible to a machine that applies the law; it is endowed with its own will and responsibility that permit it to face the unpredictable'.[83] Locke's achievement is to have brought the dictatorial power to act *extra et contra legem* that Machiavelli regarded as being an essential safeguard for the state into the general framework of the constitution.

Although credited with having devised the doctrine of the separation of powers, Montesquieu also gave due recognition to the importance of executive power. The

---

[80] The federative power (derived from *foedus*, the Latin term for treaty) is that power to deal with foreign affairs, and is accepted by Locke as being 'much less capable to be directed by antecedent, standing, positive Laws, than the Executive': Locke, above n. 77, ii. § 147. Notwithstanding the differences in function, Locke recognized that the federative power was invariably vested in the executive (ibid. § 148). Vile's commentary on the federative power is significant: 'The importance of what Locke has to say here has generally been overlooked, and the failure, particularly on the part of Montesquieu, to take up this point, has contributed greatly to the inadequacy of the classification of government functions. Locke was writing at a time when the supremacy of legislature over the policy of the government *in internal affairs* was being established. The king must rule according to law. But Locke realized . . . that the control of internal affairs, particularly taxation, presented very different problems from those of external affairs. In matters of war, and of treaties with foreign powers, it was not possible, and still is not possible today, to subject the government to the sort of prior control that is possible in domestic matters': M. J. C. Vile, *Constitutionalism and the Separation of Powers* (Indianapolis: Liberty Fund, 2nd edn. 1998), 66. The distinction between ordinary and absolute prerogative has thus, in part, been converted into a distinction between internal and external functions. This issue remains a major source of tension with respect to the continued existence of a sphere of unfettered discretionary power that governments possess to deal with emergencies: see, e.g., Jules Lobel, 'Emergency Power and the Decline of Liberalism' (1989) 98 *Yale Law Journal* 1385–1433.

[81] Locke, above n. 77, ii. § 159.   [82] Ibid. § 160.

[83] Pasquale Pasquino, 'Locke on King's Prerogative' (1998) 26 *Political Theory* 198–208, 202.

great value of the executive, he believed, was that it always is focused on 'immediate things', that is, on matters of political necessity. But he went further and suggested that if the executive power 'does not have the rights to check the enterprises of the legislative body, the latter will be despotic'.[84] Placing a modern gloss on Montesquieu's views, Harvey Mansfield has noted that executive power, 'expanding when needed, kept the rule of law from being, in effect, the rule of ambitious legislators and contrary judges'.[85] Its beauty is that it 'can reach where law cannot, and thus supply the defect of law, yet remain subordinate to law'.[86] By recognizing the need to maintain a balance between the legal and the non-legal, between rules and prudence, Montesquieu 'shows how liberty *emerges* in a whole which mixes the law with what we would call its conditioning factors in a series of "relations"'.[87]

The error, it would appear, lies not in the work of these political philosophers of liberalism. Instead, it is to be found in the modern culture of legalism. Within the framework of constitutional legalism it has proved increasingly difficult openly to acknowledge the real political function of the executive power. In Locke's thought, legislative and executive powers remained in tension, with any conflict having to be addressed politically, and ultimately being resolved through the people's residual right of rebellion.[88] Although advocating a more formal separation of powers, Montesquieu also recognized the political character of the exercise, believing that, provided each of these roles is properly acknowledged, the three branches of government 'are constrained to move by the necessary motion of things'.[89] With the growth of constitutional legalism, however, came the belief that solutions to these political questions can be found in or through the text. Consequently, whenever—as has been the case in all modern states—the executive has acted to fill those spaces which exist within constitutional documents,[90] this has been the occasion for disapprobation.

The error of constitutional legalism is of a most basic kind, that of mistaking a part for the whole. It fails to acknowledge the provisional character of constitutional arrangements and that 'the development and acceptance of a constitutional framework can occur only as the contingent result of irresolvable conflict'.[91] This must be the case, since the object of regulation—the activity of governing—is interminable. The arrangements of governing are in a permanent state of disequilibrium, since 'the system has never been designed as a whole, and such coherence as it possesses is the product of constant readjustment of its parts to one another'.[92] What Oakeshott calls 'the system of superficial order' is, of course, always 'capable of being made more

---

[84] Montesquieu, *The Spirit of the Laws* [1748], Anne M. Cohler, Basia Carolyn Miller, and Harold Samuel Stone trans. and eds (Cambridge: Cambridge University Press, 1989), xi.6.
[85] Harvey C. Mansfield, Jr., *Taming the Prince: The Ambivalence of Modern Executive Power* (Baltimore: Johns Hopkins University Press, 1993), xx.
[86] Ibid. [87] Ibid. 221.
[88] Locke, above n. 77, ii.19. [89] Montesquieu, above n. 84, xi.6.
[90] See, e.g., Richard M. Pious, *The American Presidency* (New York: Basic Books, 1979), 333: 'The president claims the silences of the Constitution'.
[91] Stephen Holmes, *Passions and Constraint: On the Theory of Liberal Democracy* (Chicago: University of Chicago Press, 1995), 217.
[92] Oakeshott, above n. 48, 34–35.

coherent'.⁹³ While this can often be a useful and positive exercise, 'the barbarism of order appears when order is pursued for its own sake and when the preservation of order involves the destruction of that without which order is only the orderliness of the ant-heap or the graveyard'.⁹⁴

Modern constitutions, especially when colonized by lawyers, are prone to this type of orderliness, presumably because one of the basic legal myths is that an answer to any issue can be found in the body of the law.⁹⁵ What we often fail to appreciate, especially when theorizing about constitutions, is that, despite their textuality,⁹⁶ constitutions are replete with gaps, silences, and abeyances. More importantly, such silences are not just the result of an oversight. They may not even be the product of a truce between opposing defined positions. Abeyances, as Michael Foley notes, are 'a set of implicit agreements to collude in keeping fundamental questions of political authority in a state of irresolution'.⁹⁷ Far from being susceptible to orderly compromise, these silences and abeyances 'can only be assimilated by an intuitive social acquiescence in the incompleteness of a constitution'.⁹⁸ Being important aspects of the exercise of managing political conflict, obscurities are functional.⁹⁹ Constitutions—and constitutional laws—are as much instruments in the on-going business of state-building as they are constraints on the practices of government.

This argument that constitutions should be viewed as instruments of state-building rests on an appreciation of the complex nature of political power. Political power is not the same as force. It is generated through authority, that is, through the acceptance by the people of the legitimacy of a governing regime.¹⁰⁰ By placing

---

⁹³ Oakeshott, above n. 48, 35.   ⁹⁴ Ibid.

⁹⁵ The most prominent contemporary advocate is Ronald Dworkin: see his *Taking Rights Seriously* (Cambridge, Mass.: Harvard University Press, 1977).

⁹⁶ See Wayne Franklin, 'The US Constitution and the Textuality of American Culture' in Vivian Hart and Shannon C. Stimson (eds), *Writing a National Identity: Political, Economic, and Cultural Perspectives on the Written Constitution* (Manchester: Manchester University Press, 1993), 9–20; Steven D. Smith, *The Constitution and the Pride of Reason* (New York: Oxford University Press, 1998).

⁹⁷ Michael Foley, *The Silence of Constitutions: Gaps, 'Abeyances' and Political Temperament in the Maintenance of Government* (London: Routledge, 1989), xi.

⁹⁸ Ibid. 10.

⁹⁹ See, e.g., Albert V. Dicey and Robert S. Rait, *Thoughts on the Union between England and Scotland* (London: Macmillan, 1920), 191–193. Here the authors analyse Art. 19 of the Treaty of Union of 1707, which seemed to protect the integrity of Scots law by refusing any jurisdictional claim of the English courts. But the position of the House of Lords was left unmentioned. Dicey and Rait comment: 'Did the Commissioners, one asks, intentionally leave a difficult question [the possibility of an appeal from the Court of Session to the House of Lords] open and undecided? The most obvious and possibly the truest reply is that such was their intention, and that prudence suggested the wisdom of leaving to the decision of future events the answer to a dangerous inquiry which after all might not arise for years. There must have seemed much good sense in leaving a curious point of constitutional law practically unsettled until by the lapse of twenty years or more every one should have become accustomed to the workings of the Act of Union'. This type of analysis could equally be applied to the Anglo-Irish Agreement (Cmnd. 9657, 1985) and the Belfast Agreement (Cm. 4292, 1999) with respect to governmental arrangements affecting Northern Ireland.

¹⁰⁰ For a sophisticated treatment see Coicaud, above n. 2. On the idea of legitimacy as a product of belief see David Beetham, *The Legitimation of Power* (London: Macmillan, 1991); Rodney Barker, *Political Legitimacy and the State* (Oxford: Clarendon Press, 1990); Rodney Barker, *Legitimating Identities: The Self-Preservation of Rulers and Subjects* (Cambridge: Cambridge University Press, 2001).

limitations on the exercise of governmental authority, it is possible to generate more political power—constraints can be enabling.[101] Consequently, although formal authority rests in the institutions of government, the extent of that authority is in reality a product of the character of the political relationship that exists between that institutional structure and the people. In this sense, the political order—the sense of political unity of a people—must precede the constitutional order understood as text. The political provides the foundation for the constitutional.[102]

It is the primacy of the political that dictates the ambiguous and provisional character of constitutional texts. By virtue of its character, the text can never grasp all the precepts underpinning the practices of politics. But even if it could, the tensions between political practices and more basic conflicts—that is, between the first and second order conceptions of the political that gives politics much of its dynamic quality—retain the potential to destabilize that accommodation.[103] Although this was well understood by early modern theorists, it seems today in danger of being submerged beneath the rhetoric of constitutional legalism. Ronald Dworkin, one of the principal exponents of this position, occasionally seems to recognize the sensitive political character of constitutional reasoning. But more commonly, the political aspects are suppressed. 'Some issues from the battleground of power politics', he argues, are called 'to the forum of principle' and in this special constitutional arena such 'conflicts' are converted into 'questions of justice'.[104] But the process of conversion from political to legal remains mysterious, and his call for 'a fusion of constitutional law and moral theory'[105] suggests that ultimately he seeks to circumvent politics by appealing to the transcendental character of law. Whilst adherence to law

---

[101] This is the theme that Elster has recently been exploring as an aspect of what he calls 'constraint theory': see Jon Elster, *Ulysses Unbound: Studies in Rationality, Precommitment, and Constraints* (Cambridge: Cambridge University Press, 2000).

[102] Cf. Carl Schmitt, *Verfassungslehre* (Munich: Duncker & Humblot, 1928), ch. 8; for French translation see Carl Schmitt, *Théorie de la Constitution*, Lilyane Deroche trans. (Paris: Presses Universitaires de France, 1993). In relation to Schmitt's argument that the political is the pre-constitutional foundation of the constitution, Preuss (above n. 50, 157–158) notes: 'This has a far-reaching consequence—probably one which, next to the notorious friend-enemy theory of the political, has instigated the most fervent resistance, at least among constitutional lawyers: the consequence that the integrity of the political order can—and sometimes even must—be sustained against the constitution, through the breach of the constitution, because the essence of the political order is not the constitution but the undamaged oneness of the people'. On occasions, Schmitt's argument seems to rely on an unresolved ambiguity between the ancient and modern usages of the term 'constitution'. But, again, where he errs is in presenting an essentialist—that is, an ethnic rather than a civic—interpretation of the idea of the unity of a people.

[103] It is for this reason that the attempt by John Rawls to resile from his earlier foundationalism—see his *A Theory of Justice* (Oxford: Oxford University Press, 1972)—and rely on an 'overlapping consensus'— 'a consensus that includes all the opposing philosophical and religious doctrines likely to persist and gain adherents in a more or less just constitutional democratic society'—fails adequately to reorientate the idea of 'justice as fairness' as one that emerges within a political tradition: see Rawls, 'Justice as Fairness: Political not Metaphysical' (1985) 14 *Philosophy and Public Affairs* 223–251, 225–226.

[104] Ronald Dworkin, 'The Forum of Principle' in his *A Matter of Principle* (Cambridge, Mass.: Harvard University Press, 1985), 33–71, 71.

[105] Ronald Dworkin, 'Constitutional Cases' in his *Taking Rights Seriously* (Cambridge, Mass.: Harvard University Press, 1977), 131–149, 149.

is vital, this must be treated as being a prudential necessity rather than some transcendental requirement.

CONCLUSION

Attempts to define politics are invariably hazardous. But the exercise cannot be avoided here since my argument about the distinctive nature of public law is founded on the autonomy of the political realm. An inquiry into the engagement of politics must therefore form a central part of the exercise. In this chapter, I have sketched three orders of the political. I do not claim this to be a comprehensive framework that defines the structure and essence of politics; it is offered simply as a heuristic device to highlight some of its key features.

What I have tried to show is that politics is rooted in human conflict arising from the struggle to realize our varying ideals of the good life. Conflict may lie at the root of the political—the first order—but this is not the end of the matter. The second order, politics as a set of practices within a state, is as much concerned with devising forms of co-operation as with conflict over them. In this role, the great value of politics lies in its deployment of a range of techniques enabling us to handle these conflicts and enmities constructively.[106] And if the first order of the political conjures an image of struggle for security or for material gain, the second order is played out primarily in terms of opinion and belief.[107]

I have tried to show that we might best understand the way in which law establishes the governing framework of a state as a continuation of the political engagement. Since the appeal to impartiality holds a great imaginative sway over us, the aspiration to establish a law-governed state is an especially powerful state-building technique. The benefits of 'the rule of law' should never be underestimated, but we must not forget that the claim can also be manipulated for political purposes. The heterogeneity of human purposes and the plasticity of human judgments in combination ensure not only that 'there is a clear surplus of conflict over co-operation in human interactions' but also that 'there will always continue to be so'.[108] If the first order of the political concerns struggle and the second order revolves around beliefs, then the third order—the order of constitutional law—is driven primarily by prudential considerations.

---

[106] Cf. John Dunn, *The Cunning of Unreason: Making Sense of Politics* (London: Harper Collins, 2000), 133: 'What exactly is politics? It is, first of all, the struggles which result from the collisions between human purposes: most clearly when these collisions involve large numbers of human beings. But it is not, of course, only a matter of struggle. It takes in, too, the immense array of expedients and practices which human beings have invented to co-operate, as much as to compete, with one another in pursuing their purposes'.

[107] Cf. Julien Freund, *L'Essence du Politique* (Paris: Sirey, 1965), esp. Pt. II; Ernest Gellner, *Plough, Sword and Book: The Structure of Human History* (London: Paladin, 1991), identifying wealth, power, and belief as the three main modes of human interaction.

[108] Dunn, above n. 106, 361.

# 4

## *Representation*

The concept of representation is such a fundamental aspect of public law that its true significance can be overlooked. All self-proclaimed modern democracies base their systems of government on the foundation of representation. But it is precisely because the representative form of democracy has been almost universally adopted that we sometimes neglect to ask certain basic questions. The most fundamental of these is: what is being represented? The answer to that question seems obvious: it is the people that form the objects of representation. In modern societies, government does not claim to rule the people; by electing politicians to act on their behalf, government is representative of the people. Representative government should therefore be viewed as the method by which the people are able to govern themselves.

However, the idea of representative government as a form of self-government is often misunderstood. Government by the people is actually a thoroughly ambiguous, even incoherent, notion. If representative government is the means by which the people rule themselves, it is a very indirect method of doing so. It is the indirect nature of this ostensible exercise in self-government that should be of particular interest to those concerned with representation in the architecture of public law.

Harvey Mansfield has pointed us in the right direction: self-government, he says, is not only 'accomplished by agents appointed out of themselves' but is also undertaken by agents who have been vested with 'sovereign powers in an artificial, public status'.[1] Both aspects of this process—form as well as agency—must be properly acknowledged. All too often it is supposed that the issue of representation in constitutional theory is concerned solely with the question of agency, thus focusing on the relationship between the people and their agents and exemplifying the modern sense of democracy. But the form of governmental authority—the way in which such 'sovereign powers' are given 'an artificial, public status'—also has important representational aspects. By considering both aspects, we will be in a position to understand how representative government, initially conceived in explicit opposition to democracy, is today seen as democracy's predominant form.[2] By examining the two together, the importance of representation in public law should become clear.

---

[1] Harvey C. Mansfield Jr., 'Hobbes and the Science of Indirect Government' (1971) 65 *American Political Science Review* 97–110, 97.

[2] See Bernard Manin, *The Principles of Representative Government* (Cambridge: Cambridge University Press, 1997), 236.

### THE REPRESENTATION OF SOVEREIGN AUTHORITY

A system of government is, as we have seen, founded on the capacity to fashion a collective order out of the unity of a people and to establish some apparatus of rule. The order that is instituted ties rulers and people together in a bond of protection and allegiance, and a set of reciprocal duties and rights. But whenever some form of governing order is established, the question remains: wherein lies the source of authority?

Answers to that question most commonly take the form of trying to identify a locus of ultimate authority, whether that be the king (as divine right theorists suggested), the people (as advocates of popular sovereignty proclaim), or (as constitutional scholars have occasionally argued) an institution such as parliament. This question troubled medieval jurists who, obliged to acknowledge the pre-eminence of monarchical authority, also asserted that the king was under the law. The most celebrated of such formulations—Bracton's statement that the king 'must not be under a man, but under God and under the law'[3]—may have satisfied medieval jurists, but it has puzzled modern scholars.[4] If Bracton had intended to suggest that certain institutional legal constraints on the powers of the king existed, he did nothing to explain how, in what circumstances, and by whom these were to be applied.[5] Much of the difficulty comes from the inherent ambiguity of concepts, a point demonstrated by the continuing influence throughout the middle ages of an elusive prescription of the ancient Romans: *Imperium in magistratibus, auctoritatem in Senatu, potestatem in plebe, maiestatem in populo.*[6] The question of ultimate authority did not receive any clear answer until the early modern period.

The first systematic treatment appears in the work of Thomas Hobbes. Hobbes built a theory of the state out of the human desire for order and security in a world of perpetual struggle. Starting from a graphic image of life in a state of nature—one of 'war of every man against every man' in which 'the life of man [is] solitary, poor, nasty, brutish and short'[7]—Hobbes demonstrated that the only way to secure peace and security would be for everyone to covenant to relinquish their natural rights and

---

[3] Henry de Bracton, *De Legibus et Consuetudinibus Angliae (On the Laws and Customs of England)* [c.1258], George E. Woodbine ed., S. E. Thorne trans. (Cambridge, Mass: Belknap Press, 1968), ii. 33: *Ipse autem rex non debet esse sub homine, sed sub deo et lege, quia facit legem.*

[4] See below, Ch. 8, 134–136.

[5] See Charles H. McIlwain, *Constitutionalism: Ancient and Modern* (Ithaca, NY: Cornell University Press, rev. edn. 1947), 73: 'It is somewhat surprising that historians have been content to leave such an apparent discrepancy as this so largely unexplained. Was Bracton, then, an absolutist or a constitutionalist, or was he just a blockhead?'

[6] 'Command [is] in the magistrates, authority in the Senate, power in the commons, and sovereignty in the people.' See Jean Bodin, *The Six Bookes of a Commonweale* [1576], Richard Knolles trans., Kenneth Douglas McRae ed. (Cambridge, Mass.: Harvard University Press, 1962), i.10. See also J. P. V. D. Balsdon, 'Auctoritas, Dignitas, Otium' (1960) 54 *The Classical Quarterly* 43–50, 43: 'Thus *auctoritas*, which was the Senate's function in government, was, as Mommsen said, "an indefinite word, evading strict definition"'.

[7] Hobbes, *Leviathan* [1651], Richard Tuck ed. (Cambridge: Cambridge University Press, 1996), 88, 89.

submit to the authority of a sovereign power. This great Leviathan, Hobbes argued, 'hath the use of so much Power and Strength conferred on him, that by terror thereof, he is inabled to conforme the wills of them all, to Peace at home and mutual ayd against their enemies abroad'.[8] The solution that Hobbes proposed to the persistence of conflict was to establish a political power equipped with an awesome authority.

Hobbes's great achievement was to have provided us with the first unequivocally modern conception of the state. It was a governmental authority differentiated not only from the people who established it but also from the personality of office-holders. In his opening words to *Leviathan*, Hobbes indicates that he intends to speak 'not of the men, but (in the Abstract) of the Seat of Power'.[9] He seeks to show how 'by Art is created that great *Leviathan* called a *Common-wealth*, or *State*'.[10] It is Hobbes 'who first speaks . . . in the abstract and unmodulated tones of the modern theorist of the state'.[11]

*Representation*

Hobbes was unequivocal in his characterization of sovereign power. He maintained that this power was in no sense personal: the power belongs entirely to the status of 'the office of the soveraign representative'.[12] Elaborating, Hobbes stated that the 'office of the soveraign, (be it a Monarch, or an Assembly,) consisteth in the end, for which he was trusted with the soveraign power, namely the procuration of *the safety of the people*'.[13] Hobbes here ties the question of the locus of political authority directly to the issue of representation. Hobbes's status as a great political philosopher is widely acknowledged. His analysis of representation reveals him also as a profound juristic thinker.

Hobbes builds his theory from the concept of the 'person'. A person is not to be equated with a human being. There are two types of personality, natural and artificial.[14] The words and actions of a natural person are his own, but those of an artificial person are the representations of another. What is especially important about this formulation is that Hobbes builds his theory of government entirely on the foundation of artificial personality. Government is established as a result of the competence of artificial persons to represent natural persons. A commonwealth thus comes into existence whenever a multitude of individuals agrees and covenants amongst themselves that an individual or group shall have 'the *right* to *present* the Person of them all, (that is to say, to be their *Representative*)'.[15]

---

[8] Ibid. 120–121.   [9] Ibid. 3.
[10] Ibid. 9.
[11] Quentin Skinner, 'The State' in Terence Ball, James Farr, and Russell L. Hanson (eds), *Political Innovation and Conceptual Change* (Cambridge: Cambridge University Press, 1989), 90–131, 126.
[12] *Leviathan*, above n. 7, ch. 30.   [13] Ibid. 231.
[14] Ibid. 111: 'A person, is he, whose words or actions are considered, either as their own, or as representing the words or actions of an other man, or of any other thing to whom they are attributed, whether Truly or by Fiction'.
[15] Ibid. 121.

The representative nature of this regime is critical. Hobbes explains that a 'multitude of men, are made *One* Person, when they are by one man, or one Person Represented' and it is 'the *Unity* of the Representer not the *Unity* of the Represented, that maketh the Person One'.[16] In the office of the sovereign 'consisteth the Essence of the Commonwealth; which . . . is *One Person*'.[17] The sovereign thus represents a single person, and to that unit we can give the name 'commonwealth' or, in modern language, 'the state'.

From this explanation, we gather that 'the people' exists only once a sovereign power is established: 'prior to the formation of a commonwealth a *People* does not exist, since it was not then a person but a crowd of individual persons'.[18] Noting the three classical types of commonwealth—monarchy, aristocracy, and democracy—Hobbes recognizes that if the people meet 'to erect a commonwealth, they are, almost by the very fact that they have met, a *Democracy*' and 'a convention whose will is the will of all the citizens has soveraign power'.[19] So an aristocracy or monarchy is created by the people as a result of the transfer of sovereign power to a small group or to a single individual. But once a sovereign is instituted, his authority knows no bounds; the sovereign is 'their Representative unlimited'.[20] This is explicit in the distinction Hobbes makes between a people and a crowd:

[M]en do not make a clear enough distinction between a *people* and a *crowd*. A *people* is a *single* entity, with *a single will*; you can attribute *an act* to it. None of this can be said of a *crowd*. In every commonwealth the *People* Reigns; for even in *Monarchies* the *People* exercises power; for the *people* wills through the will of *one man*. But the citizens, i.e. the subjects, are a *crowd*. In a *Democracy* and in an *Aristocracy* the citizens are the *crowd*, but the *council* is the *people*; in a *Monarchy* the subjects are the *crowd*, and (paradoxically) the *King* is the *people*.[21]

The crowd, in short, lacks political agency; such agency is intrinsically representative.[22]

Hobbes does nothing less than lay down the foundation for a comprehensive system of public law. The centrality of representation is evident in the allocation of responsibilities in a mature political system. In this situation, the sovereign body invariably needs to appoint representatives—executive and judicial officers—to carry out the tasks of government. The power of such representatives must always be

---

[16] *Leviathan*, above n. 7, ch. 30, 114.   [17] Ibid. 121.
[18] Hobbes, *On the Citizen* [1647], Richard Tuck and Michael Silverthorne trans. (Cambridge: Cambridge University Press, 1998), 95.
[19] Ibid. 94.   [20] *Leviathan*, above n. 7, 156.   [21] *On the Citizen*, above n. 18, 137.
[22] The formula S.P.Q.R. (*Senatus Populusque Romanus*/the Senate and People of Rome) under which the legions of Rome marched and which provides a formula of élite rule is illustrative of this point. As Bernard Crick has noted, this was not just a constitutional dictum; it could also present itself as 'a warning maxim addressed to the patrician class—do not forget the dreadful power of the people [i.e., the crowd] if things go wrong or if agitators stir them up'. See Bernard Crick, 'Introduction' to Niccolò Machiavelli, *The Discourses* (Harmondsworth: Penguin, 1970), 24. On the nature of this relationship see Elias Canetti, *Crowds and Power*, Carol Stewart trans. (Harmondsworth: Penguin, 1973), esp. 'Rulers and Paranoiacs', 475–537; Graham Maddox, 'The Limits of Neo-Roman Liberty' (2002) 23 *History of Political Thought* 418–431.

limited since 'Power Unlimited is absolute Soveraignty' and the limits of the powers of such officers are for the sovereign to determine.[23] But Hobbes is clear about the representative nature of the task:

> A Publique Minister, is he, that by the Soveraign (whether a Monarch, or an Assembly,) is employed in any affaires, with Authority to represent in that employment, the Person of the Common-wealth.[24]

Similarly with judges: those 'to whom jurisdiction is given, are Publique Ministers' because 'in their Seats of Justice they represent the person of the Soveraign; and their Sentence, is his Sentence'.[25]

For Hobbes, the public capacity of representatives (artificial persons) must be differentiated from the private role of the individual (the natural person) who exercises these responsibilities. Further, it is not only ministers who have two personalities: medieval jurists developed an intricate notion of 'the king's two bodies' precisely for the purpose of demonstrating that the monarch, the titular sovereign, also possesses two personalities or capacities, the natural and the political.[26] Following the logic of this medieval doctrine, Hobbes notes that 'they that be servants to them [the sovereign] in their naturall Capacity, are not Publique Ministers; but those onely that serve them in the Administration of the Publique businesse'.[27]

Hobbes's analysis helps us to appreciate how representation provides the key to understanding the structural unity of public law. The concept of representation requires a distinction to be drawn between the public and private aspects of a representative's personality. Since the concept suggests that certain standards are attached to, and certain limits are imposed on, the office of the representative, it emphasizes the fact that public law deals mainly with duties that attach to such offices. This is elementary so far as the executive officers of the state are concerned. But what of the office of the sovereign?

Hanna Pitkin has argued that when Hobbes calls his sovereign a representative, 'he implies that the man is to *represent* his subjects, not merely to do whatever he pleases' since the 'concept itself contains the idea that the sovereign has duties'.[28] Although this is correct, Hobbes maintains that subjects can have no rights against the sovereign. These positions are not, however, irreconcilable. The conundrum disappears when Hobbes is seen to be developing a juristic theory. The duties of the sovereign inhere in the nature of the office (to promote the *salus populi*). And to argue that subjects have no right—that is, no institutional mechanism—to enforce these duties of which the sovereign is in law the sole judge is not in the least paradoxical. But a full elaboration of this point requires discussion of its political aspects, which is deferred until the latter half of this chapter.

[23] *Leviathan*, above n. 7, 155.   [24] Ibid. 166.   [25] Ibid. 168.
[26] See Ernst H. Kantorowicz, *The King's Two Bodies: A Study in Mediaeval Political Theology* (Princeton: Princeton University Press, 1957).
[27] *Leviathan*, above n. 7, 166.
[28] Hanna Fenichel Pitkin, *The Concept of Representation* (Berkeley, Calif.: University of California Press, 1967), 33.

## The State

By building a juristic theory on the foundation of representation, Hobbes provides the foundation for a comprehensive account of the sovereign authority of the state. A core question remains: what is the state?

To answer this, we need to return to Hobbes's analysis of persons. As we have seen, he draws a basic distinction between natural and artificial persons and builds a theory of public law on the foundation of artificial personality. Certain natural persons, such as ministers, are also artificial persons. But the state is an artificial person that has no natural personality. The state does not stand alone in this category. The world can be divided into 'men' and 'things' and there are many inanimate things that are capable of being 'represented by Fiction'.[29] To illustrate, Hobbes uses the example of a church, a hospital, or a bridge which 'may be Personated by a Rector, Master, or Overseer' respectively.[30] Since inanimate things cannot give authority to their representatives to procure their maintenance, 'such things cannot be Personated, before there be some state of Civill Government'.[31] These artificial persons acquire their personality—and the ability to authorize representatives to act on their behalf—entirely through the operation of the law.

Can this analysis of artificial personality be extended to the personality of the state? Hobbes writes that a state is instituted:

> when a *Multitude* of men do Agree, and *Covenant*, *every one with every* one, that to whatever *Man*, or *Assembly of Men*, shall be given by the major part, the *Right* to present the person of them all, (that is to say, to be their *Representative*), every one, as well he that *Voted for it*, as he that *Voted against it*, shall *Authorise* all the Actions and Judgements, of that Man, or Assembly of men, in the same manner, as if they were his own, to the end, to live peaceably amongst themselves, and be protected against other men.[32]

The unity of the 'Man, or Assembly of Men'—that is, 'the *Unity* of the Representer, not the *Unity* of the Represented'[33]—is what creates the personality of the state. And the name which is given to this Representer, who 'carryeth this Person, is called SOVERAIGNE, and said to have *Soveraigne Power*, and every one besides, his SUBJECT'.[34]

Hobbes here is seeking to clarify the meaning of, and relations between, the concepts of state, sovereign, and sovereignty. Thus, the state is the name of the person created as a result of this process of authorization by a multitude.[35] The sovereign is the name given to the representative of the person of the state. Sovereignty is the name given to the relation between sovereign and subject.

---

[29] *Leviathan*, above n. 7, 113.    [30] Ibid.    [31] Ibid.    [32] Ibid. 121.
[33] Ibid. 114.    [34] Ibid. 121.
[35] In *The Logic of Leviathan: The Moral and Political Theory of Thomas Hobbes* (Oxford: Clarendon Press, 1969), ch. 4, David Gauthier argues that Hobbes's use of the notion of authorization in *Leviathan* (as compared with subjection or surrender of rights in earlier works) represents a major, and more democratic, shift in his thought. Cf. Jean Hampton, *Hobbes and the Social Contract Tradition* (Cambridge: Cambridge University Press, 1986), ch. 5.

Technically, the sovereign can be a natural or artificial person, but the important point is to recognize its intrinsically public nature: the sovereign holds an office impressed with public responsibilities and for the realization of which he is vested with absolute sovereign authority. This authority is exercised mainly through the power of law-making. And although these laws are enacted by the sovereign, the sovereign is a representative acting in the name of the state. In this purely juristic sense, then, the sovereign's acts constitute an exercise in self-government.

But what kind of person is the state? It has been suggested that because Hobbes founds juristic order on the unconditional allegiance of subjects, the idea of vesting personality in the state does not make much sense.[36] A further difficulty arises since, although Hobbes states at several points in *Leviathan* that the Commonwealth or state is a person,[37] he never articulates precisely what kind of person the state is supposed to be. Quentin Skinner has recently argued that for Hobbes the state must be viewed as analogous to a church, hospital, or bridge and treated as a 'purely artificial person'.[38] However, David Runciman's criticisms of this claim are convincing.[39] Runciman notes that although Hobbes treated the state as a single person, the state could not be a real person for the basic reason that it is not capable of acting for itself. The state cannot act other than through the person of its representative. But who does the sovereign represent? It is common ground that the state itself cannot authorize the sovereign to act and it is similarly accepted that the sovereign must represent something other than a multitude. The most sensible answer, Runciman suggests, is that the multitude 'separately perform the real actions [i.e., covenanting] which allow responsibility to be attributed to the state as a single unit'.[40] The consequence of this type of attribution of unity is that the state must be understood to be a person by fiction.

That the state is a *persona ficta* is justified by Runciman on various grounds.[41] But there is a more basic juristic reason for regarding the state as *sui generis*, and for recognizing its fictitious personality. The person of the state must first be differentiated

---

[36] David Runciman, *Pluralism and the Personality of the State* (Cambridge: Cambridge University Press, 1997), 32.

[37] It is not clear, however, that Hobbes is entirely consistent on this matter. In *Leviathan* he states that 'the Multitude so united in one Person, is called a COMMON-WEALTH' (above n. 7, 120). But later he seems to deny this: 'But the Common-wealth is no Person, nor has the capacity to doe anything, but by the Representative, (that is, the Soveraign)' (ibid. 184). This is best resolved by reading the latter as stating that the person of the Commonwealth has no independent will, but can act only through the will of the sovereign as representative.

[38] Quentin Skinner, 'Hobbes and the Purely Artificial Person of the State' (1999) 7 *J. of Political Philosophy* 1–29. Contrary to a number of commentators, Skinner thus argues (at 22) that Hobbes does not regard the state as a *persona ficta*. Cf. Michael Oakeshott, *On Human Conduct* (Oxford: Clarendon Press, 1975), 204; Runciman, above n. 36, ch. 2.

[39] David Runciman, 'What Kind of a Person is Hobbes's State? A Reply to Skinner' (2000) 8 *J. of Political Philosophy* 268–278.

[40] Ibid. 273.

[41] Runciman (ibid. 278) contends, first, that Skinner's term, 'purely artificial person', is not a phrase that Hobbes uses; secondly, that it 'does not sufficiently distinguish the person of the state from those artificial persons who are capable of action, such as assemblies'; and finally that Hobbes's own phrase, 'person by fiction', seems 'best to conjure up the kind of state we actually encounter in the political world we do inhabit, the world that Hobbes helped to create'.

from other artificial persons such as churches, hospitals, and bridges. This is not difficult: as Runciman recognizes, the state, unlike a bridge, does not exist at all before its representative is set in place.[42] Unlike a bridge, the state is entirely created from the act of representation. Even more fundamentally, the personality of the bridge is, as we have seen,[43] created as a result of the operation of law; it acquires, we might say, a form of juristic personality. This cannot be so with respect to the person of the state, however, since the state and its representative, the sovereign, are instituted precisely for the purpose of creating law. The state stands alone as a fictitious person.

The argument whether the state is a 'purely artificial person' or a 'person by fiction' is in danger of dissipating into sterile debate. But underpinning the exercise lies an attempt to clarify the basic concepts on which constitutional order is founded. In this respect, Hobbes's great achievement is to have produced a coherent explanation of the ideas of state, sovereign, sovereignty, and law, and to have demonstrated that, far from being a natural phenomenon, political power, being generated by artifice, is rooted in the principle of representation.

The specifically juristic aspects of Hobbes's work on the state have been neglected. When in the late nineteenth century they were taken up by Maitland, he complained that while a 'theory of the State . . . may be interesting to the philosophic few . . . a doctrine of Corporations, which probably speaks of fictitious personality and similar artifices, can only concern some juristic speculators, of whom there are none or next to none in this country'.[44] While continuing to focus on the practical legal questions which provoked this philosophical inquiry,[45] however, Maitland never got beyond acknowledging that 'there seems to be a genus of which State and corporation are species'.[46] But if this inquiry into representation reveals one basic insight it is that Hobbes's *Leviathan* is not only a 'masterpiece of political philosophy'[47] but also a work of profound juristic sophistication. *Leviathan* is an explication of the idea of juristic order founded on sovereignty and exercised through law. From this perspective, the state's power to command is absolute. For Hobbes, all notions of charisma, dignity, and honour are subsumed within the idea of power, honour being simply 'an argument and signe of Power'.[48]

---

[42] David Runciman, 'What Kind of a Person is Hobbes's State? A Reply to Skinner' (2000) 8 *J. of Political Philosophy* 273–274.
[43] Above 58.
[44] F. W. Maitland, 'Introduction' to Otto Gierke, *Political Theories of the Middle Age* (Cambridge: Cambridge University Press, 1900), ix.
[45] See Maitland's essays on this subject which have helpfully been collected in F. W. Maitland, *Selected Essays*, H. D. Hazeltine, G. Lapsley, and P. H. Winfield eds (Cambridge: Cambridge University Press, 1936).
[46] Maitland, above n. 44, ix; Maitland, 'Moral Personality and Legal Personality' in *Selected Essays*, above n. 45, ch. 5. See further Martin Loughlin, 'The State, the Crown and the Law' in Maurice Sunkin and Sebastian Payne (eds), *The Nature of the Crown: A Legal and Political Analysis* (Oxford: Oxford University Press, 1999), ch. 3; David Runciman, 'Is the State a Corporation?' (2000) 35 *Government & Opposition* 90–104.
[47] Michael Oakeshott, 'Introduction' in Thomas Hobbes, *Leviathan* (Oxford: Blackwell, 1946), viii: 'The *Leviathan* is the greatest, perhaps the sole, masterpiece of political philosophy written in the English language'.
[48] *Leviathan*, above n. 7, 65.

However, a juristic reading of Hobbes also highlights its limitations. In *Leviathan*, Hobbes uses the social contract—covenanting in the state of nature—to solve the question about the source of governmental authority. But it is evident that although it provides a clear analysis of the basic concepts on which a system of public law is founded, it does not resolve the issue of authority. This is not surprising, since the establishment of political order is no mere juristic exercise. By centralizing the concept of representation, Hobbes directs us along the right path. In *Leviathan*, representation sets in place the foundations of a system of positive law. But in order to find the source of governmental authority, his method must be extended and a broader conception of political representation embraced.

POLITICAL REPRESENTATION

In *Leviathan*, Hobbes sought mainly to offer an account of the person of the state and the office of the sovereign. The concept of sovereignty—the relation between sovereign and subject—remained underdeveloped. It was not squarely faced until the following century, when, as a consequence of the French revolution, the idea of covenanting by a multitude moved out of the realm of ideas and into the realm of action. The political debates which the revolution provoked demanded that the idea of covenanting to institute a state required much closer scrutiny.

Amongst the French revolutionary thinkers, the Abbé Sieyes was the one who paid closest attention to the significance of this Hobbesian moment.[49] His main achievement was to have 'transformed the modern theory of the state that had gradually been developing in the wake of the Reformation, that is to say the theory of the state as the creation of the social contract, into a practicable, realizable idea'.[50] This idea, latent in Hobbes,[51] is that of 'the people', or what Sieyes calls 'the nation', as the constituent power of political establishment. Before considering directly the relevance of sovereignty, the idea of constituent power needs closer attention.

*Constituent Power*

Sieyes emphasized the necessity of drawing a clear distinction between the constituted power (*pouvoir constitué*) and constituent power (*pouvoir constituant*). Holding an authority delegated from the people, government is a form of constituted power. But it is the government, not the nation, that is constituted. 'Not only is the nation not

---

[49] There is some confusion over the spelling of Sieyes's name and Sieyes himself does not appear to have maintained consistency. I have therefore followed Pasquino in spelling without accents: Pasquale Pasquino, 'Emmanuel Sieyes, Benjamin Constant et le "Gouvernement des Modernes"' (1987) 37 *Revue Française de Science Politique* 214–228, 214: 'L'orthographe sans accents semble la plus vraisemblable'.

[50] Murray Forsyth, *Reason and Revolution: The Political Thought of the Abbé Sieyes* (Leicester: Leicester University Press, 1987), 217.

[51] Murray Forsyth, 'Thomas Hobbes and the Constituent Power of the People' (1981) 29 *Political Studies* 191–203. Cf. Runciman, above n. 36, 12 (n. 13).

subject to a constitution', argued Sieyes, 'but it *cannot* be and *must not* be'.[52] The nation, he emphasized, must not be identified with its constitutional forms. Although constitutional law may be fundamental law with respect to the institutions of government, this simply means that no type of delegated power can alter the conditions of its delegation.[53] The constituent power remains: 'The nation is prior to everything. It is the source of everything. Its will is always legal; indeed, it is the law itself'.[54]

Although Sieyes identified 'the nation' as the constituent power, he also recognized that that body could not govern. Machiavelli's basic philosophy—that conflict is a basic feature of all collectivities and that politics exists to manage these irreducible tensions[55]—reveals the chimera that authority rests in the 'will of the people'. Accepting this basic facet of modern political conduct, Sieyes argued that the way in which such tensions can be positively addressed is through the principle of representation.[56]

Sieyes accepted both that the establishment of government is a necessary precondition for enabling citizens to realize their freedoms and also that there could never be an identity of rulers and ruled. This is a distinctively modern condition.[57] Sieyes 'saw representation as a fundamental fact of modern society, as something indelibly inscribed in the division of labour and commercial sociability, and political representation as a permanent necessity in any large and populous country in which it was virtually impossible to unite the voice of the people directly'.[58] But representation is not merely a mechanism to ensure that in mass society the views of all citizens can be heard. Representation is not simply the product of necessity. Because of its ability to manage conflict effectively, representative government is a superior form of government.[59]

---

[52] Emmanuel Joseph Sieyès, *What is the Third Estate?* [1789], M. Blondel trans. (London: Pall Mall Press, 1963), 126.

[53] Ibid. 125. [54] Ibid. 124.

[55] Niccolò Machiavelli, *The Discourses*, i.4. See further above, Ch. 3, 37–42.

[56] Cf. Joseph de Maistre, 'Study on Sovereignty' in Jack Lively (ed.), *The Works of Joseph de Maistre* (London: Allen & Unwin, 1965), 93–129, 93: 'It is said that the people are sovereign; but over whom?— over themselves, apparently. The people are thus subject. There is something equivocal if not erroneous here, for the people which *command* are not the people which *obey*. It is enough, then, to put the general proposition, "The people are sovereign", to feel that it needs an exegesis. . . . The people, it will be said, exercise their sovereignty by means of their representatives. This begins to make sense. The people are the sovereign which cannot exercise their sovereignty'.

[57] See Pasquino, above n. 49, esp. 223–225; Manin, above n. 2, esp. ch. 6. See also Bernard Manin, 'The Metamorphoses of Representative Government' (1994) 23 *Economy and Society* 133–171.

[58] Istvan Hont, 'The Permanent Crisis of a Divided Mankind: "Contemporary Crisis of the Nation State" in Historical Perspective' in John Dunn (ed.), *Contemporary Crisis of the Nation State?* (Oxford: Blackwell, 1995), 166–231, 198.

[59] Citing *Federalist* No. 52, Pitkin (above n. 28, 191) assumes that Madison, Hamilton, and Jay were of the view that 'representative government is a device adopted instead of direct democracy, because of the impossibility of assembling large meetings of people in a single place, "a substitute for the meeting of the citizens in person"'. This seems to be a not entirely faithful reading of the federalists. Madison in particular was concerned about the inability of 'a pure democracy' to deal with 'the mischiefs of faction' and suggests that a 'republic, by which I mean a government in which the scheme of representation takes place, opens a different prospect and promises the cure for which we are seeking'. James Madison, Alexander Hamilton, and John Jay, *The Federalist Papers*, No. 10 Publius (Madison). Cf. Manin, above n. 2, 3: 'For

For Sieyes, political power originates in representation. Pure or direct forms of democracy are ineffective methods of rule. A properly constituted political order must be based on the notion of 'indirect rule' in which the representative remains independent of the people. The 'people' establish a mode of government—a system of public offices to represent the 'general will'—and must then elect the persons to hold such offices. Drawing a contrast between classical and modern systems, Manin argues that representative governments have never used selection by lot, a method which ensures an equal probability of citizens being called on to perform governmental functions. This shows that the difference between representative and direct systems concerns their method of selection rather than the limited number of those selected. 'What makes a system representative', Manin concludes, 'is not that a few govern in the place of the people, but that they are selected by election only'.[60] Representation is a fundamental feature of modern government. This is not because representation legitimates power; rather it is 'because all legitimate power arises exclusively in and through political representation'.[61]

By focusing on political representation we get a much clearer perspective on the question of sovereign authority. Following Sieyes, it might be said that constituent power vests in the nation. But this does not mean that political authority is located in the people (*qua* the multitude), as theorists of popular sovereignty suggest.[62] Sieyes believed that sovereignty was fused with representation and could not be exercised without it. This does not mean that political authority is bound up entirely in the authority of an established ruler, as theorists of the authoritarian state claim. Sovereignty may be fused with representation, but—contrary to Hobbes—Sieyes argued that the people never leave the state of nature and thus retain the possibility of re-acquiring constituent power. One of the fundamental tasks of political practice is to ensure that this situation never arises. The implication of this argument is that sovereign authority does not rest in any particular locus; it is a product of the relation between the people and the state. Political power is a complex phenomenon: it is rooted in the division between governors and governed, it rests on the principle of representation, and it underpins the concept of sovereignty.

Siéyès, . . . as for Madison, representative government was not one kind of democracy; it was an essentially different and furthermore preferable form of government'.

[60] Manin, above n. 2, 41.

[61] F. R. Ankersmit, *Aesthetic Politics: Political Philosophy Beyond Fact and Value* (Stanford, Calif: Stanford University Press, 1996), 51. This point is one that recent advocates of more participatory forms of democracy often tend (erroneously) to reject: see, e.g., Benjamin Barber, *Strong Democracy: Participatory Politics for a New Age* (Berkeley, Calif.: University of California Press, 1984), 135, 145–146: 'Representation is incompatible with freedom . . . Representation is incompatible with equality . . . Representation, finally, is incompatible with social justice'. Cf. David Plotke, 'Representation is Democracy' (1997) 4 *Constellations* 19–34.

[62] Cf. G. W. F. Hegel, *Philosophy of Right* [1821], T. M. Knox trans. (Oxford: Oxford University Press, 1952), § 279: 'the sovereignty of the people is one of the confused notions based on the wild idea of the "people". Taken without its monarch and the articulation of the whole which is the indispensable and direct concomitant of monarchy, the people is a formless mass and no longer a state. It lacks every one of those determinate characteristics—sovereignty, government, judges, magistrates, class-divisions, etc.,—which are to be found only in a whole which is inwardly organized'.

Political power is thus derived from those tensions and conflicts which exist in all collectivities. These tensions must be properly handled, and it is for this purpose that the practices of politics have evolved. But such conflicts are not resolved by vesting absolute legal power in the sovereign authority since this does not eliminate the problem of generating a real, sustainable political will. Furthermore, if the concepts of juridical and political will are confused and assumed to be united, the system can collapse into tyranny. Apart from other considerations, tyranny is a grossly ineffective political regime. Hobbes was conscious of this distinction. Although an authoritarian, he was no absolutist. He recognized that 'the power of the mighty hath no foundation but in the opinion and belief of the people'[63] and acknowledged implicitly the significance of Machiavelli's belief that freedom flourishes through the maintenance of the tension between state and society.[64]

But if political authority does not derive from the establishment of a top-down system of authority, then neither does it rest in 'the will of the people', whatever this confused notion might mean. If the expression reflects a belief that this 'will' is discerned by an aggregation of the desires of the multitude,[65] then it leads not to authority but to impotence. As Sieyes's analysis of the idea of constituent power suggests, political power is the product of representation. Only through representation can conflict be positively harnessed, appropriate governing arrangements devised,[66] and real political will established.[67]

---

[63] Thomas Hobbes, *Behemoth, or the Long Parliament* [1682], Ferdinand Tönnies ed. (London: Cass, 1969), 16.

[64] See Hobbes, *Leviathan*, above n. 7, ch. 30.

[65] Cf. Jean-Jacques Rousseau, *The Social Contract* [1762], Maurice Cranston trans. (Harmondsworth: Penguin, 1968), iii. 15. See Maurice Cranston, 'The Sovereignty of the Nation' in Colin Lucas (ed.), *The French Revolution and the Creation of Modern Political Culture. Vol. 2: The Political Culture of the French Revolution* (Oxford: Pergamon Press, 1988), 97–104, 100: 'Rousseau's concept of a general will is often dismissed as a rather absurd notion, but it is a crucial element of his system. Without it, republican theory must lean heavily on a concept of representation: the senators and officers rule as representatives of the people. But Rousseau had no patience with representation'.

[66] By this, I mean the elaborate arrangements of government which have become associated with parliamentarism, deliberation, trusteeship in office, and notions of accountability for the exercise of governmental power. For classic illustrations see: Edmund Burke, 'Speech to the Electors of Bristol, 1774' in his *Speeches and Letters on American Affairs* (London: Dent, 1908), 68–75; J. S. Mill, *Considerations on Representative Government* [1861] in Mill, *Three Essays* (Oxford: Oxford University Press, 1975), 145–426. For a recent analysis of these issues see: Adam Przeworski, Susan C. Stokes, and Bernard Manin (eds), *Democracy, Accountability and Representation* (Cambridge: Cambridge University Press, 1999); F. R. Ankersmit, 'On the Origin, Nature and Future of Representative Democracy' in his *Political Representation* (Stanford, Calif.: Stanford University Press, 2002), 91–132.

[67] Cf. Carl Schmitt, *The Crisis of Parliamentary Democracy* [1923], Ellen Kennedy trans. (Cambridge, Mass: MIT Press, 1985), 34: 'The *ratio* of Parliament rests in a "dynamic-dialectic", that is, in a process of confrontation of differences and opinions, from which the real political will results'.

## Sovereignty

This analysis leads to a relational concept of sovereignty. A relational perspective enables us to draw out the nuances inherent in the concept of sovereignty.[68] However, it is necessary first to return to that critical moment when a multitude covenant to found a state. Hobbes argued that the state is the person created by the authorization of the multitude and the sovereign is the representative of the person of the state. But if sovereignty is a relational phenomenon, which is the determinative relationship—that between the state and the people, or between sovereign and subject? For Hobbes the answer is clear. Since the state has no will except through that of its representative, the critical relationship is the latter: it is the sovereign who reduces the 'plurality of voices, unto one Will' and who is 'to beare their Person',[69] and it is 'his Command, that maketh Law'.[70] But is this adequate?

Hobbes's answer is a consequence of the way in which he conceives his task as an essentially juristic exercise. The issue becomes more complicated once Sieyes makes his distinction between 'the nation' and 'the government'. It is evident that, as the bearer of constituent power, 'the nation' is a representative form to be differentiated from the people as a multitude or crowd. But this would suggest that the nation should be understood as a synonym for the person of the state. This has a certain merit, especially since this personality is capable of having an existence over and above a formal constitutional ordering. Consider, for example, Maitland's practical concern about the ability of states to borrow money.[71] Does this debt persist even if the government collapses and, as a result of a new constitutional settlement, an entirely new governmental regime is established? The answer suggested by international law is that it does: in the international arena the state has a personality which is distinct from that of the constituted governmental order.[72] Maitland in fact argues that '[w]e cannot get on without the State, or the Nation, or the Commonwealth, or the Public, or some similar entity', though he added that, given the confusions of the British system, 'this is what we are proposing to do'.[73] Despite the ambiguities of British

---

[68] In Ch. 2 above (30, n. 134) it was suggested that the idea of public law as practice had certain affinities with Bourdieu's treatment of the logic of practice. It might similarly be noted that relational thinking is central to Bourdieu's method. Bourdieu argues that substantialist thinking, which dominates positivism, privileges substances over relationships by treating the properties attached to agents as forces independent of the relationship in which they operate. The relational or structuralist mode of thinking, by contrast, 'identifies the real not with substances but with relationships' and this mode, he argues, lies at the basis of all scientific thought. See Pierre Bourdieu, *Distinction: A Social Critique of the Judgement of Taste*, Richard Nice trans. (London: Routledge, 1984), 22.

[69] *Leviathan*, above n. 7, 120.    [70] Ibid. 187.

[71] See, e.g., Maitland, 'The Crown as Corporation' in his *Selected Essays*, above n. 45, 104–140, 113–115 which discusses the idea of 'the Publick' which by statute becomes responsible for the national debt.

[72] See *Tinoco Concessions* arbitration (1923) RIAA i.369; Ian Brownlie, *Principles of Public International Law* (Oxford: Clarendon Press, 5th edn. 1998), 86–89.

[73] Maitland, above n. 71, 112. One of the complexities in the British system concerns the status of the monarch: 'It is true that "The people" exists, and "the liberties of the People" must be set over against "the prerogatives of the King"; but just because the King is no part of the People, the People cannot be the State or the Commonwealth' (ibid. 113).

arrangements, it is evident that in order to grasp the relational character of sovereignty both the state/people and sovereign/subject (or government/citizen) relationships need to be considered. Each brings out a different dimension of sovereignty; neither can be ignored.

When the sovereign/subject aspect is the focus of inquiry, the primary concern will be the question of ultimate legal authority. Sovereignty in the British system is an expression of the ability of the crown in parliament to legislate without any legal limitation on its competence.[74] There have been recent complications arising from the accession of the United Kingdom to the European Union.[75] Nonetheless, the legal doctrine of sovereignty does not usually cause conceptual difficulties. But the question of sovereignty cannot be reduced to an issue of positive law, dealing solely with the sovereign/subject relationship.

For the purpose of explaining this point, we should return to Sieyes's claim that the will of the nation 'is the law itself'. This is a peculiar statement. We get a deeper sense of its meaning when immediately following this Sieyes writes: 'Prior to and above the nation, there is only *natural* law'.[76] The claim, nevertheless, remains puzzling, since the concept of natural law does not much help us here.[77] But if we accept that the relationship between sovereign and subject is expressed in the language of positive law, what term, other than that of classical natural law, can be used for that conception of law embodied in 'the nation' that is 'the source of everything', including positive law itself? I suggest that Sieyes is here referring to the vital, but now neglected, idea of *droit politique*, political right. It is only by deploying the concept of *droit politique*, precepts of political conduct which are needed to ensure the maintenance of the state, that the juristic significance of the political concept of sovereignty can adequately be grasped.

The long-standing dominance of legal positivism—expressed most clearly in the idea that sovereignty solely concerns the relation of sovereign and subject—has eroded the conception of law understood as *droit politique*. But there is evidence that in the early modern period its logic was readily understood. Shortly after *Leviathan* was published, for example, George Lawson published his *Politica Sacra et Civilis*.[78] In this work, Lawson drew a distinction between two types of sovereignty, real and personal.

---

[74] For the classic expression of the legal doctrine, see A. V. Dicey, *Introduction to the Study of the Law of the Constitution* (London: Macmillan, 8th edn. 1915), ch. 1.

[75] See, e.g., Paul Craig, 'Britain in the European Union' in Jeffrey Jowell and Dawn Oliver (eds), *The Changing Constitution* (Oxford: Oxford University Press, 4th edn. 2000); Neil MacCormick, *Questioning Sovereignty: Law, State, and Nation in the European Commonwealth* (Oxford: Oxford University Press, 1999); Neil Walker, 'Sovereignty and Differentiated Integration in the European Union' (1998) 4 *European Law Journal* 355–388.

[76] Sieyes, above n. 52, 124; and see above, 62.

[77] But see below, Ch. 8, 134–140.

[78] George Lawson, *Politica Sacra et Civilis or, A Modell of Civil and Ecclesiasticall Government* [1660], Conal Condren ed. (Cambridge: Cambridge University Press, 1992). Lawson had earlier written an explicit critique of *Leviathan*: George Lawson, *An Examination of the Political Part of Mr Hobbs, his Leviathan* (London: privately published, 1657). See Conal Condren, *George Lawson's Politica and the English Revolution* (Cambridge: Cambridge University Press, 1989), esp. ch. 15.

Personal sovereignty is 'the power of a commonwealth already constituted',[79] the power, it might be said, of the office of the sovereign. Real sovereignty, by contrast, belongs to the community itself. And real sovereignty, Lawson claimed, is superior to personal sovereignty. Lawson noted that the holders of personal sovereignty 'cannot alter or take away the cause whereby they have their being, nor can they meddle with the fundamental laws of the constitution, which if it once cease, they cease to be a Parliament'.[80] The sovereignty vested in the community, however, 'hath the power of constitution', which includes the power 'to alter the forms of the government'.[81]

This type of statement is easily misconstrued. Today, legal scholars re-interpret its meaning either by elevating the notion of 'real sovereignty' to the language of natural law[82] or by reducing it to a positivist statement about the rule of recognition.[83] Both these tendencies are distortive. Real sovereignty, analogous to Sieyes's concept of *pouvoir constituant*,[84] is an expression of politic law. This complex notion, concerned with the intrinsically political precepts of conduct between the state and the people,[85] is a vital aspect of the subject of public law.

Once we turn to Lawson's idea of 'real' sovereignty, matters get complicated. The focus on real sovereignty, or on constituent power, helps us to understand how the institutionalized separation of powers is not a division[86] but an explication of sovereignty.[87] This helps us to understand how the institutional forms of constitutionalism

---

[79] Lawson, *Politica*, ibid. 47.    [80] Ibid. 48.    [81] Ibid. 47.

[82] See, e.g., T. R. S. Allan, *Law, Liberty, and Justice: The Legal Foundations of British Constitutionalism* (Oxford: Clarendon Press, 1993), 4: 'In the absence of a higher "constitutional" law, proclaimed in a written Constitution and venerated as a source of unique legal authority, the rule of law serves in Britain as a form of constitution'. Allan makes it clear (ibid. 5) that the rule of law 'entails the subjection of government to the law . . . in the sense of its being bound to comply with "rules of just conduct"'.

[83] See, e.g., Jeffrey Goldsworthy, *The Sovereignty of Parliament: History and Philosophy* (Oxford: Clarendon Press, 1999), ch. 10. Cf. T. R. S. Allan, *Constitutional Justice: A Liberal Theory of the Rule of Law* (Oxford: Oxford University Press, 2001), 216–225.

[84] See Pasquale Pasquino, 'The Constitutional Republicanism of Emmanuel Sieyès' in Biancamaria Fontana (ed.), *The Invention of the Modern Republic* (Cambridge: Cambridge University Press, 1994), ch. 5, 112–113.

[85] Although Dicey acknowledged the force of this point, because of his adherence to legal positivism he was unable to invest it with juristic significance. Thus, he recognized that 'the word "sovereignty" is sometimes employed in a political rather than in a strictly legal sense' and that in this political sense 'the electors of Great Britain may be said to be, together with the Crown and the Lords, or perhaps, in strict accuracy, independently of the King and the Peers, the body in which sovereign power is invested'. 'But this', Dicey concluded, 'is a political, not a legal fact'. Dicey, above n. 74, 70–71.

[86] Cf. the American revolutionary debates in which 'American thinkers attempted to depart sharply from one of the most firmly fixed points in eighteenth-century political thought [i.e. the indivisibility of sovereignty]; and though they failed to gain acceptance for their strange and awkward views, they succeeded nevertheless in opening this fundamental issue to critical discussion, preparing the way for a new departure in the organization of power'. Bernard Bailyn, *The Ideological Origins of the American Revolution* (Cambridge, Mass: Belknap Press, 1967), 198–229, 198.

[87] Sieyes, *Préliminaire de la Constitution* (July 1789): 'In a large society individual liberty has three kinds of enemies to fear. The least dangerous are malevolent citizens . . . Individual liberty is far more endangered by [the second enemy: the] undertakings of the *Officers encharged to exercise some part of public power*. . . . The separation, and a good constitution of public powers are the only guarantee that nations and citizens might be preserved from this extreme evil' (cited in Pasquino, above n. 84, 113–114) [the third threat is that of a foreign enemy].

bolster sovereignty. It also suggests that this entire framework is conditional rather than absolute.

This is a conclusion most jurists operating within modern liberal constitutionalism are unwilling to accept. Their general objective has been to suppress the idea of sovereignty and to assert the absolute supremacy of 'the rule of law'.[88] In this sense, the French revolution—the moment at which constituent power asserted itself—is an embarrassment to liberal juristic thought.[89] Thus, although the opening sentence of Carl Schmitt's *Political Theology*—'Sovereign is he who decides on the exception'[90]— is today generally considered 'infamous',[91] it is actually a fairly conventional, albeit dramatic, presentation of the concept of political sovereignty. It is not necessary to embrace Schmitt's personalistic and decisionistic interpretation of the exception to recognize that his formulation offers acute juristic insight.[92] He contends that although the sovereign 'stands outside the normally valid legal system, he nevertheless belongs to it, for it is he who must decide whether the constitution needs to be suspended in its entirety'.[93] In the turbulent politics of the Weimar republic, Schmitt's political message was highly provocative.[94] But if his work is read as an explication of (in Lawson's language) 'real' sovereignty, the general message is imperative: any coherent constitutional theory is obliged to take seriously the indivisible and absolute nature of the constituent power.[95]

---

[88] See, e.g., Allan, above n. 82, ch. 11; Allan, above n. 83, ch. 7; Ronald Dworkin, *Law's Empire* (London: Fontana, 1986), ch. 11. Although this theme appears most prominently in the work of contemporary anti-positivists, it is worth noting that this is a feature which they share with legal positivists who, by differentiating legal from political sovereignty, aim to marginalize the significance of the latter conception. Cf. Carl Schmitt, *Théorie de la Constitution* [*Verfassungslehre*, 1928], Lilyane Deroche trans. (Paris: Presses Universitaires de France, 1993), 270: 'It is imagined first, that the constitution is nothing but a system of legal norms; secondly, that it is a closed system; and thirdly that it is "sovereign"—that is to say, it can never be interfered with or even influenced by reason or necessity of political existence'.

[89] Cf. Jacques Derrida, 'Declarations of Independence' (1986) 15 *New Political Science* 7–15, who states (at 10), in relation to the 'We the People' statement in the American declaration, that 'this people does not yet exist. They do *not* exist as an entity, it does *not* exist, *before* this declaration, *as such* . . . The signature invents the signer'.

[90] Carl Schmitt, *Political Theology: Four Chapters on Sovereignty* [1922], George Schwab trans. (Cambridge, Mass: MIT Press, 1988), 5.

[91] See, e.g., John P. McCormick, *Carl Schmitt's Critique of Liberalism: Against Politics as Technology* (Cambridge: Cambridge University Press, 1997), 213.

[92] See, e.g., Franz L. Neumann, *The Rule of Law: Political Theory and the Legal System in Modern Society* [1936], Matthias Ruete intro. (Leamington Spa: Berg, 1986). Neumann argues that: 'Decisionist legal thought has, in fact, nothing to do with law. . . . In this kind of legal thinking, law is nothing but a technique for translating political will into legal form' (285). But Neumann, a German Jewish refugee from Nazism, also follows Schmitt to the extent of arguing that sovereignty and the rule of law are irreconcilable and whenever an attempt is made to do so 'we come up against insoluble contradictions' (4). And, as has recently been observed: 'The fact that Neumann writes of Schmitt's discussion of sovereignty after three years of Hitler's rule . . . illustrates an engagement that remains under-explored'. See Duncan Kelly, 'Rethinking Franz Neumann's Route to *Behemoth*' (2002) 23 *History of Political Thought* 458–496, 464.

[93] Schmitt, above n. 90, 7.

[94] See Peter C. Caldwell, *Popular Sovereignty and the Crisis of German Constitutional Law: The Theory and Practice of Weimar Constitutionalism* (Durham, NC: Duke University Press, 1997), esp. ch. 4.

[95] Schmitt, above n. 88, 215: 'The people, the nation, remains the true origin of all political events. It is the source of all those energies which manifest themselves in ever-new forms, and although it generates new forms and organisations, it is never able conclusively to subordinate its political existence to a particular form'.

If the constitutional form is not definitive, we need not descend into pure decisionism, in which concrete will is substituted for abstract form. The fact that the exception is not rule-governed does not mean that it is resolved through arbitrary will.[96] This was Schmitt's basic error, an error which stemmed from his scepticism about the intrinsically representative character of the constituent power.[97] Once the representative dimensions of the constituent power are taken seriously, we understand *droit politique* as a set of precepts and maxims enabling the state to maintain itself and to flourish. From the perspective of *droit politique*, sovereignty is as much concerned with capacity as with competence, with power not just authority. On this basis, we can appreciate how institutional restraints on the powers of government enhance the state's capacity to mobilize public power for common purposes. By reassuring the people that state power will promote public welfare and by establishing checking and reviewing mechanisms, the significance of constitutionalism is clear. Constitutionalism is neither a set of fundamental moral principles nor the 'unpolitical principles of the bourgeois *Rechtstaat*', but 'one of the most effective philosophies of state building ever contrived'.[98] Constitutional values are conditional, not absolute; constitutional discourse is political, not moral.

CONCLUSION

The objective of this chapter has been to reveal the extent to which our understanding of constitutional ordering—and indeed the division of all associations into governors and governed—is dependent on the concept of representation. The foundations of this understanding were laid bare primarily by Hobbes's remarkable exposition of the subject. By building a theory of government on the foundation of representation, Hobbes was able to offer a clear and coherent explanation of the concepts of state, sovereign and sovereignty, concepts which lie at the heart of modern political order.

However, once *Leviathan* is viewed as a work of jurisprudence, and therefore as an early elaboration of legal positivism, certain limitations in Hobbes's treatment of the

---

[96] See Ernest Gellner, *Reason and Culture: The Historic Role of Rationality and Rationalism* (Oxford: Blackwell, 1992), 149–150: 'Unreason is an essential part of social control, of group definition and status ascription. In a rational world, such traps for the unwary would not exist: reason has no favourites, and is available to all. But in social worlds as we know them, in cultures, unreason is an important gatekeeper. Even the irregularity of verbs may have its role to play in the social deployment of speech and the maintenance of social order. Grammar may, like military discipline or etiquette or protocol, actually *need* its arbitrariness. He who has not mastered the exceptions betrays his outsider status. Irregular verbs make their contribution to social discipline. It is good, from a social viewpoint, that some people should feel insecure all of the time, and that all should feel insecure some of the time. It keeps them on their toes, and helps maintain respect for the established order'.

[97] From this perspective, Schmitt does not present himself consistently. Notwithstanding his tendency to treat political authority as personal, in *Verfassungslehre* he appears to modify his position and acknowledges the representative character of the constituent power of the people: above n. 88, ch. 18.

[98] Stephen Holmes, *Passions and Constraint: On the Theory of Liberal Democracy* (Chicago: University of Chicago Press, 1995), xi.

concept of sovereignty are evident. These have been highlighted with the aid of Sieyes's exploration of the concept of constituent power. Sieyes agrees with Hobbes's contention that representation is a foundational concept. But by drawing on a broader notion of political representation—one which recognizes the role of representation in the management of conflict—Sieyes provides us with the basis for understanding sovereignty as a political concept.

We are now able to recognize that sovereignty is relational. Sovereignty does not reside in any particular locus; it is generated as a product of the political relationship between the people and the state. Here too the idea of representation is pivotal, especially in fashioning both the relationship between governors and governed and the way in which government acquires an 'artificial, public status'. This relational perspective enables us to appreciate the legal and political aspects of sovereignty, and especially to grasp the relation between the two. It suggests that legal analysis of sovereignty that does not acknowledge the inextricable links with the political remains in danger of leading to distortion.

The concept of representation lies at the root of public power. It is only through representation that those exercising governmental power are given certain responsibilities; similarly, it is only through representation that the people are transformed into citizens.[99] In this sense, it might be said that public power is both generated and utilized through representation. The notion of pure or direct democracy must as a consequence be recognized as a thoroughly ineffective method of rule. Drawing a distinction between 'aesthetic' and 'mimetic' representation, Ankersmit has captured the essence of this concept of political representation. Mimetic representation, or representation as a mirror of society, finds its expression in calls for direct democracy, a concept that 'dishonours democracy by extraditing it to the boundless and unlimited desires of a collective political libido'.[100] Only through aesthetic representation, a symbolic form that acknowledges that political actors possess some duty of trusteeship but also have the power of creative political action, can social conflict properly be managed.[101]

---

[99] One of the main thrusts behind the growing contemporary interest in such themes as civic republicanism and deliberative democracy, it might be noted, has been precisely to remind governors of their civic duties in the exercise of their public offices, and to educate the people in the responsibilities of the office of citizenship. See Philip Pettit, *Republicanism: A Theory of Freedom and Government* (Oxford: Oxford University Press, 1997); John S. Dryzek, *Deliberative Democracy and Beyond: Liberals, Critics, Contestations* (Oxford: Oxford University Press, 2000).

[100] Ankersmit, above n. 61, 347. It follows that those seeking to promote mimetic representation—the aim of ensuring that government and its agencies (including the judiciary) somehow mirror society—fail to appreciate the vitally important role which aesthetic representation—and the maintenance of a division between state and society—plays in the constitution of political authority. This is not to deny that there are important questions to be addressed concerning political exclusion: on which see Anne Phillips, *The Politics of Presence: The Political Representation of Gender, Ethnicity, and Race* (Oxford: Clarendon Press, 1995). But the politics of inclusion must be recognized also to constitute a form of symbolic representation.

[101] See George Kateb, 'The Moral Distinctiveness of Representative Democracy' (1981) 91 *Ethics* 357–374.

Finally, if the juristic aspects of this exercise in state-building are to be understood, each of the predominant conceptions of law in contemporary jurisprudence—both those that treat law as the command of the sovereign and those promoting an image of law as a moral force that transcends the political—must be severely qualified. The juristic dimensions to constitutional ordering can be grasped only by resurrecting a conception of law which draws on the affinities between the legal and the political—that is, by adopting a concept of public law as *droit politique*.

# 5

## *Sovereignty*

Sovereignty has been given such a variety of ambiguous and confused meanings that many have suggested that, in the interests of precision and rigour, the concept should be altogether abandoned. During the early decades of the twentieth century, an influential movement devoted to the promotion of pluralism in political thought wanted to jettison sovereignty,[1] and replace it with such notions as 'polyarchism'.[2] In the mid-century, the influence of positivism and behaviourism in legal and political studies was such that studies of sovereignty often recognized 'a tendency among present-day political theorists to work without the aid of the concept'.[3] At the century's end, many scholars assessing the impact of contemporary trends like globalization, flexibilization and emerging multi-level governance argued that we were now living in an era of post-sovereignty.[4]

My argument will be that efforts to erode, evade, or move beyond sovereignty[5] are invariably based on a misunderstanding of the concept and the roles it performs. Sovereignty stands as a representation of the autonomy of the political and is the

---

[1] See, e.g., Francis W. Coker, 'The Technique of the Pluralist State' (1921) 15 *American Political Science Review* 186–213; Harold J. Laski, 'The Pluralistic State' in his *The Foundations of Sovereignty and Other Essays* (London: Allen & Unwin, 1921), 232–249. The implications of pluralism for sovereignty had been illustrated in John Dewey, *Outlines of a Critical Theory of Ethics* [1891] (New York: Hilary House, 1957), 172: 'Every institution . . . has its sovereignty, or authority, and its laws and rights. It is only a false abstraction which makes us conceive of sovereignty, or authority, and law and rights as inhering only in some supreme organization, as the national state'. Cited in Jens Bartelson, *The Critique of the State* (Cambridge: Cambridge University Press, 2001), 89.

[2] See, e.g., Ernest Barker, 'The Discredited State' (1915) 5 (o.s.) *Political Quarterly* 101–121, 120. Cf. Joshua Cohen and Charles Sabel, 'Directly Deliberative Polyarchy' (1997) 3 *European Law Journal* 313–342; Oliver Gerstenberg, 'Law's Polyarchy: A Comment on Cohen and Sabel' (1997) 3 *European Law Journal* 343–358.

[3] W. J. Rees, 'The Theory of Sovereignty Restated' (1950) 59 *Mind* 495–521, 495. See also Stanley I. Benn, 'The Uses of "Sovereignty"' (1955) 3 *Political Studies* 109–122, 122: 'it would be a mistake to treat "sovereignty" as denoting a genus of which the species can be distinguished by suitable adjectives, and there would seem to be a strong case for giving up so Protean a word'. Cf. Raia Prokhovnik, 'The State of Liberal Sovereignty' (1999) 1 *Brit. J. of Politics & International Relations* 63–83, 63: 'The initial aim of this paper is to counter the claim that sovereignty is a bankrupt concept'.

[4] See Neil Walker, 'Late Sovereignty in the European Union', European Forum Discussion Paper, Robert Schuman Centre, EUI (2001); Michael Keating, *Plurinational Democracy: Stateless Nations of the United Kingdom, Spain, Canada and Belgium in a Post-Sovereign World* (Oxford: Oxford University Press, 2001).

[5] See, e.g., Henry Shue, 'Eroding Sovereignty: The Advance of Principle' in Robert McKim and Jeff McMahon (eds), *The Morality of Nationalism* (New York: Oxford University Press, 1997), 340–359; Richard Falk, 'Evasions of Sovereignty' in R. B. J. Walker and Saul H. Mendlovitz (eds), *Contending Sovereignties: Redefining Political Community* (Boulder, Colorado: Lynne Rienner, 1990), 61–78; Keating, above n. 4.

foundational concept of modern public law. Many of the difficulties in grasping the idea are linked to the failure to recognize public law as a practice with its own distinctive methods and objectives. The resulting confusions flow either from an attempt to place sovereignty within a formal, analytical, and positivist frame[6] or to devise transcendental principles of right conduct to which all legal and political behaviour must be subject.[7]

In order to explain this argument, I will explicate the concept by presenting ten tenets of sovereignty. These are: (1) sovereignty is a facet of the modern state; (2) political relationships do not derive from property relationships; (3) public power must be differentiated from private power; (4) public power is not personal but official; (5) public power is a product of a political relationship; (6) sovereignty is an expression of public power; (7) sovereignty is relational; (8) rights are not antagonistic to sovereignty but are the product of its expression; (9) the system of public law is an expression of sovereignty; and (10) public law is not solely a matter of positive law. These tenets—ideas translated into concrete practices—define the essence of the modern concept of sovereignty.

Concepts lose their intelligibility when they are burdened with a plethora of contradictory meanings. By retrieving an understanding of modern sovereignty, I hope to show that sovereignty is a coherent concept of continuing relevance. This position depends both on the recognition that sovereignty is socially constructed[8] and on an acknowledgement of the utility of sovereignty as an expression of contemporary juridico-political discourse.

## SOVEREIGNTY IS A FACET OF THE MODERN STATE

Being 'entirely inseparable from the state',[9] sovereignty is a modern concept. Although the terminology of sovereignty was used during the medieval period, the concept in a true sense did not then exist.[10] In the words of Bertrand de Jouvenel,

---

[6] The most egregious recent illustration from political science has been Krasner's labelling of sovereignty as 'organized hypocrisy': see Stephen D. Krasner, *Sovereignty: Organized Hypocrisy* (Princeton, NJ: Princeton University Press, 1999).

[7] See, e.g., Shue, above n. 5, 349: 'I want to argue . . . against sovereignty directly. . . . I shall argue that there ought to be external limits on the means by which domestic economic ends may be pursued by states, limits that ought to become binding on individual sovereigns irrespective of whether those sovereigns wish to acknowledge them, just as sovereigns are already bound by both legal rights and moral rights against the domestic use of torture whatever their own opinions on the subject of torture may be'.

[8] See, e.g., Thomas J. Biersteker and Cynthia Weber (eds), *State Sovereignty as Social Construction* (Cambridge: Cambridge University Press, 1996).

[9] Charles Loyseau, *Traicté des Seigneuries* (Paris: Abel l'Angelier, 1614), ii.4: 'la Souveraineté est du tout inseparable de l'Estat'.

[10] See Walter Ullmann, 'The Development of the Medieval Idea of Sovereignty' (1949) 64 *English Historical Review* 1–33; J. W. McKenna, 'The Myth of Parliamentary Sovereignty in Late-Medieval England' (1979) 94 *English Historical Review* 481–506.

although people in the middle ages had 'a very strong sense of that concrete thing, hierarchy; they lacked the idea of that abstract thing, sovereignty'.[11]

During the middle ages, sovereignty was used simply to signify a superior. But despite the common etymological root, sovereignty and suzerainty must be distinguished. Feudal power, the power of lordship or property, should not be confused with sovereignty. Although the Holy Roman Emperor might have been recognized 'as the suzerain of suzerains and the seignior of seigniors—as, it might even be said, the king of kings' this status only implied 'command over those who were best placed to disobey'.[12] For a variety of reasons, technological, geographical, fiscal, and military, the central authority possessed only a limited hold over the governed. Until these basic obstacles could be overcome, the activity of governing could not emerge as an autonomous practice. This was achieved only as a consequence of the formation of the modern state. Bound up with this movement, sovereignty was always part of a modernizing project.

This project was realized in stages. Royalty was first obliged to acquire the *plenitudo potestatis*, the supreme power, and this necessitated the destruction of all authorities that sought to challenge it. By breaking the political power of feudal magnates, an internal coherence of governing authority was established. The English situation was unusual since, after the conquest, Norman statecraft ensured that, although the chief barons became major landlords, they did not assume the tasks of government. Conditions therefore favoured the growth of a unified and highly centralized polity.[13] Elsewhere in western Europe, the struggle was longer.[14]

The establishment of internal authority had to be bolstered by the assertion of the territorial autonomy of the kingdom. The movement to acquire independence from external authority is exemplified by the actions of the kings of England and France who, challenging the authority of the Pope and the Holy Roman Emperor, claimed to be emperor in their own realm.[15] The emergence of sovereignty thus manifests

---

[11] Bertrand de Jouvenel, *Sovereignty: An Inquiry into the Political Good*, J. F. Huntington trans. (Cambridge: Cambridge University Press, 1957), 171.

[12] Jouvenel, ibid. 173.

[13] See W. L. Warren, *The Governance of Norman and Angevin England, 1086–1272* (London: Edward Arnold, 1987); James Campbell, 'The Significance of the Anglo-Norman State in the Administrative History of Western Europe' in his *Essays in Anglo-Saxon History* (London: Hambledon Press, 1986), ch. 11.

[14] See Wolfgang Reinhard (ed.), *Power Elites and State Building* (Oxford: Clarendon Press, 1996); Thomas Ertman, *Birth of the Leviathan: Building States and Regimes in Medieval and Early Modern Europe* (Cambridge: Cambridge University Press, 1997), chs 2, 3, 5.

[15] From the mid-thirteenth century onwards, jurists began to refer to the king's authority in terms of the maxim, *rex in regno suo imperator est* (a king is emperor within his own kingdom): see Gaines Post, *Studies in Medieval Legal Thought: Public Law and the State, 1100–1322* (Princeton, NJ: Princeton University Press, 1964), 453–482. For the source of the maxim, see Peter N. Riesenberg, *Inalienability of Sovereignty in Medieval Political Thought* (New York: Columbia University Press, 1956), 82–83. This line of thought culminates in the opening words of the Act in Restraint of Appeals 1533 which declared that 'This realm of England is an empire, and so hath been accepted in the world, governed by one supreme head and king having the dignity and royal estate of the imperial crown . . .'. See Walter Ullmann, 'This Realm of England is an Empire' (1979) 30 *J. of Ecclesiastical History* 175–203.

itself primarily as an assertion of royal authority and the subversion of the medieval order.

An important aspect of this modernizing project was the manner in which law was deployed as an instrument of royal power. In his account of the establishment of sovereignty in France in the early modern period, Bernard Durand highlighted the use of law as an instrument of authority:

'The central power', Mousnier wrote, 'only had a limited hold on the governed.' Distances (it took ten days to travel from Paris to Toulouse), the variety of spoken languages, the lack of administrators, the vague knowledge of the kingdom, everything contributed to the need for a strong message in order to compensate for material weaknesses. Only legal instruments (skilfully used) were able to bring cohesion to and ensure obedience from populations accustomed, since the Middle Ages, to a juridical message. Legislation, justice, law, were the instruments which made authority possible and efficacious. They showed themselves not only through the services they rendered and the rules they laid down but also through the justification they conveyed and the message they reinforced. The progress of state power was obviously made possible by these legal instruments: the very foundations of sovereignty were concerned, as well as the available instruments, justice and legislation.[16]

The project of forging a modern state required the promotion of a conception of law as an instrument of command. For this purpose, jurists drew heavily on such Roman law maxims as *quod principi placuit legis habet vigorem* (what pleases the prince has the force of law), which provided the intellectual source of such contemporary expressions as *si veut le roi, si veut la loi; car tel est notre plaisir* (what the king wills, the law wills; for such is our pleasure).[17]

Oakeshott has indicated that the modern state was a 'free' or 'sovereign' association in respect of three main characteristics: first, because its government was 'not subject to any superior external authority'; secondly, 'in virtue of being association in terms of law'; and thirdly, because its government possessed 'the authority and the procedures to emancipate itself continuously from its legal past', in the sense that 'there was no law so ancient and so entrenched that it could not be amended or repealed'.[18] Put slightly differently, sovereignty expresses three basic features of the modern state: internal coherence, external independence, and supremacy of the law.[19]

---

[16] Bernard Durand, 'Royal Power and its Legal Instruments in France, 1500–1800' in Antonio Padoa-Schioppa (ed.), *Legislation and Justice* (Oxford: Clarendon Press, 1997), 291–312, 293. The role of the common law in the processes of state formation in England was of particular importance: see, e.g., Paul Brand, 'The Formation of the English Legal System, 1150–1400' in Padoa-Schioppa, ibid. 103–121; R. C. van Caenegem, *The Birth of the English Common Law* (Cambridge: Cambridge University Press, 2nd edn. 1988).

[17] See Justinian, *Digest* [534], Alan Watson trans. (Philadelphia: University of Pennsylvania Press, 1998), i.4.1.

[18] Michael Oakeshott, 'On the Character of a Modern European State' in his *On Human Conduct* (Oxford: Clarendon Press, 1975), 182–326, 229.

[19] See Blandine Kriegel, *The State and the Rule of Law*, Marc A. LePain and Jeffrey C. Cohen trans. (Princeton: Princeton University Press, 1995), 29.

### POLITICAL RELATIONSHIPS DO NOT DERIVE FROM PROPERTY RELATIONSHIPS

The argument that political relationships do not derive from property relationships arises from the struggle to differentiate the feudal patrimonial rights of monarchs from their political rights as sovereigns.[20] Because the English monarchy centralized its power so early, it was able to prevent the build-up of political feudalism which afflicted much of continental Europe.[21] It is perhaps for this reason that English jurists undertaking inquiries into the foundations of state power felt no great need to differentiate between political and proprietary power.

For explicit acknowledgement of the importance of this distinction it is necessary to turn to French scholars who grappled with the issue of sovereignty. Jurists like Bodin and Loyseau defined sovereign authority as a phenomenon directly opposed to the exercise of feudal power.[22] Although Hobbes built upon and in certain respects radicalized the insights of the early modern French jurists, he developed his theory of sovereignty from basic precepts of political reasoning. Hobbes felt no need explicitly to unravel the proprietorial from the political; for Hobbes, a system of property (the rules of *Meum* and *Tuum*) was the product of an exercise of the sovereign power of prescribing the rules of civil law.[23]

This distinction between the political and proprietorial is rooted in classical political thought, the Greeks differentiating between the spheres of the *polis* and the *oikos*, and the Romans between *res publica* and *dominium*.[24] Hobbes too recognized this distinction between the household of the king and those that served the sovereign in the discharge of political responsibilities.[25] But this classical distinction was later suppressed in English political thought, not least because of Whig assumptions,

---

[20] See esp., Kriegel, ibid. ch. 2.

[21] The Norman kings also strengthened their position by requiring an oath of allegiance to be sworn by all holders of land and not simply the chief vassals. This ensured that, over and above the feudal relationship, a political bond of obedience between the subject and the crown was forged. See Émile Boutmy, *The English Constitution*, Isabel M. Eaden trans. (London: Macmillan, 1891), 10.

[22] See Jean Bodin, *The Six Bookes of a Commonweale* [1576], Richard Knolles trans., Kenneth Douglas McRae ed. (Cambridge, Mass: Harvard University Press, 1962), i. 8–10; Loyseau, above n. 9, chs 1 and 2. See also Charles Loyseau, *A Treatise of Orders and Plain Dignities* [1610], Howell A. Lloyd trans. (Cambridge: Cambridge University Press, 1994), vii.2.14: 'According to its true etymology, "prince" signifies the supreme head, that is, he who has the sovereignty of the state . . . [but] the dukes and counts of France had long since called themselves princes because they had usurped the rights of sovereignty. Thus they were really subject princes'.

[23] Thomas Hobbes, *Leviathan* [1651], Richard Tuck ed. (Cambridge: Cambridge University Press, 1996), 125. For a contrasting interpretation, however, see C. B. Macpherson, *The Political Theory of Possessive Individualism: Hobbes to Locke* (Oxford: Oxford University Press, 1962), 265: 'For Hobbes the model of the self-moving, appetitive, possessive individual, and the model of society as a series of market relations between these individuals, were a sufficient source of political obligation'.

[24] See above, Ch. 2, 6.

[25] Hobbes, above n. 23, 166. See above, Ch. 4, 57.

underpinned by the work of Locke, that property is a pre-political category and that the chief end of government is to ensure its preservation.[26]

The maintenance of this distinction between political power and the power exercised through property is essential to an understanding of sovereignty. This needs reiterating today because of a modern tendency to reduce all arguments of power to a matter of economics.[27] An aspect of this propensity sees the modern state as an instrument of the dominant classes in society.[28] But although this largely Marxist debate has generated an extensive literature,[29] it has never been able to provide an account of political order that dislodges the underlying sense of the distinctive unity of the state.[30] From this perspective, the second tenet of sovereignty asserts the autonomy of the political in the face of such modern socio-economic reductionism.

PUBLIC POWER MUST BE DIFFERENTIATED FROM PRIVATE POWER

The idea that public power must be differentiated from private power highlights an important feature of the political relationship: political power derives neither from force nor from the power that property confers. Political power cannot be possessed like property, nor applied like force. As Hannah Arendt has argued, political power is always 'a power potential and not an unchangeable, measurable, and reliable entity like force or strength'.[31] Political power is 'to an astonishing degree independent of material factors', since the only material factor required in the generation of political power 'is the living together of people'.[32] Political power maintains the public realm.[33]

Private power is the product of an exclusive relationship between a person and other persons with respect to an object, such as land and other forms of property. It

[26] See John Locke, *Two Treatises of Government*, ii, §§ 28, 124. See *Entick* v. *Carrington* (1765) 19 St. Tr. 1029, *per* Lord Camden CJ: 'The great end, for which men entered into society, was to secure their property. That right is preserved sacred'.
[27] See Kriegel, above n. 19, 65–67, criticizing the tendency of historians such as Perry Anderson whose 'economistic approach [to the development of the modern state] is preoccupied with surplus value and class struggle, but it is blind to the juridico-institutional forms that engendered a new state organization at an early date in England and later on and only in part in France'.
[28] The classic expression is that of Marx in *The German Ideology*: 'Through the emancipation of private property from the community, the State has become a separate entity, beside and outside civil society; but it is nothing more than the form of organisation which the bourgeois necessarily adopt both for internal and external purposes, for the mutual guarantee of their property and interests'. See Karl Marx and Frederick Engels, *Selected Works* (Moscow: Progress Publishers, 1969), i.16–80, 77.
[29] For an overview see Martin Carnoy, *The State and Political Theory* (Princeton, NJ: Princeton University Press, 1984), esp. chs 2–4. Although largely a debate within Marxism, it might be noted that it is not confined to that tradition of thought: see, e.g., Charles A. Beard, *An Economic Interpretation of the Constitution of the United States* [1913] (New York: Macmillan, 1954).
[30] See Bartelson, above n. 1, ch. 4.
[31] Hannah Arendt, *The Human Condition* (Chicago: University of Chicago Press, 1958), 200.
[32] Ibid. 200–1.
[33] For an analysis of this understanding of political power (as 'power to') and which differentiates it from domination (or 'power over') see: Angus Stewart, *Theories of Power and Domination* (London: Sage, 2001).

is the power of mastery or *dominium*. Private power is exercised through the ownership and control of material resources. Political power, by contrast, is a product of a relationship between individuals (natural persons) that, in form at least, conceives them to be equals. This power, a product of the world-building capacity of humans, 'comes into being only if and when men join themselves together for the purpose of action'.[34] But this political power becomes public power only when assuming an institutional form. As Arendt notes, the Romans 'knew that the principle of *potestas in populo* is capable of inspiring a form of government only if one adds, as the Romans did, *auctoritas in senatu*, authority resides in the senate, so that government itself consists of both power and authority, or, as the Romans put it, *senatus populusque Romanus*'.[35] Public power is formed by harnessing political power through the institutionalization of authority.

Public power is thus the product of a form of partnership. This is what Oakeshott calls *societas*, a formal relationship constituted by a system of rules.[36] The power generated is therefore a consequence of the loyalty of individuals to the system. Public power may thus be said ultimately to rest on opinion and belief.[37] Even Hobbes, the greatest of the theorists of the authoritarian state, recognized that 'the power of the mighty hath no foundation but in the opinion and belief of the people'.[38]

The public/private distinction also suggests that, notwithstanding the Whig belief that the object of government was the preservation of property, the political relationship has no precise object at which it is aimed. Although some have expressed the objective rather grandiosely as being the maintenance and extension of human freedom, it is better summed up by the more ambiguous idea that the object is to promote the *salus populi*.[39] In formal terms, the political relationship is simply born of

---

[34] Hannah Arendt, *On Revolution* (Harmondsworth: Penguin, 1973), 175. Arendt adds (ibid.): 'The grammar of action: that action is the only human faculty that demands a plurality of men; and the syntax of power: that power is the only human attribute which applies solely to the worldly in-between space by which men are mutually related, combine in the act of foundation by virtue of the making and keeping of promises, which, in the realm of politics, may well be the highest human faculty'.

[35] Ibid. 178.

[36] Oakeshott, 'On the Character of the Modern European State', above n. 18, 199–203. See above, Ch. 2, 16–17.

[37] James Madison, Alexander Hamilton, and John Jay, *The Federalist Papers* [1788], Isaac Kramnick ed. (Harmondsworth: Penguin, 1987), No. 49 (Madison): 'If it be true that all governments rest on opinion, it is no less true that the strength of opinion in each individual, and its practical influence on his conduct, depend much on the number which he supposes to have entertained the same opinion'.

[38] Thomas Hobbes, *Behemoth, or the Long Parliament* [1682], Ferdinand Tönnies ed. (London: Cass, 1969), 16. See also Joseph de Maistre, 'Study on Sovereignty' in Jack Lively (ed.), *The Works of Joseph de Maistre* (London: Allen & Unwin, 1965), 93–129, 110: 'Any *institution* is only a political edifice. In the physical and the moral order, the laws are the same; you cannot build a great edifice on narrow foundations or a durable one on a moving or transient base. Likewise, in the political order, to build high and for centuries, it is necessary to rely on an opinion or belief broad and deep: for if the opinion does not hold the majority of minds and is not deeply rooted, it will provide only a narrow and transient base'.

[39] Hobbes, *On the Citizen* [1647], Richard Tuck and Michael Silverthorne eds (Cambridge: Cambridge University Press, 1998), 143. See above, Ch. 2, 7–8.

'the activity of attending to the general arrangements of a set of people whom chance or choice have brought together'.[40]

Seeking to define the characteristics of this public relationship, Oakeshott, following Aristotle, posited four basic features of what he called 'the civil condition'. These are that it is a relationship of human beings, that it is a relationship of equals, that it is a 'constituted' condition, and that it is a self-sufficient relationship.[41] Following this line of argument, we might say that public power is a product of the civil condition and is generated by the establishment of a system of government, the setting to work of an apparatus of rule.

PUBLIC POWER IS NOT PERSONAL BUT OFFICIAL

Charles Loyseau identified both the essence of this tenet and its connections with tenets 2 and 3 in the distinction he drew between lordship and office. Lordship, he argued, can be defined as 'dignity with power in property'; office, by contrast, connotes 'dignity with public function'.[42] This concept of office (*officium*) was derived from ecclesiastical institutions and 'drew concurrently upon the dual Roman and canonical tradition of service to the public realm and the common good'.[43] *Officium* signified a position of some permanence; the position assumes the status of an institution.[44]

This concept of office transforms our understanding of public power: in a strict sense, power vests not in the individual but in the office itself.[45] The distinction between the personal and official nature of the task has deep roots. It is already manifest in the distinction that medieval jurists drew between the king's two bodies: between the natural and the politic, the private and the public, the personal and the official, the king and the crown.[46] From here, it is a short step to acknowledge that

---

[40] Michael Oakeshott, 'Political Education' in his *Rationalism in Politics* (London: Methuen, 1962), 111–136, 112.
[41] Oakeshott, 'On the Civil Condition' in his *On Human Conduct*, above n. 18, 108–184, 109–110.
[42] Loyseau, above n. 22, i.6.
[43] Hélène Millet and Peter Moraw, 'Clerics in the State' in Reinhard (ed.), above n. 14, 173–188, 179. For the Roman influence see: Myron Piper Gilmore, *Argument from Roman Law in Political Thought, 1200–1600* (Cambridge, Mass: Harvard University Press, 1941), ch. 3. And for the work of medieval publicists on the concept of office see Riesenberg, above n. 15, ch. 2.
[44] See Udo Wolter, 'The *officium* in Medieval Ecclesiastical Law as a Prototype of Modern Administration' in Padoa-Schioppa (ed.), above n. 16, 17–36, 23.
[45] For a modern account of the significance of office see Dennis F. Thompson, *Political Ethics and Public Office* (Cambridge, Mass: Harvard University Press, 1987).
[46] See above, Ch. 2, 20–23. Note might also be made of the work of Sir John Fortescue in the fifteenth century who, in characterizing the English regime as *dominium politicum et regale*, emphasized the fact that although the king possessed authority to rule, he was unable to pass whatever measures he pleased but was required to work through the institutional arrangements of parliament. See Sir John Fortescue, *De Laudibus Legum Anglie* [1468–71], S. B. Chrimes ed. (Cambridge: Cambridge University Press, 1942).

power is entrusted to the institutional framework of government.[47] Consequently, although in Britain we continue to pay lip-service to the notion that justice emanates from Her Majesty or that the Queen's fiat makes law, it is evident that royal will is in no sense personal. This power can only be exercised through specific institutional and official forms.[48]

The official character of public power was fully understood by early modern theorists of sovereignty. Bodin argued that the sovereign could be identified by knowing his attributes, these being those properties that are not shared by subjects. The principal 'marks' of sovereignty were defined by Bodin as: the power of law-making, the power to declare war and make peace, the power to establish offices of state, the ultimate right of judgment, the power of pardon, the right of coining money, and the right of taxation.[49] The sophisticated character of these attributes suggests that such rights and powers are unlikely to be personal; Bodin here seems to be contemplating the establishment of an elaborate institution. This point is developed by Hobbes, who insists that sovereigns are not proprietors of their sovereignty. Sovereign power is in no sense personal; it resides entirely in a representative office.[50]

The power exercised through this institutional framework is generally referred to as the sovereignty of the state. Further (referring back to tenet 1), it would be inaccurate to suggest that this institutional notion of sovereignty came into being because parliament succeeded in wresting sovereignty from the king. Before the formation of the institutional framework of the state, sovereignty did not exist. In his study of the evolution of parliament, A. F. Pollard pins this down: 'The crown had never been sovereign by itself, for before the days of parliament there was no real sovereignty at all: sovereignty was only achieved by the energy of the crown in parliament, and the fruits of conquest were enjoyed in common'.[51] Sovereignty is a function of the institutional arrangements established as a consequence of the formation of the modern state.[52]

---

[47] This is nevertheless a shift that, because of an inability to separate the king from his crown, the English have never been able cleanly to make. But many seventeenth century constitutional conflicts can be understood in this light: see, e.g., Janelle Greenberg, 'Our Grand Maxim of State, "The King Can Do No Wrong"' (1991) *History of Political Thought* 209–228.

[48] See, e.g., A. V. Dicey, *Introduction to the Study of the Law of the Constitution* (London: Macmillan, 8th edn. 1915), 322: 'the Royal will can, speaking generally, be expressed in one of three different ways, viz. (1) by Order in Council; (2) by order, commission, or warrant under the sign-manual; (3) by proclamations, writs, patents, letters and other documents under the Great Seal'.

[49] Bodin, above n. 22, i.10. Cf. Hobbes, *On the Citizen*, above n. 39, vi.18.

[50] Hobbes, *Leviathan*, above n. 23, ch. 30. See above, Ch. 4, 58–61.

[51] A. F. Pollard, *The Evolution of Parliament* (London: Longmans, 1920), 230.

[52] This provides one answer to Lord Cooper's puzzle, expressed in *MacCormick* v. *Lord Advocate* 1953 SC 396, 411: 'The principle of the unlimited sovereignty of Parliament is a distinctively English principle which has no counterpart in Scottish constitutional law . . . Considering that the Union legislation extinguished the Parliaments of Scotland and England and replaced them by a new Parliament, I have great difficulty in seeing why it should have been supposed that the new Parliament of Great Britain must inherit all the peculiar characteristics of the English Parliament but none of the Scottish Parliament . . .'.

PUBLIC POWER IS A PRODUCT OF A POLITICAL RELATIONSHIP

Although public power vests in the arrangement of offices rather than the individuals who hold office (tenet 4), when distinguishing public and private power (tenet 3) it was suggested that this apparatus of rule ultimately derives its power from a political relationship between a government and its subjects. This aspect of sovereignty must now be directly addressed. Properly understood, political power does not reside in any specific locus, whether that be the king, the people or an institution such as parliament. Political power is generated from the particular relationship that evolves between the sovereign and subject, government and citizens. Political power generated through the apparatus of rule must be conceived as relational.

The point here is that the state's capacity for effective command depends on its ability to establish its authority. This requires the harnessing of power, which derives from the degree of loyalty of the citizens. Authority, notes Lester Ruiz, 'is the giving and receiving of confidence and commitment between persons who recognize and affirm a common community; it is not an independent variable that creates or imposes the values that constitute this common community'.[53] Legitimacy is conferred by authority rather than the reverse, and relationality precedes authority.[54] As Arendt explains, the term authority (*auctoritas*) is derived from the verb *augere* (to augment) and 'what . . . those in authority constantly augment is the foundation'.[55] Authority therefore 'has its roots in the past';[56] the question of authority 'is fundamentally a question of tradition' and 'the question of tradition is inextricably related to the question of *the people*'.[57]

This insight into the nature of authority highlights the significance of a growing body of scholarly work that analyses the development of the modern state.[58] In the case of Britain, for example, a highly centralized agency of government was established at an early stage of development. Consequently, when a parliament strongly linked to local government emerged, it was unable to prevent the process of state-building, and therefore came to focus its activities on ensuring that the central authority operated within an acceptable constitutional framework. The framework of authority established proved to be both effective and durable.[59] Historical work of

[53] Lester Edwin J. Ruiz, 'Sovereignty as a Transformative Practice' in Walker and Mendlovitz (eds), above n. 5, 79–96, 85.
[54] See Ruiz, ibid.
[55] Hannah Arendt, 'What is Authority?' in her *Between Past and Future: Eight Exercises in Political Thought* (Harmondsworth: Penguin, 1977), 91–141, 122.
[56] Ibid.   [57] Ruiz, above n. 53, 85.
[58] See, e.g., Charles Tilly (ed.), *The Formation of Nation States in Western Europe* (Princeton: Princeton University Press, 1975); Otto Hintze, *The Historical Essays of Otto Hintze*, Felix Gilbert ed. (New York: Oxford University Press, 1975); Michael Mann, *The Sources of Social Power. Vol. 1: A History of Power from the Beginning to AD 1760* (Cambridge: Cambridge University Press, 1986), *Vol. 2: The Rise of Classes and Nation-States, 1760–1914* (Cambridge: Cambridge University Press, 1994); Martin van Creveld, *The Rise and Decline of the State* (Cambridge: Cambridge University Press, 1999).
[59] This thesis is presented in Ertman, above n. 14, esp. ch. 4. See also John Brewer, *The Sinews of Power: War, Money and the English State, 1688–1783* (London: Unwin Hyman, 1989).

this character—showing how the growth of representative assemblies was closely bound up with the furtherance of the state's objectives—suggests the need to revise more idealized accounts of the system of parliamentary democracy. More generally, it helps us to bring authority and liberty into appropriate alignment. Contrary to certain interpretations, liberty and authority should not be conceived as being in direct antagonism. As Benedetto Croce put it: 'Liberty struggles against authority, yet desires it; and authority checks liberty, yet keeps it alive or awakens it, because neither would exist without the other'.[60]

The authority invested in the institutional framework of government is founded on a political relationship. Although the involvement of the people in the activity of government is an effective state-building strategy, once it is recognized that political power rests ultimately in the people, it is evident that this power must be actively managed. Governmental authority rests on the allegiance of the people. Once support is withdrawn, the authority of governors dissipates.

SOVEREIGNTY IS AN EXPRESSION OF PUBLIC POWER

Public power, it has been argued, is different from private power; it is a form of official power which is the product of a distinctively political relationship. It has further been argued that this type of public power acquires autonomous status only with the establishment of the modern idea of the state. Once these tenets have been set in place, sovereignty can be understood as an expression of public power.

In the formative period, the emergence of the concept of sovereign gave effect to a monistic conception of the state. Sovereignty, in the words of Jean Bodin, 'is the absolute and perpetual power of a commonwealth', it is 'the highest power of command'.[61] As the source of law, the sovereign cannot be subject to the laws.[62] Sovereignty thus seems to provide a justification for absolutism. If we focus solely on the monistic and absolutist features of sovereignty, however, we are liable to misunderstand its character. The concept certainly borrows some of its authority from such Roman maxims as *princeps legibus solutus est* (the prince is freed from the laws) and *quod principi placuit*,[63] and the sovereign does provide the source of all positive law. Sovereign authority possesses what in the German tradition of public law is called *Kompetenz-Kompetenz*, 'the competence of its competence', or the competence to determine the limits, if any, of its own competence.[64] But those who highlight its absolutist features often fail to recognize that sovereignty makes sense only once the public, official character of governmental power has been acknowledged.

---

[60] Benedetto Croce, *Politics and Morals* [1925], Salvatore J. Castiglione trans. (New York: Philosophical Library, 1945), 14.
[61] Jean Bodin, above n. 22, i.8.     [62] Bodin, ibid. i.8.
[63] Justinian, *Digest*, above n. 17, i.3.31; i.4.1.
[64] See, e.g., Paul Laband, *Das Staatsrecht des Deutschen Reiches* (Tübingen: Mohr, 1901), ii. 64–67, 85–88; Georg Jellinek, *Allgemeine Staatslehre* (Berlin: Springer, 1900), 483–484.

Once this aspect of sovereignty is grasped, the classical categorization of the forms of government must be questioned. Within the modern state, Aristotle's claim that there are three basic forms of government—monarchy, aristocracy, and democracy[65]—can no longer be conceived as alternative forms of political rule. In the modern state these forms do not provide realistic alternatives: the notion that a single individual could exercise a boundless right of rule is virtually incomprehensible, and the idea of direct democracy in the classical sense[66] has almost entirely been superseded by an indirect, representative version.[67] Modern government is aristocratic. To the extent that the classical forms continue to be relevant they should now be conceived as three phases in the activity of ruling: consultation, which involves all; counsel, which involves few; and decision, which is singular.[68]

Understood as an expression of public power, sovereignty resides in the established institutional framework of the state. However, since it is accepted (tenet 5) that public power is an expression of a political relationship, it would be a mistake to assume that sovereignty resides in a specific locus, whether that be the king, the people or an institution such as parliament. Sovereignty ultimately inheres in the form which the political relationship takes.

### SOVEREIGNTY IS RELATIONAL

Sovereignty is quintessentially an expression of a political relationship and, from a juristic perspective, sovereignty constitutes the essence of the modern state. The state, argued Hobbes, is the person that is created as a result of the authorization through covenant of the people (a multitude). The sovereign is the representative of the person of the state.[69] Sovereignty, it follows, is the name given to express the quality of the political relationship that is formed between the state and the people, or the sovereign and the subject. This relational aspect of sovereignty is highlighted by Croce. 'In the relationship between ruler and ruled', he argues, 'sovereignty belongs to neither but to the relationship itself'.[70]

What is the nature of this relational aspect of sovereignty? Is it rooted in the relation between sovereign and subject or between the state and the people? In Hobbesian theory this remains ambiguous, because it is axiomatic that the state is able to act only through the person of the sovereign. But once a conceptual distinction is drawn between the state and the office of the sovereign,[71] it is evident that this question may throw light on two principal facets of sovereignty that have often caused confusion. These two facets are the legal and the political conceptions of sovereignty.

---

[65] Aristotle, *The Politics* [c.335–323 BC], T. A. Sinclair trans., Trevor J. Saunders ed. (Harmondsworth: Penguin, 1981), Bks IV–VI.
[66] See M. H. Hansen, *The Athenian Democracy in the Age of Demosthenes* (Oxford: Blackwell, 1991).
[67] See Bernard Manin, *The Principles of Representative Democracy* (Cambridge: Cambridge University Press, 1997).
[68] Cf. Croce, above n. 60, 17.
[69] Hobbes, *Leviathan*, above n. 23, 120–121.
[70] Croce, above n. 60, 17.
[71] See above, Ch. 4, 65–69.

These two conceptions of sovereignty reflect a differentiation between the public and the political.

It has been argued that public power is not personal but official (tenet 4), that public power is the product of a political relationship (tenet 5) and that sovereignty is an expression of public power (tenet 6). This suggests that sovereignty is both an expression of official power and is the product of a political relationship. The former, focusing on the institutional and public, depicts the legal conception of sovereignty; the latter expresses the political conception. These legal and political conceptions of sovereignty in turn reflect concerns about the issues of competence and capacity, of authority and power.

Competence is an official or institutional matter. As a facet of sovereignty, competence is an expression of the absolute power of the state to enact law. In a technical jurisdictional sense, competence reflects both internal coherence (that is, the existence of a viable system of rule) and external independence (the identity of the state as an entity in the international arena). The external aspect, which expresses the basic principle of state sovereignty, is widely understood.[72] But especially in Britain, the internal aspect sometimes causes confusion. Under the British constitution, the internal aspect is classically understood as the right of the crown in parliament 'to make or unmake any law whatever', with no person or body being recognized 'as having the right to override or set aside the legislation of Parliament'.[73] This is commonly stated to be the legislative sovereignty of parliament. In the British context, the structure of official power is unusually simple. And the reason for this is that, as a consequence of maintaining a Hobbesian framework, the crown in parliament, the ultimate law-making institution, is also the sole representative of the person of the state. In this respect, the British constitution is almost unique.

Most modern states have, through the exercise of the constituent power of 'the people' or 'the nation', established a formal constitutional framework which allocates legislative, executive, and judicial powers of the state to designated institutions. This constitutional framework generally defines and delimits the competence of the legislative assembly to enact laws and, if a federal regime is established, may divide legislative powers between federal and provincial institutions. Such a limitation or division of legislative power does not, however, amount to a division of sovereignty: sovereignty divided is sovereignty destroyed. The constitutional framework instituted for the exercise of governmental power of the state must be understood as an explication rather than a division of sovereignty. The supreme power to enact law is exercised through the power of 'the nation' to constitute a system of government. The constitutional framework provides the measure of internal coherence; the constitution can thus be understood to be an elaboration of legal sovereignty. In this arrangement, sovereignty as an expression of official power exists in the relation between the

---

[72] See, e.g., R. B. J. Walker, *Inside/Outside: International Relations as Political Theory* (Cambridge: Cambridge University Press, 1993).

[73] Dicey, above n. 48, 38.

form of institutional authority established and the subjects of that power (i.e., the citizenry).

However, in addition to expressing a relation of jurisdictional competence, sovereignty is also an expression of the basic political relationship between the people and the institutional framework of state power. This aspect of sovereignty is concerned not so much with competence but with capacity, not with authority but with power. This political conception of sovereignty focuses on the capacity of a people to overcome social division and conflict by establishing a sense of political unity. Political sovereignty is what George Lawson termed 'real' sovereignty, 'the power to constitute, abolish, alter, reform forms of government'.[74] Real or political sovereignty, which is synonymous with what Sieyes called the 'constituent power',[75] is 'a power to model a state'.[76]

This underlying relationship between rulers and ruled is one that lawyers—working on the assumption of the ultimate authority of the normative framework—tend to suppress. On rare occasions, as when a new state is formed through a process of decolonization, the judiciary is obliged to recognize that the doctrines of legal sovereignty must march alongside political reality.[77] But this conception of political sovereignty generally remains below the level of legal consciousness. It nevertheless remains basic to an understanding of sovereignty, even in the juristic sense. Political sovereignty provides the ultimate basis for the belief that the holders of official power 'do not exercise it as a right inherent in themselves, but as a right pertaining to other people; the common will is confided to them in trust'.[78]

The official power entrusted by the people must be used to promote the wellbeing—to enhance the capacity—of the state. As has been argued (tenet 6), this capacity depends on strengthening the bonds of allegiance between governors and governed. Although this can be achieved in a number of ways, one of the most effective is to impose checks on the exercise of governmental power. Such constraints, which ensure that public power is wielded only for public purposes, bolster the confidence of the people in the integrity of government and this greatly enhances the capacity of public power. In this way, authority (competence) is directly linked to power (capacity), and legal sovereignty connected with 'real' sovereignty.

The relational aspect of the political conception of sovereignty is mainly concerned with elaborating the ways in which constitutional arrangements serve state-building

---

[74] George Lawson, *Politica Sacra et Civilis or, A Modell of Civil and Ecclesiasticall Government* [1660], Conal Condren ed. (Cambridge: Cambridge University Press, 1992), 47. See above, Ch. 4, 66–68.

[75] Emmanuel Joseph Sieyès, *What is the Third Estate?* [1789], M. Blondel trans. (London: Pall Mall Press, 1963), 124–128. See Ch. 4 above, 61–64.

[76] Lawson, above n. 74, 47.

[77] See, e.g., *British Coal Corporation* v. *The King* [1935] AC 500, 520: 'It is doubtless true that the power of the Imperial Parliament to pass on its own initiative any legislation it thought fit extending to Canada remains in theory unimpaired [as a consequence of the Statute of Westminster 1931]. But that is theory and has no relation to realities'. Cf. *Madzimbamuto* v. *Lardner-Burke* [1969] AC 645.

[78] Sieyes, above n. 75, 122–123.

purposes. This feature of political sovereignty is the product of the peculiarly communal character of political power, which requires individuals to act in concert. Political power, Arendt notes, 'can be divided without decreasing it, and the interplay of powers with their checks and balances is even liable to generate more power, so long, at least, as the interplay is alive and has not resulted in a stalemate'.[79] Viewed in this light, constitutional constraints should not be seen simply as limitations on the exercise of public power; they simultaneously act as a method of generating political power.

### RIGHTS ARE NOT ANTAGONISTIC TO SOVEREIGNTY BUT ARE THE PRODUCT OF ITS EXPRESSION

A correlation existed within classical political thought between law and right; law was conceived as an expression of equity, of rightness, within the natural order of things. Classical political thought did not therefore possess a subjective concept of right, a right which an individual maintained against other individuals or the collectivity.[80] Although the status of subjective rights in medieval thought has been extensively debated,[81] the concept appeared to receive its first systematic formulation by early modern writers who built their political theories on the foundation of the individual as a bearer of rights. Such theories are not antagonistic to the idea of sovereignty: the idea of individual vested rights was elaborated in conjunction with the articulation of the concept of sovereignty.

This is highlighted in the work of Hobbes, who constructed his entire system of political order from the foundation of natural rights. But what Hobbes argued was that the natural rights that inhere in the individual are relinquished in the process of covenanting to establish an all-powerful sovereign authority. These natural rights are given up in exchange for the security offered by the establishment of a common power. Consequently, the sovereign, as bearer of supreme power, is not subject to any rights claims. To the extent that individuals hold rights under political order, these are conferred solely through the law-making action of the sovereign. Individual rights-bearers do not possess rights because they are inscribed in nature or because they can be understood to be expressions of human reason, but only because they have been conferred by the sovereign's legislation.

---

[79] Arendt, above n. 31, 201. For an elaboration of this theme see: Stephen Holmes, *Passions and Constraint: On the Theory of Liberal Democracy* (Chicago: University of Chicago Press, 1995); Jon Elster, *Ulysses Unbound: Studies in Rationality, Precommitment, and Constraints* (Cambridge: Cambridge University Press, 2000).

[80] See, e.g., Michel Villey, 'L'idée du droit subjectif et les systèmes juridiques romains' (1946) 24–25 *Revue historique de droit* 201–228, who argues that the concept of *ius* in Roman law meant right in an objective sense: that which is right. Cf. Richard Tuck, *Natural Rights Theories: Their Origin and Development* (Cambridge: Cambridge University Press, 1979), 7–13.

[81] See, e.g., Tuck, ibid. Cf. Brian Tierney, 'Tuck on Rights: Some Medieval Problems' (1983) 4 *History of Political Thought* 429–441; Tierney, 'Origins of Natural Rights Language: Texts and Contexts, 1150–1250' (1989) 10 *History of Political Thought* 615–646.

Such notions as rights, duties, and powers must therefore be understood as relational concepts operating within an institutional framework of sovereign authority.[82] Most modern accounts, even those which inspired liberalism, operate within the frame of sovereignty. Consider, for example, the work of Montesquieu, one of the most powerful expositions influencing modern liberalism. Reworking the classical forms of rule as aspects of the activity of governing, Montesquieu argued that liberty is the product of political and legal arrangements which operate to ensure that governors do not abuse their powers. But Montesquieu argues that only in a system of state sovereignty governed by law is liberty able to flourish. Political liberty, Montesquieu contends, 'in no way consists in doing what one wants'; rather it must be seen as 'the right to do everything the laws permit'.[83]

Fundamental rights are often touted today as expressions of universal moral claims, and therefore as claims which transcend and restrict the political. This assertion is essentially rhetorical; rights claims are intrinsically partial and political.[84] Another way of expressing this would be to say that rights are a product of the expression of sovereignty. Rights are the consequence of political values being given legal recognition, whether by legislative enactment or designation in constitutional arrangements, and protected by the governing authorities.

THE SYSTEM OF PUBLIC LAW IS AN EXPRESSION OF SOVEREIGNTY

The absolutist aspect of sovereignty can properly be understood only from the perspective of law. Since sovereign authority is expressed through those established institutional forms which enable the general will to be articulated, that general will, although absolute, has nothing in common with the exercise of an arbitrary power.[85] Sovereign will is the antithesis of subjective will.[86] And since the expression of this will takes the form of law, sovereignty in reality means the sovereignty of law.[87]

There is, however, another aspect of the relationship between sovereignty and law to be considered. In the perspective of sovereignty, law is the command of the sovereign. But since the sovereign is an office that exercises an official power, the will of the sovereign can be expressed only through certain institutional forms. And these

---

[82] For the classic juristic account within the frame of sovereignty see Wesley N. Hohfeld, *Fundamental Legal Conceptions as Applied in Judicial Reasoning* (New Haven: Yale University Press, 1923).

[83] Montesquieu, *The Spirit of the Laws* [1748], Anne M. Cohler, Basia Carolyn Miller, and Harold Samuel Stone trans. and ed. (Cambridge: Cambridge University Press, 1989), xi.3.

[84] See Michael Ignatieff, *Human Rights as Politics and Idolatry* (Princeton, NJ: Princeton University Press, 2001), 3–52.

[85] This is one of the key themes of Montesquieu, who argues that, being rooted in fear, despotism is one of the least powerful forms of government: above n. 83, i.9.

[86] Arendt expresses this point by drawing a distinction between power and violence: see Hannah Arendt, *On Violence* (San Diego, Calif.: Harcourt, Brace & Co., 1970), 42: 'The extreme form of power is All against One, the extreme form of violence is One against All'.

[87] Bodin, above n. 22, i.8: 'For law is nothing but the command of a sovereign making use of his power'.

institutional forms must also be laid down in law. The constitution of authority, it might be said, is conditioned by law. This means not only that the omnipotent power of the state can be expressed only in the form of law but also that it can be expressed only through those institutional forms which are recognized by law. Sovereignty, in the words of Jellinek, 'has the exclusive capacity to determine itself and to restrain itself from the perspective of the law'.[88]

The capacities and restraints that give expression to a particular arrangement of the sovereign authority of the state form the subject matter of public law.

PUBLIC LAW IS NOT SOLELY A MATTER OF POSITIVE LAW

Many of the most intractable problems in juristic thought arise as a result of misunderstandings about sovereignty. Some of the difficulties flow from a failure to recognize the official or institutional nature of sovereign authority, but others stem from an inability to grasp the relational character of sovereignty. Sovereignty is doubly relational (tenet 7) and these two aspects, the legal and political conceptions, reflect twin concerns with competence and capacity. It has been argued that the legal conception, which focuses on the authority of the sovereign to enact law, has the tendency to suppress the political conception, which is mainly concerned with the capacity to generate political power through the relationship between the state and the people. In order to understand the juristic significance of sovereignty, we need to examine a third relational aspect, that is, the relation between the legal and the political conceptions.

This issue can first be addressed by considering the theoretical framework of legal positivism, the predominant tendency in modern jurisprudence. In the English tradition, positivism has invariably accepted that legal validity rests on the existence of governmental authority. Whether those foundations are expressed as habitual obedience to a sovereign power,[89] as 'ultimate legal principles' which have historical but not legal sources,[90] or as a 'rule of recognition' whose existence is 'an empirical, though complex, question of fact',[91] the legal is conceived ultimately as being based on the political. It is, however, in the characterization of both the legal and the political, and hence of the relation between the two, that this tradition of thought commits errors. The legal error is to adopt an essentially command- or rule-based conception of law (law as the will of the sovereign) which is unable to offer an adequate account of the constitutive aspects of public law.[92] The error made concerning

---

[88] Jellinek, cited in Kriegel, above n. 19, 32.
[89] John Austin, *The Province of Jurisprudence Determined* [1832], Wilfrid E. Rumble ed. (Cambridge: Cambridge University Press, 1995), 166.
[90] John W. Salmond, *Jurisprudence*, P. J. Fitzgerald ed. (London: Stevens, 12th edn. 1966), 111–112.
[91] H. L. A. Hart, *The Concept of Law* (Oxford: Clarendon Press, 1961), 245.
[92] This error stems mainly from treating law as being founded on the bedrock of fact: see Dicey, above n. 48, 37: 'My aim in this chapter is . . . to explain the nature of Parliamentary sovereignty and to show that its existence is a legal fact'. See also H. W. R. Wade, 'The Basis of Legal Sovereignty' [1955]

the political is to assume that political power is an empirical rather than a relational phenomenon.

The consequential difficulties are highlighted in the work of Neil MacCormick, who has recently sought to re-assess sovereignty from within the positivist tradition.[93] Starting from the standard positivist account which maintains that a 'political sovereign' undergirds the 'legal sovereign', MacCormick suggests that, while this account may be useful for 'some types of politico-legal order', it has been 'found wanting in respect of those situations in which there is a standing constitutional tradition'.[94] This is a peculiar—and peculiarly English legal positivist—understanding of sovereignty. For MacCormick, once 'the powers of state are effectively divided according to a constitutional scheme' then there is 'a difficulty in identifying any sovereign being or sovereign entity holding power without any legal limitation'.[95]

We can make sense of this argument only if we recognize that it is based on an Austinian definition of sovereignty as 'power not subject to limitation by a higher or co-ordinate power, held independently over some territory'.[96] From this rather loose formulation, which is applied both to legal and political conceptions of sovereignty, a series of errors flow. MacCormick thus suggests that since 'all power holders', whether in a political or legal sense, are subject to 'some legal or political checks or controls', it follows that 'there is no single sovereign internal to the state, neither a legal nor a political sovereign'.[97] Building on this erroneous assumption, MacCormick argues that since a 'well-ordered Law-State or *Rechtstaat* is not subordinated to any political sovereign outside or above the law', this shows 'that sovereignty is neither necessary to the existence of law and state nor even desirable'.[98] He concludes his analysis by suggesting that we have moved 'beyond the sovereign state'[99] and into an era of 'post-sovereignty'.[100]

Many of these errors stem from a misconception concerning the nature of political power. MacCormick believes that political power is 'power-in-fact', that is, 'power to make sure that somebody in fact acts in a certain way'.[101] But this notion of power as coercive force overlooks the intrinsically relational aspect of political power.[102] It

---

*Cambridge Law Journal* 172–197, 189: 'What Salmond calls the "ultimate legal principle" is therefore a rule which is unique in being unchangeable by Parliament—it is changed by revolution, not by legislation; it lies in the keeping of the courts, and no Act of Parliament can take it away from them . . . It is simply a political fact'.

[93] Neil MacCormick, *Questioning Sovereignty: Law, State and Nation in the European Commonwealth* (Oxford: Oxford University Press, 1999), 75: 'I shall suggest that there is . . . a theoretical structure available, one built out of different materials presented to us by other strands within the positivist tradition'.
[94] Ibid. 128.   [95] Ibid.   [96] Ibid. 129, 128.   [97] Ibid. 129.   [98] Ibid.
[99] Ibid. 133. See also Neil MacCormick, 'Beyond the Sovereign State' (1993) 56 *Modern Law Review* 1–18.
[100] MacCormick, above n. 93, ch. 8, 'On Sovereignty and Post-Sovereignty'.   [101] Ibid. 12.
[102] In an earlier article on this subject, MacCormick, implicitly recognizing the limitations of this empirical conception of political power, stated that 'political power, to be sustained over time, requires legitimacy. Law is a significant source of legitimacy': Neil MacCormick, 'Sovereignty: Myth and Reality' in Nils Jareborg (ed.), *Towards Universal Law: Trends in National, European and International Law-making* (Uppsala: Iustus Förlag, 1995), 227–248, 235. This point has been subjected to critical analysis by Hans

is the failure to acknowledge that political power is generated by the relationship between rulers and ruled that lies at the root of the inability of positivists to accept the idea of the 'constituent power'—the people or 'the nation'—as being the repository of sovereignty in those regimes that adopt formal constitutions and allocate legal authority to designated organs of government. For want of this concept of constituent power, constitutionalist regimes are assumed to have 'divided' or moved 'beyond' sovereignty. But if sovereignty is taken as a representation of the autonomy of the political, the challenge for positivist jurisprudence is to offer an answer to the question of what sort of political world we inhabit once sovereignty is eliminated from our conception of law and state.

Some, though not all, of these difficulties stem from the peculiarities of the English approach to legal positivism. The general problem can be highlighted by considering the more abstract, neo-Kantian version of positivism expounded by Hans Kelsen. In contrast to Austin and the English analytical jurists, Kelsen rejected the idea that law was based on state power. His objective was to present a theory of law as a normative order which was not only 'purified of all political ideology' but, since it did not rest on empirical phenomena, also of 'every element of the natural sciences'.[103] Since in Kelsen's universe, the state is conceived to be the personification of legal order, the dualism between state and law that underpins Austinian legal science is dissolved.[104] And since Kelsen's scheme rests legal order on a hypothesis—the basic norm as that presupposition which gives expression to the autonomy of legal order—his theory remains unaffected by historical or sociological investigation. While this may be acceptable as a theory of legal validity, on the vital question of sovereignty Kelsen's theory leads only to a circularity in which the state, which on the one hand exists prior to law, also presents itself as a presupposition of law. As an insight into the juristic issues surrounding sovereignty, the pure theory has little to offer. Carl Schmitt's assessment—that Kelsen tried to resolve the issue simply by 'negating it'[105]—seems correct. Focusing on the issue of legal validity, Kelsen is able to maintain the purity

Lindahl, who argued that this means that political power must present itself as being conditioned and therefore not sovereign. Lindahl contended both that MacCormick's account contained a contradiction and that he had proved less than he claimed since the implication of his concession about legitimacy was that 'legitimate powers within a polity represent the sovereign'. Lindahl concluded, persuasively, that: 'While [MacCormick] has shown that there may be no individual or group of individuals in a legal and political order who enjoys undisputed superiority over all others, he has not demonstrated that sovereignty is contingent. In fact, his analysis suggests that sovereignty is a necessary legal and political concept'. See Hans Lindahl, 'The Purposiveness of Law: Two Concepts of Representation in the European Union' (1998) 17 *Law and Philosophy* 481–505, 484–487. In rewriting this essay for *Questioning Sovereignty* (above n. 93, ch. 8), MacCormick seeks to evade this criticism by retreating to an essentially empirical conception of political power and omitting his original statement concerning the relationship between legitimacy and political power.

[103] Hans Kelsen, *Introduction to the Problems of Legal Theory*, Bonnie L. Paulson and Stanley L. Paulson trans. of first edn. [1934] of *Reine Rechtslehre* (Oxford: Clarendon Press, 1992), 1.

[104] See Hans Kelsen, 'God and the State' [1922] in his *Essays in Legal and Moral Philosophy*, Ota Weinberger intro. (Dordrecht: Reidel, 1973), ch. 3.

[105] Carl Schmitt, *Political Theology: Four Chapters on the Concept of Sovereignty* [1922], George Schwab trans. (Cambridge, Mass: MIT Press, 1988), 21.

of the normative order only by conceding that 'the concept of sovereignty must be radically repressed'.[106]

The fundamental difficulty with positivist theories of law is that they are more or less explicitly devised for the purpose of presenting positive law—law as a system of enacted rules—as an autonomous practice. And because sovereignty is an essentially political concept, this means that once such jurists come to provide an explanation of the foundations of legal authority, they almost inevitably distort or suppress this foundational concept. Thus, although Kelsen was able to finesse the law/state dichotomy, he was obliged to fall back on another distortive duality, that between the legal and the political. Kelsen was explicit about this; he recognized that the maintenance of a duality of the concepts of the legal and the political 'performs an ideological function of extraordinary significance'.[107] This, he suggested, was because legal theory is obliged both to assume that 'the state, as a collective unity that is originally the subject of will and action, exists independently of, and even prior to, the law' and also to recognize that the state 'is a presupposition of the law . . . beholden to the law, because obligated and granted rights by the law'.[108]

The problem is that positivist theories focus on the issue of competence. While this may help to explain positive law as a structure of civil obligation, it distorts the attempt to understand law's role in establishing and maintaining the state. In relation to this latter function—the singular undertaking of public law—the issue of capacity must be drawn into an appropriate relation to that of competence; the political aspects of sovereignty must not be suppressed.

Within the security of a stable political order, within what MacCormick calls a 'standing constitutional tradition',[109] it is evident that law has 'its own relatively independent domain . . . [which] can be utilized to support or refute other domains'.[110] But it should not be forgotten that this legal sovereignty of competence is linked to a political sovereignty of capacity.[111] Whenever critical issues concerning the interests of the state are presented as matters of law, we should not forget that law's function—and the duty of all officers of the law—is to maintain and bolster the sovereignty of the state. The constitution, as Justice Robert Jackson once explained, is not a suicide pact.[112]

---

[106] Hans Kelsen, *Das Problem der Souveränität und die Theorie des Völkerrechts* (Tübingen: Mohr, 1920), 320; cited in Schmitt, ibid. 21.
[107] Kelsen, above n. 103, 96–97.   [108] Ibid.   [109] Above, 89.
[110] Carl Schmitt, *The Concept of the Political* [1932], George Schwab trans. (Chicago: University of Chicago Press, 1996), 66.
[111] See Schmitt, above n. 105, 5.
[112] *Terminiello* v. *City of Chicago* 337 US 1 (1949), 37(diss). Cf. Koskenniemi's synopsis of Jellinek's views: 'The State . . . is a purposeful community. Among its purposes is the wish to engage in contacts with other States. To break one's compacts would go against this. It would make social life impossible. To have a purpose is to will the presence of the conditions under which the purpose may be fulfilled. If a State can fulfil its purpose only by participating in international life, then it must keep its promises unless there is a reasonable motive . . . for disregarding them. No State can be reasonably assumed to commit suicide'. See Martti Koskenniemi, *The Gentle Civilizer of Nations: The Rise and Fall of International Law* (Cambridge: Cambridge University Press, 2001), 205–206.

This explanation may disconcert those who seek some insurance against the threat of abuse of official power. Although their concerns are not unfounded—and certainly we should not overlook the state's potential to act as a force of domination—the standard remedy proposed by many, that of maintaining faith in the transcendent quality of law, is misconceived. To the question of how in practice sovereign authority can be prevented from using public power oppressively, it must openly be acknowledged that ultimately there can be no juridical solution.

This does not mean that the institutional arrangements of law offer no protection. To the contrary, once sovereignty is understood, it is evident that law performs a vital role in seeking to ensure that such power is properly exercised. Though absolute (i.e., absolute from the perspective of its own particular way of conceptualizing the world), sovereignty incorporates certain intrinsic constraints. These limitations derive from the basic tenets of sovereignty, which identify sovereignty as being generated through an institutional framework established for the purpose of maintaining and promoting the peace, security, and welfare of citizens. Without the limits implied by those tenets, sovereignty could not be identified as a representation of the autonomy of the political and thereby distinguished from the power that economic wealth, feudal dominion or despotism confers.[113]

Law plays a critical role in explicating in the form of rules, regulations, rights, and responsibilities the character of sovereign authority. But if public law is to be taken seriously, we need to recognize that, notwithstanding certain rhetorical flourishes about the appeal to 'higher', 'fundamental' or even 'natural' law, the determination of the limits to sovereign authority, even when articulated by courts, must be political.[114] It is political because it is in the nature of sovereignty that a political system must be capable of authoritatively expressing its will on any issue. This sovereign will is expressed through institutional forms and arrangements which are generally laid down in law, and adherence to these forms gives meaning to the idea of the rule of law. But thus constituted, there can be no legal limitation on competence, and in this

---

[113] Cf. Montesquieu's project in *The Spirit of the Laws* (above n. 83) which can be understood as an extended essay on the threat that despotism poses to sovereign authority: 'republican government is that in which the people as a body, or only as a part of the people, have sovereign power; monarchical government is that in which one alone governs, though by fixed and established laws; whereas, in despotic government, one alone, without law and without rule, draws everything along by his will and his caprices' (ibid. ii.1). Despotism is the 'other'—a deviant form which lacks law, counsel, and politics and eradicates the distinction between public and private—which Montesquieu uses to throw into relief the achievements of political order. Nevertheless, it might be noted that, by projecting an Oriental image of despotism, Montesquieu the aristocrat masks the degree to which it flourished in Europe as feudal dominion: on which see Kriegel, above n. 19, 18–19. Cf. Arendt, above n. 31, 202: 'Tyranny prevents the development of power . . . it generates, in other words, impotence as naturally as other bodies politic generate power'.

[114] In *The Concept of the Political* (above n. 110), Schmitt illustrates this point at the same time as highlighting the limitations of his interpretation of Hobbes. He states: '[Hobbes] has emphasized time and again that the sovereignty of law means only the sovereignty of men who draw up and administer this law. The rule of a higher order, according to Hobbes, is an empty phrase if it does not signify that certain men of this higher order rule over men of a lower order' (ibid. 67). What Schmitt here overlooks is the intrinsically representational aspects of Hobbes's sovereign, which have the effect of impressing public responsibilities in that institution.

sense it might be said that the sovereign is above the law.[115] Between these two basic propositions, however, lies a sphere of ambiguity. On the one hand, it could be said that since the sovereign will is omnipotent there can be no legal limitations whatsoever, because established institutional forms can always be changed. On the other hand, it might be argued that the sovereign is above the law only in the way that a building is above its foundation; tamper with the foundation (the fundamental laws/the distinctive political relationship) and the building could collapse. Utilizing this architectural metaphor, some try to transform these foundational issues into matters of law (hence the point about transcendence). But these issues, going to the core of the relational aspect of sovereignty, must be acknowledged to be political. Cicero might say that such issues are resolved by *prudentia*, Aquinas by practical reason, and Montesquieu by the necessary relationships which stem from the nature of things. Whatever the precise characterization, the point is that these are not matters which are susceptible to formulaic, rule-based prescription. To pretend that there are answers above the cut and thrust of the necessity of decision in the face of conflicting views is to do a disservice both to the value of law and the arts of politics.

CONCLUSION: SOVEREIGNTY IN TRANSITION?

Sovereignty is the foundational concept underpinning public law and it stands as a representation of the autonomy of the political. By drawing on an intrinsically collective notion of political power—what Arendt referred to as 'the worldly in-between space by which men are mutually related'[116]—sovereignty can be identified as a relational phenomenon. This relational idea of sovereignty enables us to identify both the public and political aspects of the concept, which concern the issues of competence (authority) and capacity (power) respectively. Lawyers need to be able to locate the authority structure of the state with some precision. When focusing on the issue of jurisdictional competence, however, it should never be forgotten that the regime draws its power from a political relationship between state and citizens, that competence and capacity are inextricably linked.

Understood in this light, it is difficult to conceive how the present era is one that may be characterized as moving 'beyond' sovereignty. Such analyses are based on a misunderstanding of the concept. But since the contemporary trends that provide the basis for such an assessment are important, the potential impact of these developments on the idea of relational sovereignty should be assessed.

Most analyses focus on the likely impact of newly emerging institutional configurations on the status of the modern, territorially organized, state. The tendencies of states to promote greater institutional differentiation in the domestic sphere, leading

---

[115] The complexity of this formulation can be discerned by considering the history of the maxim that 'the king can do no wrong': see Greenberg, above n. 47.
[116] Arendt, above n. 34, 175.

to a devolution of authority from the centre,[117] and greater institutional integration in the international arena, leading to transfers of jurisdictional competence to supra-national bodies,[118] both appear to challenge their pre-eminent position. Such responses to contemporary political challenges do not amount to a division or transfer of sovereignty (tenet 7), and can just as easily be explained as an augmentation of sovereignty. Provided the question of 'ultimate' authority is not affected by these novel institutional arrangements, they do not entrench on sovereignty. That is, provided these institutional arrangements can be explained as an elaboration of internal coherence or as the promotion of more efficacious external action, the basics of sovereignty remain unaffected. And the reason for this is that issues of jurisdictional competence are not determinative of questions of sovereignty.

This point can be illustrated by considering the most innovative arrangement, that of the evolving structure of the European Union (EU). The project now known as the EU was formed by the member states of western Europe for the purpose of better advancing their traditional objectives of maintaining the security, prosperity, and welfare of their citizens.[119] To assist in the realization of this objective, an elaborate supra-national authority structure was established. In the words of the European Court of Justice (ECJ), one of the newly-formed institutions, the Union constitutes 'a new legal order of international law for the benefit of which the states have limited their sovereign rights'.[120] But shared competence or transferred jurisdiction does not entail shared or transferred sovereignty, even if, with the acquiescence of the member state, European law assumes priority in any conflict with a provision of domestic law.[121] With the extending range of EU competences, however, deliberation over the autonomy of the EU legal order has been transmuted into a debate over the 'constitutionalization' of the entity[122] and this has generated analyses concerning the formation of a 'post-state polity'.[123] Despite this flurry of activity, the critical question of sovereignty remains that which was most directly addressed by the German Federal

---

[117] Note, e.g., recent reforms affecting the governmental arrangements of the several parts of the United Kingdom: see Alan J. Ward, 'Devolution: Labour's Strange Constitutional "Design"' in Jeffrey Jowell and Dawn Oliver (eds), *The Changing Constitution* (Oxford: Oxford University Press, 4th edn. 2000), ch. 5.

[118] See, e.g., David Held, Anthony McGrew, David Goldblatt, and Jonathan Perraton, *Global Transformations: Politics, Economics and Culture* (Cambridge: Polity Press, 1999).

[119] See Alan S. Milward, *The European Rescue of the Nation-State* (London: Routledge, rev. edn. 1994), esp. ch. 1.

[120] Case 26/62, *Van Gend en Loos* v. *Nederlandse Administratie der Berlastingen* [1963] ECR 1, 12. See also Case 6/64, *Costa* v. *ENEL* [1964] ECR 585, which asserts the supremacy of European Community law over the domestic law of member states (EC law cannot 'be overridden by domestic legal provisions, however framed, . . . without the legal basis of the Community itself being called into question') and declares that state accession entails 'a permanent limitation of their sovereign rights'.

[121] See Bruno de Witte, 'Direct Effect, Supremacy, and the Nature of the Legal Order' in Paul Craig and Gráinne de Búrca (eds), *The Evolution of EU Law* (Oxford: Oxford University Press, 1999), 177–213.

[122] See J. H. H. Weiler, *The Constitution of Europe: 'Do the New Clothes have an Emperor?'* (Cambridge: Cambridge University Press, 1999); Dieter Grimm, 'Does Europe Need a Constitution?' (1995) 1 *European Law Journal* 282–302; Jürgen Habermas, 'Remarks on Dieter Grimm's "Does Europe Need a Constitution?"' (1995) 1 *European Law Journal* 303–307.

[123] See Neil Walker, 'The Idea of Constitutional Pluralism' (2002) 65 *Modern Law Review* 317–359.

Constitutional Court in 1993 in the case of *Brunner*.[124] In *Brunner*, the court declared that, with respect to matters of German constitutionality and sovereignty, it was for the constitutional court, and not the ECJ, to determine the limits of the powers of the EU.[125] The court also stated that, 'given the right [of the people] guaranteed by Article 38 of the Constitution to participate in the legitimation of state power'[126] (the principle of democracy), it followed that:

If the peoples of the individual States provide democratic legitimation through the agency of their national parliaments (as at present) limits are then set by virtue of the democratic principle to the extension of the European Communities' functions and powers.[127]

Although the court did not preclude the possibility of the democratic bases of the EU being built up in tandem with continuing integration, it maintained that presently 'the exercise of sovereign power through a federation of States like the European Union is based on authorisations from States which remain sovereign and which in international matters generally, act through their governments and control the integration process thereby'.[128] What the German constitutional court recognized was the essentially political character of sovereignty. Sovereignty, it implied, is not directly affected by increasingly elaborate institutional arrangements of governance, since sovereignty is an expression of a political relationship between the people and the state.[129] Jurisdictional questions of competence ultimately rest on the political issue of capacity, the norm on the exception. And in an exceptional state of crisis, there seems little doubt that the state retains ultimate power and authority.

Concerns about sovereignty that are geared to issues of competence presented by the emergence of new institutional frameworks invariably turn out to be misplaced. This is not to say that contemporary trends do not present major challenges for the idea of sovereignty. But such challenges are not orientated to institutional matters. Rather, they are threats to capacity which are directed at the political conception of sovereignty. This is a much more serious threat, one that presents a challenge to the continuing viability of the modern political project.

This radical challenge to the concept of sovereignty is rooted in an analysis of power in the contemporary world. The argument here is not merely that, as a consequence of new institutional configurations, the power of the modern state to impose its authority is diminishing. Although significant economic limits to the conduct of modern politics exist,[130] so long as the political realm is able to be conceptualized as

---

[124] *Brunner* v. *European Union Treaty* [1994] 1 CMLR 57.
[125] Ibid. para. 49.   [126] Ibid. para. 34.   [127] Ibid. para. 44.   [128] Ibid. para. 46.
[129] In this sense, the 'devolutionary' arrangements of the Scotland Act 1998, which establish a Scottish parliament able to give institutional expression to Scots political identity, potentially provide the more radical challenge to the sovereignty of the United Kingdom state. For comparison with the Canadian situation, see *Reference by the Governor in Council, pursuant to section 53 of the Supreme Court Act, concerning the secession of Quebec from Canada* [1998] 2 SCR 217; Mark D. Walters, 'Nationalism and the Pathology of Legal Systems: Considering the *Quebec Secession Reference* and its Lessons for the United Kingdom' (1999) 62 *Modern Law Review* 371–396.
[130] See John Dunn (ed.), *The Economic Limits to Modern Politics* (Cambridge: Cambridge University Press, 1990).

a discrete sphere of human activity, such economic constraints do not directly undermine the idea of sovereignty. The argument is that power in late modernity has so fundamentally altered in character that the modern concept of sovereignty as a representational idea founded on the autonomy of the political is now redundant.

This radical claim is most closely associated with the work of Michel Foucault, who has argued that, as a consequence of technological, economic, and social change, the political power generated by sovereignty is, through the processes of bureaucratization, being transformed into a general economy of discipline that now pervades society.[131] This is what Foucault refers to as 'the paradox of the relations between capacity and power'.[132] A synthesis having been effected between political and economic power, Foucault contends that disciplinary power not only shapes social and political practices but is able also to structure human thought.[133] As a consequence, the relationship between society and power—between the people and government—has been inverted and the regulatory force of governmental power, as a form of bio-power, is now applied to humanity itself.[134] This new paradigm of governance without government marks the death of the subject, the destruction of the autonomy of the political and the end of sovereignty.[135]

The juridical implications of Foucault's thesis have been elaborated by Michael Hardt and Antonio Negri.[136] Hardt and Negri argue that this decline in the modern political conception of sovereignty as a result of the emergence of 'governmentality' is better conceived 'as a passage *within* the notion of sovereignty'.[137] Sovereignty, they claim, should now be understood to have assumed a new form 'composed of a series of national and supranational organisms united under a single logic of rule'.[138] And this 'new global form of sovereignty' is what they call 'imperial sovereignty' or simply 'Empire'.[139]

---

[131] Michel Foucault, 'Governmentality' in Graham Burchell, Colin Gordon, and Peter Miller (eds), *The Foucault Effect: Studies in Governmentality* (Hemel Hempstead: Harvester Wheatsheaf, 1991), 87–104.

[132] Michel Foucault, 'What is Enlightenment?' in Paul Rabinow (ed.), *The Foucault Reader* (Harmondsworth: Penguin, 1986), 32–50, 47.

[133] Michel Foucault, *Discipline and Punish: The Birth of the Prison*, Alan Sheridan trans. (Harmondsworth: Penguin, 1977).

[134] Michel Foucault, *The History of Sexuality*, Robert Hurley trans. (Harmondsworth: Penguin, 1981), i.135–145. For a study that explores further Foucault's argument that this 'politicization of bare life' constitutes the decisive event of modernity and signals a radical change in political categories see: Giorgio Agamben, *Homo Sacer: Sovereign Power and Bare Life*, Daniel Heller-Roazen trans. (Stanford, Calif.: Stanford University Press, 1998).

[135] Michel Foucault, *Power/Knowledge* (Brighton: Harvester, 1980), 121: '[Political] theories still continue today to busy themselves with the problem of sovereignty. What we need, however, is a political philosophy that isn't erected around the problem of sovereignty, nor therefore around the problems of law and prohibition. We still need to cut off the King's head: in political theory that has still to be done'.

[136] Michael Hardt and Antonio Negri, *Empire* (Cambridge, Mass: Harvard University Press, 2000).

[137] Ibid. 88. In this sense, the authors remain close to Foucault's argument that the discourse of sovereignty and governmentality run in tandem: see Michel Foucault, 'Governmentality' in Graham Burchell, Colin Gordon, and Peter Miller (eds), *The Foucault Effect: Studies in Governmentality* (Hemel Hempstead: Harvester Wheatsheaf, 1991), 87–104, 102. See further above, Ch. 2, 14–15.

[138] Hardt and Negri, above n. 136, xii.      [139] Ibid. xii, 8.

# Sovereignty

Imperial sovereignty is, however, a rather different creature. It presents itself as nothing less than the nemesis of modern sovereignty: imperial sovereignty reflects a fusion of economic and political power (cf. tenet 2),[140] the elimination of the distinction between public and private (cf. tenet 3),[141] the erosion of civil order which underpins the idea of official power (cf. tenet 4),[142] and the disintegration of a distinctive political relationship (cf. tenets 5 and 6).[143] More generally, imperial sovereignty signals the end of the idea of the modern state (cf. tenet 1)[144] and of a relational sovereignty based on a territorial unit (cf. tenet 7).[145] It marks the triumph of institutional competence, of legal sovereignty severed from political capacity and, in a return to classical political thought (cf. tenet 8), leads to the emergence of 'imperial right'.[146] Empire is the sovereign power that governs the world, the consummation of a capitalist project of fusing economic and political power. And in the process, the modern idea of public law is replaced by a systems-orientated framework of regulatory law operating in accordance with a 'single logic of rule' (cf. tenets 9 and 10).[147]

Imperial sovereignty directly challenges modern sovereignty. Modern sovereignty, it claims, is a juridico-political fiction that no longer offers an adequate representation of power in late modern societies, and therefore legitimates an authority structure whose dynamic it is unable to grasp.[148] If modern sovereignty symbolizes the past, then imperial sovereignty, a process that 'is materializing before our very

---

[140] Ibid. 354: 'Empire constitutes the ontological fabric in which all the relations of power are woven together—political and economic relations as well as social and personal relations'.

[141] Ibid. 188–189.

[142] Ibid. 187: 'In the imperial world, this dialectic of sovereignty between the civil order and the natural order has come to an end'.

[143] Ibid. 307: 'Today a notion of politics as an independent sphere of the determination of consensus and a sphere of mediation among conflicting social forces has very little room to exist. . . . Politics does not disappear; what disappears is any notion of the autonomy of the political'.

[144] Ibid. 306: 'the state has been defeated and corporations now rule the earth!'

[145] Ibid. 139–140: 'there is no longer an outside that can bound the place of sovereignty. . . . In this smooth space of Empire, there is no *place* of power—it is both everywhere and nowhere'.

[146] Ibid. 62, referring to 'the frustration and continual instability suffered by imperial right as it attempts to destroy the old values that served as reference points for international public law (the nation-states, the international order of Westphalia, the United Nations and so forth) along with the so-called turbulence that accompanies this process'. From this perspective, it seems clear that bodies such as the European Court of Justice are to be conceived as being agencies of imperial right.

[147] Ibid. 13–14: 'The new paradigm is both system and hierarchy, centralized construction of norms and far-reaching production of legitimacy, spread out over world space. It is configured *ab initio* as a dynamic and flexible systemic structure that is articulated horizontally. We conceive the structure in a kind of intellectual shorthand as a hybrid of Niklas Luhmann's systems theory and John Rawls's theory of justice. . . . The development of the global system (and of imperial right in the first place) seems to be the development of a machine that imposes procedures of continual contractualization that lead to systemic equilibria—a machine that creates a continuous call for authority'. See further, Niklas Luhmann, *Social Systems*, John Bednarz Jr. trans. (Stanford, Calif: Stanford University Press, 1995); Gunther Teubner, *Law as an Autopoietic System* (Oxford: Blackwell, 1993); Gunther Teubner (ed.), *Global Law without a State* (Aldershot: Dartmouth, 1997).

[148] Hardt and Negri, above n. 136, 375: 'European virtue—or really its aristocratic morality organized in the institutions of modern sovereignty—cannot manage to keep pace with the vital powers of mass democracy'.

eyes',[149] represents the future. Hardt and Negri believe not only that the emergence of Empire is inevitable, but that it should be embraced. This is essentially because they place their faith in the constituent power of the multitude.[150] The emergence of Empire, they argue, highlights the fact that 'the multitude is the real productive force of our social world' and that Empire is 'a mere apparatus of capture that lives only off the vitality of the multitude'.[151] Empire therefore creates a greater potential for revolutionary action—constituent power in all its radicalness and strength—as 'all the exploited and the subjugated' come face to face with 'the machine of command' with 'no mediation between them'.[152]

In its final expression, Empire is revealed to be a normative theory which rests on a controversial belief in the constituent power of the multitude. We will examine the use they make of constituent power in the chapter that follows. But since both the empirical analysis of the emergence of global sovereignty[153] and the theoretical construction of imperial power[154] remain questionable, there is no case on positive grounds for abandoning the claim that the modern state is an unresolved tension between two irreconcilable dispositions (expressed as *societas* and *universitas*).[155] Although the processes that Foucault describes under the rubric of 'the governmentalization of the state' heighten the tension, they have not led to a creation of a world in which 'power over' has totally overcome the representative claims of 'power to'. The modern idea of sovereignty remains the most appropriate framework for grappling with the tensions between power and domination in the contemporary world.

---

[149] Hardt and Negri, above xi.

[150] See Antonio Negri, *Insurgencies: Constituent Power and the Modern State*, Maurizia Boscagli trans. (Minneapolis: University of Minnesota Press, 1999).

[151] Hardt and Negri, above n. 136, 62.            [152] Ibid. 393.

[153] See, e.g., Held *et al.*, above n. 118.

[154] See, e.g., Charles Taylor, 'Foucault on Freedom and Truth' in his *Philosophy and the Human Sciences: Philosophical Papers, vol. 2* (Cambridge: Cambridge University Press, 1985), 152–184, 175–176: 'There are empirical obstacles, and some very deep-lying ones in man's historical situation. But that is not Foucault's point. He wants to discredit as somehow based on a misunderstanding the very idea of liberation from power. But I am arguing that power, in his sense, *does not make sense* without at least the idea of liberation'. See also Michael Walzer, 'The Lonely Politics of Michel Foucault' in his *The Company of Critics: Social Criticism and Political Commitment in the Twentieth Century* (New York: Basic Books, 1988), 191–209.

[155] See above, Ch. 2, 13–19.

# 6

## Constituent Power

One might be forgiven for thinking that the concept of constituent power offers lawyers nothing but problems. Although it helps us locate the source of modern political authority, and therefore identify the base upon which the structure of legal authority rests, this apparently all-powerful concept is one that jurists suppress. This is achieved by drawing a rudimentary distinction between constituent power and constituted power. Only the latter, it is implied, that which is situated within the established framework of constitutional authority, falls within the sphere of juristic competence. Constituted power is contained within a hierarchy of norms, and legal knowledge is concerned solely with this form of normative ordering. While jurists recognize that the hierarchy of norms must rest on some foundation, political questions concerning the nature of the foundation tend to be avoided. Such questions are replaced either with a postulated fact like 'the rule of recognition' or with a hypothesis such as the 'basic norm'.[1] Reflecting on the political foundations of legal order, David Dyzenhaus has commented on 'the oddness of a metaphor which says that a norm is both the foundation and the apex of a structure'.[2] But he does not follow this through. What analytical jurists have done is invert the foundation. And this inversion—the replacement of a base with an apex—serves the purpose of overcoming the concept of constituent power.

A consequence of this manoeuvre is that although constituent power presents itself as a vibrant force that drives constitutional development, it appears in juristic thought only as a formal principle, one whose dynamic remains shielded from legal cognition. If jurisprudence were concerned solely with the structure of civic obligations derived from the rules, then a construction operating under the presupposition of an extant authority structure might be understandable. For those seeking to understand public law, however, this approach is difficult to defend; denying juristic significance to the concept of constituent power is tantamount to rejecting the idea of public law.

This approach to constituent power has dominated modern Anglo-American jurisprudence. Given that the British constitution lacks the formal constraints of modern constitutional frameworks this seems odd. The character of the constitution makes it more difficult for British jurists to draw a clear line between constituted power and constituent power—that is, between the formal and the material, between

---

[1] H. L. A. Hart, *The Concept of Law* (Oxford: Clarendon Press, 1961), esp. ch. 6; Hans Kelsen, *Introduction to the Problems of Legal Theory* (trans. of first edn. [1934] of *Reine Rechtslehre* by Bonnie L. Paulson and Stanley L. Paulson) (Oxford: Clarendon Press, 1992).

[2] David Dyzenhaus, *Legality and Legitimacy: Carl Schmitt, Hans Kelsen and Herman Heller in Weimar* (Oxford: Oxford University Press, 1997), 103 (n. 4).

competence and capacity, between the distributive and the generative, between the legal and the political. The attempt to do so has resulted in the projection of a rather desiccated notion of the constitution, skewing our perception of the activity of governing and preventing us from viewing constitutional arrangements dynamically.

In this chapter, my objective will be to assess the contribution made by the concept of constituent power to an understanding of public law. It is a complex task because constituent power resists simple absorption into juristic categories. 'The strength hidden in constituent power', Georges Burdeau notes, 'refuses to be fully integrated in a hierarchical system of norms and competencies'.[3] But reflecting on this is a useful starting point. The main reason for it is the fact that constituent power articulates the power of the multitude: constituent power is the juristic expression of the democratic impetus. The concept expresses the tensions between democracy and law.

Democracy is not easily reconciled to law. It is an expression of an expansive or innovative movement that asserts the capacity of the people to decide for themselves the type of ordering under which they might live. As the primary legitimating principle of modern political order, democracy fixes on the present and is orientated to the future. Democracy reflects a principle of openness. Law, by contrast, seeks to control, regulate and divide this expansive force. Although addressing the concerns of the present, law is orientated to the past. Law seeks the closure of that which democracy tries to keep open. The relationship between democracy and law is never going to be easy, expressing as it does ambivalence between innovation and conservation, change and stability, openness and closure, the inheritance of the past against the possibilities of the future.

This difficult relationship between democracy and law helps us to understand constituent power as the concept through which such pressures are mediated. Constituent power is the generative principle of modern constitutional arrangements. It gives juristic expression to those forces that constantly irritate the formal constitution, thereby ensuring it is able to perform its political function. In order to appreciate how this concept has become a basic building block of public law, we begin by outlining its emergence in modern political thought.

THE EMERGENCE OF THE MULTITUDE

Constituent power emerges as a theme in political thought alongside the conviction that the authority of government rests on the consent of the people. The idea of the 'consent of the people' initially makes a rather tentative appearance. At first, consent was not understood to be an active undertaking; as Sheldon Wolin notes, it was much less risky 'to adopt the myth that political society was founded *on* the people rather

---

[3] Georges Burdeau, *Traité des sciences politique*, vol. 4 (Paris: Librairie générale de droit et de jurisprudence, 1983), 171: cited in Antonio Negri, *Insurgencies: Constituent Power and the Modern State*, Maurizia Boscagli trans. (Minneapolis: University of Minnesota Press), 1.

than *by* them'.[4] The notion of 'the people' being invoked was that of an inert and symbolic collectivity, such as that mythologized within the idea of 'one Body Politick'.[5] But gradually 'the people' insinuated itself into modern political thought as representing some form of active political agency. And the origins of constituent power are found in the process through which 'the people' are converted from a passive to an active force.

In tracing this process, it is helpful to return to the work of Machiavelli, which sought to instruct ruling elites in the arts of government. At the core of his thought lies a tension between virtue (*virtù*) and fortune (*fortuna*), or in a modern idiom between freedom and necessity, the realms of ought and is. For Machiavelli, virtue, like law, has its limits. Since the 'distance between how one lives and how one should live is so great', he explains, 'he who discards what he does for what he should do, usually learns how to ruin rather than maintain himself'.[6] This, for Machiavelli, is the tragedy of the political. But it must be acknowledged and openly embraced. Effective political conduct thus requires the prince 'to develop the ability to be not good, and use or not use this ability as necessity dictates'.[7]

For our purposes, the main significance of this tension between freedom and necessity lies in the recognition of an unbridgeable gulf between governors and governed. This points to a central problem of politics. The 'contrasting humours' of virtue and fortune, Machiavelli notes, 'result in the nobles desiring to control and oppress the people whilst the people desire not to be controlled or oppressed by the nobles'.[8] He draws out the implications of this theme in *The Discourses*. In every republic, he suggests, 'there are two different dispositions, that of the populace and that of the upper class and . . . all legislation favourable to liberty is brought about by the clash between them'.[9] Machiavelli's solution to the problem is, in Quentin Skinner's summation, 'to frame the laws relating to the constitution in such a way as to engineer a tensely-balanced equilibrium between these opposed social forces, one in which all the parties remain involved in the business of government, and each "keeps watch over the other" in order to forestall both "the rich men's arrogance" and "the people's licence"'.[10]

Machiavelli's work is important precisely because this dialectic between authority and liberty—between the will to power and the desire for freedom—exposes the driving principle of constituent power. Without descending into a romantic notion

---

[4] Sheldon S. Wolin, *Tocqueville between Two Worlds: The Making of a Political and Theoretical Life* (Princeton, NJ: Princeton University Press, 2001), 177.

[5] John Locke, *Two Treatises of Government* [1680], Peter Laslett ed. (Cambridge: Cambridge University Press, 1988), ii. § 97: 'And thus every Man, by consenting with others to make one Body Politick under one Government, puts himself under an Obligation to every one of that Society, to submit to the determination of the *majority*'.

[6] Niccolò Machiavelli, *The Prince* [1513] (London: Dent, 1995), ch. 15.   [7] Ibid.

[8] Ibid. ch. 9. For an elaboration of this theme, see Harvey C. Mansfield, *Machiavelli's Virtue* (Chicago: University of Chicago Press, 1996), ch. 1.

[9] Niccolò Machiavelli, *The Discourses* [1531], Leslie J. Walker trans., Bernard Crick ed. (Harmondsworth: Penguin, 1983), i.4.

[10] Quentin Skinner, *Machiavelli* (Oxford: Oxford University Press, 1981), 74.

of its potential, Machiavelli identifies the power of the people as an active force. Though the populace may be ignorant, he notes, 'it is capable of grasping the truth'.[11] He also recognizes that, notwithstanding his own desires, the prince must 'be sufficiently prudent that he knows how to avoid the infamy of those vices that will deprive him of his state'.[12] Antonio Negri has argued that the theme lying at the heart of *The Prince* is that of 'the tragedy of constituent power'[13] and that *The Discourses* is to be interpreted as demonstrating 'that the only content of the constituent form is the people, that the only constitution of the Prince is democracy'.[14] By undertaking the hazardous task of seeking 'new modes and orders',[15] Machiavelli was the first thinker to insinuate the concept of constituent power into the core of a modern conception of politics.

The contrast with Hobbes here is instructive. Although Hobbes is claimed to be the first systematic theorist of the modern state,[16] the idea of constituent power does not figure prominently in his work.[17] Hobbes constructs a theory of the state from the notion that the people covenant to form a commonwealth. He also recognizes that, whatever the precise framework of government that the people institute, the fact of their meeting means that power is rooted in democracy.[18] For Hobbes, however, the idea of 'the people' is created only as a consequence of establishing the state. Before the formation of the commonwealth there is only a multitude, or a crowd. And once the crowd is transformed into a people as a result of the establishment of the commonwealth, it ceases to perform any active political role.[19] Hobbes argues that 'the Common-peoples minds . . . are like clean paper, fit to receive whatsoever by Publique Authority shall be imprinted in them'.[20] One of the primary functions of the state, therefore, is to instil in the people the habits of obedience;[21] the people must, through the use of a political variant of a catechism, be instructed 'in the Essential Rights (which are the Naturall, and Fundamental Lawes) of Soveraignty'.[22]

Once the critical moment at which the state is instituted has passed, Hobbes denies the people any active role in the exercise of constituent power. This was partly because his objective was to construct a juristic theory of the state.[23] Focused on the necessity of establishing and maintaining the authority of constituted power, Hobbes denied

---

[11] Machiavelli, above n. 9, i.4.     [12] Machiavelli, above n. 6, ch. 15.
[13] Negri, above n. 3, 54.     [14] Ibid. 66.
[15] Machiavelli, above n. 9, Bk. 1: 'Although owing to the envy inherent in man's nature it has always been no less dangerous to discover new ways and methods than to set off in search of new seas and unknown lands . . .'. Cf. Harvey C. Mansfield, *Machiavelli's New Modes and Orders: A Study of the Discourses on Livy* (Chicago: University of Chicago Press, 2001), 26.
[16] See above, Ch. 4, 55.
[17] Cf. Murray Forsyth, 'Thomas Hobbes and the Constituent Power of the People' (1981) 29 *Political Studies* 191–203.
[18] Thomas Hobbes, *On the Citizen* [1647], Richard Tuck and Michael Silverthorne trans. (Cambridge: Cambridge University Press, 1998), vii.5.
[19] See above, Ch. 4, 55–57.
[20] Thomas Hobbes, *Leviathan* [1651], Richard Tuck ed. (Cambridge: Cambridge University Press, 1996), 233.
[21] Ibid. 233–236.     [22] Ibid. 233.
[23] See above, Ch. 4, 57.

the people any continuing political role.[24] Within the Hobbesian scheme, political power is presented not only as transcendental but also as absolute. It is a power which, knowing nothing of constitutional constraint, has the potential to re-shape the social as well as the political realm.

In the work of John Locke, however, the division between social and political power—between civil society and the state—forms the centrepiece of his philosophy. Reworking the idea of the social contract as a covenant concerned with the delegation and not the alienation of original authority, Locke suggests that there are inherent limitations to the exercise of constituted power. But what protection exists if the government acts contrary to the terms of this delegation and attempts to oppress the people? Locke believes that no institutional mechanism is capable of resolving this issue.[25] Rather, he asserts that 'the *Community* perpetually *retains a Supream power* of saving themselves' from the foolish or wicked actions of their governors.[26] If governors act in breach of the trust that has been placed in them, the bond of obligation is forfeited 'and the Power devolve[s] into the hands of those that gave it, who may place it anew where they shall think best for their safety and security'.[27]

By acknowledging the continuing political role of the people, Locke implicitly accepts the distinction between constituted authority and constituent power.[28] However, pressing questions remain. Who, for example, decides whether the governors are acting in breach of trust? Locke's answer is unequivocal:

*The People shall be Judge*, for who shall be *Judge* whether his Trustee or Deputy acts well, and according to the trust reposed in him, but he who deputes him, and must, by having deputed him have still a Power to discard him, when he fails in his Trust?[29]

At the same moment as he asserts this basic right of the multitude, Locke expresses concern about its destabilizing potential. He accepts that the legitimate exercise of authority could be undermined as a result of the influence that 'ill affected and factious Men may spread amongst the People'[30] and that this residual power is capable of 'lay[ing] a ferment for frequent rebellion'.[31] Being concerned to limit the influence

---

[24] See, e.g., Hobbes, above n. 20, 234: 'Take away in any kind of State, the Obedience, (and consequently the Concord of the People,) and they shall not onely not flourish, but in short time be dissolved. And they that go about by disobedience, to doe no more than reforme the Common-wealth, shall find they do thereby destroy it; like the foolish daughters of *Peleus* (in the fable;) which desiring to renew the youth of their decrepit Father, did by the Counsell of *Medea*, cut him into pieces, and boyle him, together with strange herbs, but made not of him a new man'.

[25] John Locke, above n. 5, ii.§ 168.   [26] Ibid. ii.§ 149.   [27] Ibid.

[28] This division is most clearly drawn in the distinction which Locke draws between 'the dissolution of government' and 'the dissolution of society': ibid. ii. ch. 19.

[29] Ibid. ii.§ 240. It might be noted that earlier theorists—such as Philippe du Plessis Mornay in *Vindiciae contra tyrannos* [1579]—who had suggested the existence of this right of resistance, rather than placing it in 'the people', had invested it in corporate bodies of the elite: see Quentin Skinner, *The Foundations of Modern Political Thought* (Cambridge: Cambridge University Press, 1978), ii. ch. 9.

[30] Locke, above n. 5, ii.§ 240.

[31] Ibid. ii.§ 224. Cf. Hobbes, above n. 18, 133–134: 'One may easily see how dangerous this belief [i.e., tyrannicide] is to commonwealths, and particularly to *Monarchies*, by recognizing that it exposes any *King*, good or bad, to the risk of being condemned by the judgement, and murdered by the hand, of one solitary assassin'.

of this power, Locke argues that the people have an innate 'slowness and aversion ... to quit their old Constitutions'.[32] The people being tolerant, '*great mistakes* in the ruling part ... will be *born by the People*, without mutiny or murmur'.[33] Revolutions, in short, 'happen not upon every little mismanagement in public affairs'.[34] This great power of 'dissolution of government', in short, must be placed at the extreme margins of legitimate political action.

Locke maintained that constituent power is residual only through the deployment of an ingenious argument. He suggested that the very existence of this power of legitimate rebellion ensures that it will rarely be used, since its existence guarantees that those vested with governmental authority will never be tempted to abuse their powers.[35] For Locke, then, the gulf that Machiavelli identified between governors and governed is one that must be bridged. That bridge is provided by the modern theory of constitutionalism. The vital function of the established framework of constituted authority is that of being able to generate trust between governors and governed.[36] For this confidence to be maintained, governors must act in accordance with the will of the majority.[37]

Locke's contribution was, as Wolin has expressed it, 'to rescue the notion of the people from the opprobrium of a destructive mob whose only modes of action were revolutionary violence and expropriation of private property and to put in its stead a theory of majority rule, which, potentially, could become annexed to a democratic politics'.[38] But Locke's deliberations over the relationship between the people and their governors reveal a paradox in the construction of contractual arguments concerning the foundation of a state. How is it that a multitude—a crowd of uneducated common people—is able to deliberate the appropriate structure of constituted authority? Hobbes altogether avoids this issue; if, as he believed, the minds of the common people are like blank sheets, how could the activity of covenanting to establish a sovereign authority be understood as an expression of democracy? Locke does not fare much better: 'Locke's majority was, successively, a constituent power, a form of rule, and a revolutionary actor'.[39] In an effort to resolve this difficulty, Locke was obliged to recognize that this formally sovereign people needs to be tutored and guided to ensure that it did not resort to the destructive actions of a revolutionary mob. This is the problem that Jean-Jacques Rousseau directly addresses.

Although Rousseau is often cited as a theorist of democracy, he openly acknowledged difficulties concerning its founding. In *The Social Contract*, he states that:

For a newly formed people to understand wise principles of politics and to follow the basic rules of statecraft, the effect would have to become the cause; the social spirit which must be the

---

[32] Locke, above n. 5, ii.§ 223.   [33] Ibid. ii.§ 225.   [34] Ibid.   [35] Ibid. ii.§ 226.
[36] See John Dunn, '"Trust" in the politics of John Locke' in his *Rethinking Modern Political Theory* (Cambridge: Cambridge University Press, 1985), 34–54.
[37] Locke, above n. 5, ii.§ 212: 'For the Essence and Union of the Society consisting in having one Will, the Legislative, when once established by a Majority, has the declaring, and as it were keeping of that Will'. See further ibid. ii.§ 95.
[38] Wolin, above n. 4, 243.   [39] Ibid.

product of social institutions would have to preside over the setting up of those institutions; men would have to have already become before the advent of law that which they become as a result of the law.[40]

Rousseau recognizes that 'the enterprise of setting up a people' required the transformation of each solitary individual into 'a part of a much greater whole', the conversion of a multitude of individuals into a body of citizens.[41] Democracy, Rousseau indicates, is a regime that presupposes the existence of certain skills and virtues necessary for its flourishing. And the consequence of this is that the idea of the foundation within contractualist thinking must be treated simply as a hypothetical rather than a historical condition, or as Kant put it 'merely an *idea* of reason'.[42]

Consequently, although social contract theorists place the idea of the people as the originating source of political power at the centre of their analyses of government, they invariably deploy a range of devices to avoid having to address the question of the role of the multitude as an active political presence. Rousseau's innovation was to have shifted the focus of the question of political virtue, which in classical thought had been addressed solely to the governing élite, to that of the multitude. Having done so, however, he then retreated into the abstraction of the general will. Although particular wills may err, 'the general will is always rightful and always tends to the public good'.[43] Rousseau's concept of the general will amounts to an expression of constituent power as a pure act of the intellect, with all passions subdued. Negri treats Rousseau's conception of the general will as a 'metaphysical transformation of the constitutive action of the masses', and argues that it is only in this ideal form that constituent power enters the modern discourse of public law.[44]

From a Machiavellian perspective that treats constituent power as an active practice rather than a formal principle, the social contract theorists limit democracy at the moment of embracing it. That is, they pay lip service to the idea that power resides in the people, while at the same time employing a variety of devices to keep the creative strength of the multitude at bay.[45]

---

[40] Jean-Jacques Rousseau, *The Social Contract* [1762], Maurice Cranston trans. (Harmondsworth: Penguin, 1968), ii.7.
[41] Ibid.
[42] Immanuel Kant, 'On the common saying: "This may be true in theory, but it does not apply in practice"' [1793] in his *Political Writings*, Hans Reiss ed. (Cambridge: Cambridge University Press, 2nd edn. 1991), 61–92, 79.
[43] Rousseau, above n. 40, ii.3.  [44] Negri, above n. 3, 201.
[45] The most sophisticated of the recent attempts is that of John Rawls, *A Theory of Justice* (Oxford: Oxford University Press, 1972). For the purpose of transforming his general principles of justice into an institutional framework of just government Rawls invokes a four-stage sequence (195–201). However, as Negri notes (above n. 3, 6–7), having introduced constituent power as part of the second stage, this power 'is reabsorbed into constituted law through a multi-staged mechanism that, by making constituent power immanent to the system, deprives it of its creative originality'.

## REVOLUTION AND CONSTITUTION

The revolutionary upheavals of the seventeenth and eighteenth centuries transformed the importance of constituent power. These movements challenged the belief that authority was constituted from above. Since they generally resulted in an overthrow of the established legal order, 'the people' were acknowledged as the originating source of political power not simply as a tenet of belief but also as a matter of political practice.

The English revolution made the vital though faltering first steps, in which the principal actors had to locate the power to establish a constitution in the hands of the people. But the American and French revolutions of the following century mark a more decisive break. Through the establishment of free-standing republics, the eighteenth century revolutions were expressions of the general principle that, rather than relying on custom and tradition, democracy provided the foundation of modern political legitimacy.

The English revolution symbolized by the execution of Charles I in January 1649 placed the question of constituent power onto the political agenda almost by accident. The men who executed the king in fact retained their belief in the office of the king. Consequently, although there was a pressing need to establish a new framework of government, this was 'not a liberating discovery of democratic principle, but a harsh and painful discovery' of political necessity.[46] The republican theories of government that flourished during the revolutionary period, then, 'were a consequence, not a cause or even a pre-condition of the execution of the King and the temporary abolition of the monarchy'.[47] It was perhaps for this reason that in 1748 Montesquieu felt able to comment that:

> It was a fine spectacle in the last century to see the impotent attempts of the English to establish democracy among themselves . . . the people, stunned, sought democracy and found it nowhere. Finally, after many movements and many shocks and jolts, they ended up with the very government that had been proscribed.[48]

Notwithstanding the Restoration and subsequent Glorious Revolution of 1688, however, it would be wrong to conclude, as Burke appeared to, that the old order was re-established, albeit with 'a small and a temporary deviation from the strict order of a regular hereditary succession'.[49] Too much had happened in the intervening period for the authority of the traditional order to be reconstituted. Although the English revolution did not express an unequivocal belief in the power of democracy, it did

---

[46] J. G. A. Pocock, 'Introduction' to James Harrington, *The Commonwealth of Oceana* [1656] (Cambridge: Cambridge University Press, 1992), vii–xxix, xii.

[47] Ibid. xi.

[48] Montesquieu, *The Spirit of the Laws* [1748], Anne M. Cohler, Basia Carolyn Miller, and Harold Samuel Stone eds (Cambridge: Cambridge University Press, 1989), iii.3.

[49] Edmund Burke, *Reflections on the Revolution in France* [1790], Conor Cruise O'Brien ed. (London: Penguin, 1968), 101.

highlight the necessity of forging a closer link between the bases of social and political order. That link was property.

This argument is most clearly expressed in James Harrington's *The Commonwealth of Oceana* of 1656. Harrington's argument was not only that the people are the foundation of power but that the constitutional order must be based on the 'balance of property'.[50] It is unnecessary to enter the debate over the meaning of 'property' in his scheme.[51] What is clear is that Harrington, 'England's premier civic humanist and Machiavellian',[52] vigorously asserted the power of the people through property relations to establish governmental authority. With the removal of the more radical aspects of Harrington's argument,[53] this became the dominant motif in British constitutional discourse in the eighteenth century.[54]

But restoration of the monarchy meant that the English retained a monarchical form of the constitution, which had an effect on the form that constituent power assumed. Traditional reflections on English constitutional arrangements were rooted in the idea of mixed government—that royal integrity, aristocratic wisdom, and popular sentiment would check one another and ensure that a balance of order and liberty would be achieved.[55] This traditional theme was now jettisoned; henceforth, the counter-balance to executive government would not be found in the constitutional arrangements of government but in social ordering in general.[56] Constituent power, whether taking the form of public opinion[57] or the power of the crowd, was exogenous to law. Law was a species of command, and the constituent power of the people reflected a configuration of political forces that irritated the legal order. It is in this sense that we understand the English tradition of civil liberty as an appeal to those 'natural rights of the freeborn Englishman' that protect him from the potentially restrictive impact of the law. Within the English tradition, constituent power,

---

[50] Harrington, above n. 46, 13.

[51] Cf. C. B. Macpherson, *The Political Theory of Possessive Individualism* (Oxford: Clarendon Press, 1962), ch. 4; J. G. A. Pocock, *The Machiavellian Moment: Florentine Political Thought and the Atlantic Republican Tradition* (Princeton, NJ: Princeton University Press, 1975), 383–400.

[52] J. G. A. Pocock, 'Historical Introduction' in *The Political Works of James Harrington* (Cambridge: Cambridge University Press, 1977), 15.

[53] For an analysis of the more radical implications of Harrington's thought see Negri, above n. 3, 111–128.

[54] See, e.g., Adam Smith, *Lectures on Jurisprudence* [1766], R. L. Meek, D. D. Raphael, and P. G. Stein eds (Oxford: Oxford University Press, 1978), 401: 'Property and civil government very much depend on one another. The preservation of property and the inequality of possession first formed it, and the state of property must always vary with the form of government'. See further, John Millar, *Historical View of the English Government* [1787] (London: J. Marmon, 3rd edn. 1803), iv. 226–310; Jeremy Bentham, *A Fragment on Government* [1776], Wilfrid Harrison ed. (Oxford: Blackwell, 1948).

[55] See M. J. C. Vile, *Constitutionalism and the Separation of Powers* (Indianapolis: Liberty Fund, 2nd edn. 1998), ch. 2.

[56] Mark Francis with John Morrow, 'After the Ancient Constitution: Political Theory and English Constitutional Writings, 1765–1832' (1988) 9 *History of Political Thought* 232–302, 294–295.

[57] See, e.g., A. V. Dicey, *Lectures on the Relation between Law and Public Opinion in England during the Nineteenth Century* (London: Macmillan, 1905); Cecil S. Emden, *The People and the Constitution* (Oxford: Clarendon Press, 1933); Jürgen Habermas, *The Structural Transformation of the Public Sphere: An Inquiry into a Category of Bourgeois Society*, Thomas Burger trans. (Cambridge, Mass: MIT Press, 1989).

although refracted through the practices of parliamentary representation,[58] retains its Machiavellian form as a counter-balance to that of the constituted power of government.

The American revolution significantly altered this conception of constituent power. The Declaration of Independence presents itself as a supreme act of constituent power: governments are instituted to secure the basic rights of life, liberty, and the pursuit of happiness and 'whenever any form of government becomes destructive to those ends, it is the right of the people to alter and abolish it, and to institute new government, laying its foundation upon such principles, and organizing its powers in such form, as to them shall seem most likely to effect their safety and happiness'.[59] The Declaration led to the establishment of a new framework of government and to a novel sense of the constitution. The American constitution incorporated two major innovations.

First, the constitution provided the basis not just for a new framework of government but also for a new nation. The constitution not only constitutes a structure of governmental authority but also 'constitutes a people in a certain way'.[60] The American constitution, in Wolin's words, 'proposed a distinctive identity and envisions a form of politicalness for individuals in their new collective capacity'.[61] The identity of the American people remains highly contested; despite the claim *E pluribus unum*, Americans remain sceptical of metaphysical notions of 'the people'. But to an unusual degree, this identity is tied to debates over constitutional understandings. And this is the reason why the discourse of American constitutional law continues to generate such controversy: constitutional adjudication is not an argument over the meaning of positive law, but an argument about the true character of American political identity.

This point brings us to the second innovatory aspect of the American foundation: the extent to which the constituent power of the people, expressed in the language of fundamental rights, is written into the framework of constituted power. The justification for doing so is clearly expressed in *The Federalist Papers*. Hamilton and Madison explicitly defend republican over democratic government by extolling the ability of republican arrangements—'the regular distribution of power into distinct departments; the introduction of legislative balances and checks; the institutions of courts composed of judges holding their offices during good behaviour; the representation of the people in the legislature by deputies of their own election'—to

---

[58] See Edmund Burke, 'Speech to the Electors of Bristol, 1774' in his *Speeches and Lectures on American Affairs* (London: Dent, 1908), 68–75; J. R. Pole, *Political Representation in England and the Origins of the American Republic* (Berkeley, Calif.: University of California Press, 1971), 441–442.

[59] American Declaration of Independence, 4 July 1776: see Carl Becker, *The Declaration of Independence: A Study in the History of Political Ideas* (New York: Harcourt, Brace & Co., 1922), ch. 1. For a study of its rhetorical dimensions see Jay Fliegelman, *Declaring Independence: Jefferson, Natural Language, and the Culture of Performance* (Stanford, Calif.: Stanford University Press, 1993).

[60] Sheldon S. Wolin, 'Collective Identity and Constitutional Power' in his *The Presence of the Past: Essays on the State and the Citizen* (Baltimore: Johns Hopkins University Press, 1989), 8–31, 9.

[61] Ibid.

overcome the irrational proclivities of the crowd.[62] Constituent power is conceived not as the engine of a constitution, but 'as the fuel of its engine'.[63] Constituent power is inscribed in a 'model of political society', a society 'that forms the people through representation, through the division of powers, through all the cogs of the constitutional machine'.[64] As a consequence, Negri argues, *homo politicus* 'is redefined by the constitution: without constitution there is no constituent power'.[65]

Negri's argument raises important issues that will be taken up in the following section. At this stage we might note that the absorption of constituent power into formal juristic categories has a profound effect on our understanding of constitutional law. Constituent power is no longer a counter-power to positive law. Rather, it manifests itself as an endogenous criterion of law's efficacy.[66] 'In framing a government', Madison argues, 'you must first enable the government to control the governed; and in the next place oblige it to control itself'.[67] Madison's first axiom inverts the relationship between constituent power and constituted power promoted by the claims of popular democracy, and the second highlights the central importance of formal legal constraints. Consequently, although conceding that 'a dependence on the people is, no doubt, the primary control on the government', he also emphasizes that 'experience has taught mankind the necessity of auxiliary precautions'.[68]

The contrast between the American and the French revolutions on this issue is illuminating.[69] Although aspects of the Declaration of the Rights of Man and the Citizen imply similar curbs on the will of the multitude,[70] the French revolution seemed more clearly to express the idea of constituent power in all its direct, historical specificity. In contrast to Rousseau's metaphysical abstraction of 'the general will', and of Sieyes's belief that constituent power could be entirely expressed through the principle of representation,[71] constituent power seemed to unfold as an unbounded force. In Negri's colourful prose, 'the actors enter it dressed as ancient Romans and exit dressed in bourgeois garb or in blue collar; they penetrate into it thinking as men of the Enlightenment and are expelled from it either as modern revolutionaries, or as new conservatives, ambiguously divided between historicism and reformism'.[72] From

---

[62] James Madison, Alexander Hamilton, and John Jay, *The Federalist Papers* [1788], Isaac Kramnick ed. (Harmondsworth: Penguin, 1987), No. 9 (Hamilton). See further No. 10 (Madison).
[63] Negri, above n. 3, 160.    [64] Ibid.
[65] Ibid. This argument has parallels with Christodoulidis's containment thesis: see Emilios Christodoulidis, *Law and Reflexive Politics* (Dordrecht: Kluwer, 1998), esp. ch. 6.
[66] This aspect of the American revolutionary settlement, that which mainly concerns the juristic character of basic rights, is taken up below in Ch. 7.
[67] Madison, above n. 62, No. 51.    [68] Ibid.
[69] See further, Patrice Higonnet, *Sister Republics: The Origins of French and American Republicanism* (Cambridge, Mass.: Harvard University Press, 1988).
[70] See, e.g., Declaration of the Rights of Man and the Citizen, 1789, art. 16: 'Every community in which a separation of powers and a security of rights is not provided for, wants a constitution'.
[71] Emmanuel Joseph Sieyès, *What is the Third Estate?* [1789], M. Blondel trans. (London: Pall Mall Press, 1963); see above, Ch. 4, 61–64.
[72] Negri, above n. 3, 231. See also J. L. Talmon, *The Social Origins of Totalitarian Democracy* (London: Mercury, 1961), Pt. II.

the experience of the French revolution, we discern a conception of constituent power founded on a raw principle of democracy.[73]

Edmund Burke's *Reflections* are instructive here. Despite being a stout defender of the rights of the American colonists,[74] Burke vigorously opposed the French revolutionaries. He advocated reform over revolution, and a respect for history ('our liberties as an *entailed inheritance*'[75]) over the appeal to metaphysical ideas of liberty and equality. For Burke, 'human nature cannot be found in those shaky metaphysical principles on which the French revolutionaries liked to found their *droits de l'homme et du citoyen*, but only in how human nature articulated itself in the historical institutions human beings gave themselves in the course of time'.[76] Being antithetical to politics—a practice that requires craft, nuance, and experience—Burke believed that abstract principles provided no constraint, so that an order constituted solely on such noble principles would soon dissipate into violence, terror, and despotism. France, Burke accurately predicted in 1790, 'affects to be a pure democracy, though I think it in a direct train of becoming shortly a mischievous and ignoble oligarchy'.[77]

Burke's argument was that the idea of constituent power must take into account the existence of those 'real rights' that inhere in the existing social order. Such rights include the right of property, whose 'characteristic essence ... formed out of the combined principles of its acquisition and conservation, is to be *unequal*'.[78] Here, perhaps, we are able to identify the source of Arendt's conviction that the social and the political must be kept distinct.[79] The revolutionary error, Arendt suggested, was to assume that the principles of the Declaration were designed to establish 'not the control but the foundation-stone of the body politic'.[80] Failure to distinguish between society and politics led to a belief that all the errors of the world could be solved by political means, so that, she concluded, 'when Saint-Just out of these experiences exclaimed, *Les malheureux sont la puissance de la terre*, we might as well hear these grand and prophetic words in their literal meaning'.[81]

The important point is that state formation constitutes a considerable achievement of political imagination such that 'no man should approach to look into its defects or corruptions but with due caution' and, further, that 'he should never dream of beginning its reformation by its subversion'.[82] But this is precisely the arrogance of the unrestrained democratic impetus:

[W]here popular authority is absolute and unrestrained, the people have an infinitely greater, because far better founded confidence in their own power. They are themselves, in great meas-

---

[73] See Biancamaria Fontana, 'Democracy and the French Revolution' in John Dunn (ed.), *Democracy: The Unfinished Journey 508 BC to AD 1993* (Oxford: Oxford University Press, 1992), 107–124, esp. 112–113; see further George Rudé, *The Crowd in the French Revolution* (Oxford: Clarendon Press, 1959).
[74] See Edmund Burke, *Speeches and Letters on American Affairs* [1774–1781] Hugh Law ed. (London: Dent, 1908).
[75] Burke, above n. 49, 119.
[76] F. R. Ankersmit, 'Edmund Burke: Natural Right and History' in his *Political Representation* (Stanford, Calif.: Stanford University Press, 2002), 35–59, 44.
[77] Burke, above n. 49, 228.  [78] Ibid. 140.
[79] Hannah Arendt, *On Revolution* (Harmondsworth: Penguin, 1973), ch. 2.
[80] Ibid. 109.  [81] Ibid. 112.  [82] Burke, above n. 49, 194.

ure, their own instruments. They are nearer to their objects. Besides, they are less under responsibility to one of the greatest controlling powers on earth, the sense of fame and estimation. The share of infamy that is likely to fall to the lot of each individual in public acts, is small indeed; the operation of opinion being in inverse ratio to the number of those who abuse power. Their own approbation of their own acts has to them the appearance of a public judgment in their favour. A perfect democracy is therefore the most shameless thing in the world. As it is the most shameless, it is also the most fearless.[83]

By promoting the cause of reform over revolution, Burke directly opposed the notion of constituent power as an expression of the will of the multitude. The unrestrained principle of democracy, he argued, must be accommodated to the realities of social order—reason must be constrained by history. This was a message later taken up by Tocqueville in *Democracy in America*.[84] Ostensibly writing about America, his main theme—that freedom generates an equality with the potential to undermine freedom—was mainly aimed at a European audience. If constituent power is intrinsically democratic, how are the destructive, conformist, faddist, and despotic tendencies of democratic societies to be avoided? Tocqueville posed the problem of the contemporary significance of constituent power with great clarity. He suggested that the demos, rather than being the organizing power, was itself in need of organization. Only by rejuvenating aristocratic techniques in government could the destructiveness of the social power of democracy be minimized.

CONSTITUENT POWER AND POSITIVE CONSTITUTIONALISM

When the idea that political power resides in the people is transformed into practice, it becomes a dynamic and liberating force, but also potentially dangerous and destructive. Revolutionary rhetoric is suffused with the noble rhetoric of 'the people' or 'the nation' as proud bearers of ultimate sovereignty. But parallel to this is the image of the people as an unruly force, revealing a savage world in which irrational passions hold sway. Is it possible to move beyond these contrasting images? To do so we must address the misunderstandings that have exacerbated these tensions.

We might start with Tocqueville's observation that although 'the principle of the sovereignty of the people . . . is always to be found, more or less, at the bottom of almost all human institutions', it invariably 'remains there concealed from view', and 'if for a moment it is brought to light, it is hastily cast back into the gloom of the sanctuary'.[85] This remark has particular force within legal discourse, in which constituent power, although occasionally acknowledged to be an all-embracing force that ensures the legal order remains responsive to 'the will of the people', tends to be closed off as quickly as possible. It gets contained inside vague abstractions, such as that of 'the

[83] Ibid. 190–191.
[84] Alexis de Tocqueville, *Democracy in America* [1835], Henry Reeve trans., Daniel J. Boorstin intro. (New York: Vintage Books, 1990).
[85] Ibid. i.55.

nation',[86] or in sanitized juridical categories, by treating it simply as the norm of the production of law.[87] Constituent power's expansive and dynamic aspects are due more consideration.

There is considerable antagonism pervading the literature on democracy and constitutionalism. Democracy is often presented as a theory of absolute government opposed to any attempt to impose institutional limitations over the exercise of democratic will. From this perspective, constitutionalism becomes a series of devices—the principle of representation, the division of governmental power, the establishment of a bounded framework of constituted power in the form of higher law—designed to curb the power of majorities.[88] Constitutionalism, this line of argument runs, seeks to limit, contain, and institutionalize the manifestation of constituent power. Viewed thus, constitutionalism seems to be built on a contradiction: that is, the acknowledgement of the ultimate power of 'the people' sits alongside institutional arrangements that divide, restrain, and even override the exercise of that power.

But this is a distortion of both democracy and constitutionalism. Democracy and constitutionalism are not contradictory movements. In developing this argument, I hope to be able to uncover the juristic significance of the concept of constituent power.

Constituent power is a political concept. This means that the concept can only be understood once political power is differentiated from economic power or force. Political power as 'power to' is different from 'power over', the type of domination that the control of material resources produces. While political power is concerned with the production of power in the sense of strength, this is a power of concerted action that is generated by harnessing a multitude into some form of collective agency.[89] Two things follow. The first is that this type of power derives from some principle of representation.[90] The second is that, being relational, political power does not reside in any particular locus.[91]

It follows that democracy cannot be understood in terms of some unmediated notion of popular will. The aspirations of the multitude inevitably conflict, which is precisely why the practice of politics has emerged. The aggregation of interests and opinions implicit in the concept of a democratic will can be recognized only when absorbed into some representative form.[92] But if this idea of democracy can only be

---

[86] See Guillaume Bacot, *Carré de Malberg et L'Origine de la Distinction entre Souveraineté du Peuple et Souveraineté Nationale* (Paris: CNRS Éditions, 1985).

[87] See Émile Boutmy, *Studies in Constitutional Law: France, England, United States*, E. M. Picey trans. (London: Macmillan, 1891), 250: 'Constituent power is an imperative act of nation, rising from nowhere and organising the hierarchy of powers'.

[88] See, e.g., Jeremy Waldron, 'A Rights-Based Critique of Constitutional Rights' (1993) 13 *Oxford J. of Legal Studies* 18–51, esp. 44: 'If a majority of judges in the House of Lords ... strikes down legislation passed by majoritarian processes in parliament, then the voting powers of a few judges are being held to prevail over the voting powers of the people's representatives. To provide a *democratic* justification for the judges' prevailing, one has to show not only that they have democratic credentials but that they have a *better* democratic claim than that asserted in the legislative action in question'.

[89] See above, Ch. 5, 76–79.    [90] See above, Ch. 4.

[91] See above, Ch. 5, 81–86.

[92] See J. H. Burns, 'Majorities: An Exploration' (2003) 24 *History of Political Thought* 66–85, 85: 'Does this far from complete exploration of a complex subject [the 'history of the majority'] lead to any kind of

expressed through a representative form, and therefore through certain institutional arrangements, it also follows that constitutions are not simply devices that impose restraints on the exercise of power. Like all representational frameworks, a constitution is a way of organizing, and hence also of generating, political power. A constitution is not essentially an act of authorization; it is a mode of generating and orchestrating the public power of a state. The constitution is not a segment of being but a process of becoming.[93]

Although the power of the state is to some degree a product of the material resources that a people is able to create through their labour power, constituent power must be differentiated from that social or economic power. Constituent power, the generative dimension of political power, derives from the transmutation of that social power into institutional forms through will, consent, and allegiance. Constituent power cannot be absorbed into some basic norm, for this would be to deny the continuity of the political dynamic that provides the state with its most basic energy. This is the normativist fallacy—the conflation of constituent and constituted power. But neither can constituent power be reduced to the power of a multitude since, contrary to Negri's thesis,[94] political power must take some representational form. This is the materialist fallacy, the reduction of constituent power to fact, or to the existence of strength or force.

Constituent power cannot be entirely absorbed into norms nor wholly reduced to fact. It emerges because of the unbridgeable gulf that exists between governors and governed, and it expresses a form of power that mediates between the three orders of the political.[95] Constituent power is the power that gives constitutions their open, provisional, and dynamic qualities, keeping them responsive to social change and reminding us that the norm rests ultimately on the exception. Constituent power expresses a belief that the interdependence of democracy and constitutionalism is a paradox not a contradiction,[96] and recognizes the need for agencies of the state to work actively to maintain the allegiance of their citizens. We must not idealize these political relationships by underestimating the power of domination expressed in constituted power. But at a time when social and economic power is assuming new, more broadly-encompassing forms, it remains important accurately to identify constituent power as the generative principle of public law.

general conclusion? Perhaps to the conclusion that the notion of majority rule is a myth, in the sense of being an essentially imaginative "device men adopt in order to come to terms with [political] reality"'.

[93] Cf. Lon L. Fuller, *The Law in Quest of Itself* (Boston: Beacon Press, 1940), 10.

[94] Negri, above n. 3, ch. 7, esp. 322: 'The political form of constituent power that we call disutopia ... we can also call "democracy". But we must specify something: here *democracy* means the omnilateral expression of the multitude, the radical immanence of strength, and the exclusion of any sign of external definition, either transcendent or transcendental and in any case external to this radical, absolute terrain of immanence. This democracy is the opposition of constitutionalism. Or better, it is the negation itself of constitutionalism as constituted power—a power made impermeable to singular modalities of space and time, and a machine predisposed not so much to exercising strength but, rather, to controlling its dynamics, its unchallengeable dispositions of force'.

[95] See above, Ch. 3.

[96] See Stephen Holmes, 'The Positive Constitutionalism of John Stuart Mill' in his *Passions and Constraint: On the Theory of Liberal Democracy* (Chicago: University of Chicago Press, 1995), 178–201, 178.

# 7

# *Rights*

We live today in an 'age of rights'.[1] Although the idea of rights constitutes an important strand of modern political thought, it generally has remained subservient to other claims of sovereignty, nationalism, and democracy. Since the Second World War, however, rights discourse has now established itself as a common currency of both politics and law. Contemporary public discourse, especially that which appeals to such core values as liberty, equality, and justice, is invariably cast in the language of rights.

This contemporary 'rights revolution'[2] is linked to the triumph of social power over political power, to the emergence of a more individualistic conception of society, and, at least in an ideological sense, to the formation of a political order built on the foundation of the rights-bearing individual. Rights discourse has therefore acquired its thrust from a radical shift in our understanding of the political relationship between state and citizen. The traditional focus of political thought—on the rights of sovereigns and the duties of subjects[3]—has been inverted, the emphasis now being placed on the rights of citizens and the obligations of government. Since rights and duties are twin aspects of a reciprocal relationship,[4] this looks like a distinction without a difference. But in practice, this inversion has had an important effect on the way governmental authority is constituted. It is when rights are given positive institutional effect that this effect is disclosed. This positivization of the basic rights of citizens has the potential to reconfigure the architecture of public law.

To assess this potential, it is necessary to trace the intellectual source of the modern rights movement and chart its influence on contemporary legal and political practice. Although the rights revolution is a recent phenomenon, its intellectual origins go back quite a way. Most roads lead back to the Enlightenment, and this particular one charts the re-constitution of governmental authority after the American and French revolutions. At its centre runs a belief in some notion of natural rights.[5]

---

[1] See Norberto Bobbio, *The Age of Rights*, Allan Cameron trans. (Cambridge: Polity Press, 1996); Louis Henkin, *The Age of Rights* (New York: Columbia University Press, 1990).

[2] Charles R. Epp, *The Rights Revolution: Lawyers, Activists, and Supreme Courts in Comparative Perspective* (Chicago: University of Chicago Press, 1998); Michael Ignatieff, *The Rights Revolution* (Toronto: Anansi, 2000).

[3] See, e.g., Thomas Hobbes, *On the Citizen* [1647], Richard Tuck and Michael Silverthorne ed. and trans. (Cambridge: Cambridge University Press, 1998), 7, 10: 'This book sets out men's duties, first as men, then as citizens and lastly as Christians' and is intended to investigate 'the right of a commonwealth and the duties of its citizens'.

[4] See, e.g., Max Radin, 'Natural Law and Natural Rights' (1950) 59 *Yale Law Journal* 214–237.

[5] See, e.g., Bernard Bailyn, *The Ideological Origins of the American Revolution* (Cambridge, Mass: Belknap Press, 1967), 27: 'In pamphlet after pamphlet the American writers cited Locke on natural rights and on the social and governmental contract'.

Writing in 1767, Rousseau commented that: 'The great problem of politics, which I compare to the problem of squaring the circle in geometry . . . [is]: How to find a form of government which puts the law above man'.[6] The need for a transcendent principle was acutely felt in the late eighteenth century, when the Americans and the French overthrew their established orders and were obliged to devise new frameworks of government. These revolutions, paradoxically, 'drove the very "enlightened" men of the eighteenth century to plead for some religious sanction at the very moment when they were about to emancipate the secular realm fully from the influences of the churches and to separate politics and religion once and for all'.[7] While this led some, such as Robespierre, to promote a cult of the Supreme Being,[8] many of the most influential figures of the period appealed to 'nature'. This was a conception of nature occupying a key location between man and God. For the American colonists in particular, the only route to knowledge of God's will was through the discovery of the laws of nature, and these, as Jefferson said, would doubtless be 'the laws of "nature's God"'.[9]

Although this belief in the existence of inalienable natural rights has had a contentious history, natural rights discourse has certainly had a significant impact on modern public law thought. Our concern, however, is less with the history than with the pattern of juristic thought. The objective will be to investigate how a political discourse of natural rights has permeated legal discourse and then, through positivization—that is, through the institutionalization of a conception of law as an expression of basic rights—has reconfigured the relationship between law and government. This should help us to assess the impact of rights discourse on contemporary public law.

NATURAL RIGHTS AND POLITICAL ORDER

The source of natural rights doctrines can be tracked back beyond the revolutionary documents of the late eighteenth century to the early modern period, when the foundations of political authority, rooted in classical natural law, were first questioned.[10]

---

[6] Jean-Jacques Rousseau, letter to the Marquis de Mirabeau, 26 July 1767; cited in Hannah Arendt, *On Revolution* (Harmondsworth: Penguin, 1973), 183.

[7] Arendt, ibid. 185–186. Cf. Peter Gay, *The Enlightenment: An Interpretation* (New York: Knopf, 1966), 322: 'The philosophes' claim to distance themselves from their Christian world has rarely been fully honoured. Instead, the philosophes have been sarcastically commended for "merely" secularizing religious ideas and caricatured as medieval clerks in modern dress, ungrateful and forgetful heirs of the Christian tradition who combated the pious wish for salvation in the name of a secular salvation disguised as progress . . . who laughed at religious idolatry but had their own saints—Bacon, Newton and Locke'.

[8] See Arendt, above n. 6, 184–185; François Furet, *The French Revolution, 1770–1814*, Antonia Neill trans. (Oxford: Blackwell, 1996), 147–149.

[9] See Carl Becker, *The Declaration of Independence: A Study in the History of Political Ideas* (New York: Harcourt, Brace & Co., 1922), 37.

[10] Richard Tuck, *Natural Rights Theories: Their Origins and Development* (Cambridge: Cambridge University Press, 1979). Cf. Brian Tierney, *The Idea of Natural Rights: Studies on Natural Rights, Natural Law and Church Law, 1150–1625* (Atlanta, Ga.: Scholars Press, 1997), chs 1 and 2.

In classical natural law, law was conceived as a catalogue of duties. On the premiss that all beings have a natural end, natural law derived a basic duty of humans to realize their destiny. Humans were thus placed under a duty to pursue the virtuous life. In this classical image, law did not establish general norms of conduct: 'the law is . . . merely society's medicine which re-establishes order, putting each person in his place when this cosmic order, like a diseased organ, is disturbed'.[11] With an image of law as that which is right, classical natural law did not recognize the idea of subjective rights, of rights vested in the individual and enforceable against the collectivity.

The altered world-view which made possible the emergence of the idea of subjective rights happened during the early modern period, when the classical structure of duties was challenged by a conception of political order based on individual rights. This shift was recorded most dramatically in the work of Hobbes. Since Hobbes is best known to lawyers as a theorist who promoted a conception of law as the command of the sovereign authority, thereby becoming one of the most influential authors of legal positivism, this claim might seem surprising. However, it is not his solution to the question of political order that is relevant, but his method of characterizing the problem.

Hobbes began with the individual as a bearer of natural rights within a state of nature, a depiction of the natural state of existence that was innovative.[12] His sense of the natural was distilled from his understanding of how people actually live. Arguing that people are mainly driven by passion rather than reason, Hobbes derived natural law from the most powerful of all passions—that of self-preservation. He argued that the one fundamental natural right that people possess is the right to preserve themselves. It is this need to maintain their personal security that makes people entering civil society give up their natural rights in favour of an all-powerful sovereign.

Hobbes argued that in the compact which marks the transition from the state of nature to the establishment of civil society, this natural right is extinguished.[13] His analysis therefore suggests that obligation to others arises from contract: justice basically requires individuals to fulfil their contractual commitments. It was this aspect of Hobbes's theory of natural right that Locke modified and extended. Presenting a more benign account of the natural state, in which people acquire ownership of commodities through the expenditure of their labour, Locke argues that the main reason people contract with one another to place themselves under a governing authority is the preservation of their property.[14] When a system of government is established,

---

[11] Luc Ferry, *Rights—The New Quarrel between the Ancients and the Moderns. Political Philosophy, vol. 1*, Franklin Philip trans. (Chicago: University of Chicago Press, 1990), 21.

[12] See Thomas Hobbes, *Leviathan* [1651], Richard Tuck ed. (Cambridge: Cambridge University Press, 1996), ch. 13.

[13] But see Hobbes, ibid. ch. 14, where he indicated that 'not all rights are alienable' (93). Since the covenant establishing political order is designed to promote security, the entire surrender of all natural rights (e.g. by pledging not to resist force) would, he argued, be absurd.

[14] John Locke, *Two Treatises of Government* [1680], Peter Laslett ed. (Cambridge: Cambridge University Press, 1988), ii. § 124.

natural rights are not alienated but are exchanged for state-sanctioned civil rights. For Locke, private autonomy is secured through property and contract and the function of government is to preserve and protect this right. Government fulfils a defined and limited set of tasks, and if it fails properly to discharge these responsibilities power devolves back to the people. For the purpose of preserving their natural rights, the people retain a right of rebellion.[15]

The early modern political theorists thus devised schemes of government based not on an objective natural order which humans have a duty to preserve, but on the centrality of the individual as a rights-bearing subject. But if individuals are liberated from the frame of a natural ordering, where are they to obtain instruction on the good? If a political theory rests on subjective right, especially in a Lockean scheme where natural rights are retained in the commonwealth, this surely will lead to mere licence, as each individual pursues what he or she most desires.

Recognizing this problem, natural rights theorists have argued that once the link with a pre-ordained natural order is broken, guidance is supplied by our power of reason. Rousseau's attempt to supply a solution has been especially influential. He argued that the limits of liberty are not determined vertically, by appealing to some transcendental standard, but horizontally.[16] In Leo Strauss's concise formulation of Rousseau's position: 'I am just if I grant to every other man the same rights which I claim for myself, regardless of what these rights may be'.[17] Rousseau's insight reaches its apogee in Kant's objective principle of morality, the categorical imperative: act according to that maxim which we can will should become a universal law.[18]

For natural rights theorists, political order is justified by some form of social contract entered into by rights-bearing individuals: individuals give up a portion of their natural rights to secure civil order. Government does not reflect a natural order imposing duties on subjects; it is a juridical order established for the protection of subjective rights. And once the foundation of political order is conceived as a Kantian imperative, the affinity between morality and politics is readily identified.

NATURAL RIGHTS AND MODERN CONSTITUTIONS

Natural rights theories have flourished in European political thought for only short periods. Richard Tuck has indicated that rights theories have prospered only in two

---

[15] Ibid. ii. § 149.
[16] Jean-Jacques Rousseau, *The Social Contract* [1762], Maurice Cranston trans. (Harmondsworth: Penguin, 1968), ii.4: 'The commitments which bind us to the social body are obligatory only because they are mutual; and their nature is such that in fulfilling them a man cannot work for others without at the same time working for himself'.
[17] Leo Strauss, *What is Political Philosophy? and other Studies* (New York: Free Press, 1959), 51.
[18] In his *Groundwork of the Metaphysics of Morals* Kant also reformulated the categorical imperative thus: 'Act always so that you treat humanity whether in your person or in that of another always as an end, but never as a means only'. See Immanuel Kant, *Political Writings*, H. B. Nisbet trans., Hans Reiss ed. (Cambridge: Cambridge University Press, 1970), 22–23.

significant historical periods: from 1350 to 1450 and from 1590 to 1670.[19] Placed in the context of European thought, Tuck suggests not only that these periods 'are freakish and fitful', but that 'their dismantling has been a matter of high priority for succeeding generations'.[20] Nonetheless, Lockean rights theory, formulated at the tail-end of the latter period, has had a real impact on the modern political world.

Locke's influence on political practice was certainly not due to the rigour and lucidity of his philosophical analysis. In Carl Becker's assessment, Locke's work 'is not particularly cogent unless you accept his assumptions as proved, nor lucid until you restate it to suit yourself'. Rather, continued Becker, 'it is lumbering, involved, obscured by innumerable and conflicting qualifications—a dreary devil of an argument staggering from assumption posited as premise to conclusion implicit in that assumption'.[21] Locke's influence was essentially fortuitous. For various circumstantial reasons, his theories exerted a powerful hold on the leaders of the two great revolutions of the late eighteenth century. This can be gauged by the form and phrasing of Thomas Jefferson's draft of the American Declaration of Independence, which closely followed Locke's *Second Treatise*.[22] But Locke's conclusions needed little argument, since to the colonists they were simply an expression of common sense.[23]

Although the language of rights constituted the American colonists' 'native tongue', such rights claims 'came in many forms—and anyone who set out to catalogue them faced an exhausting task'.[24] Can, then, a differentiation be made between inalienable natural rights and bundles of conventional rights whose exercise was subject to regulation by the state? During the revolutionary era, such a division was both impractical and unnecessary. This political work was, after all, undertaken by practical reformers, not professional philosophers. It is sufficient to recognize that the appeal to nature provided the most powerful rhetorical justification in defence of these higher-order claims. The language of natural rights was deployed regularly in debate and explicitly invoked in the early declarations.[25]

---

[19] Tuck, above n. 10. For criticism of this periodization see: Brian Tierney, 'Tuck on Rights: Some Medieval Problems' (1983) 4 *History of Political Thought* 429–441.
[20] Tuck, above n. 10, 177.    [21] Becker, above n. 9, 72.
[22] 'We hold these truths to be self-evident', Jefferson declared, 'that all men are created equal; that they are endowed by their Creator with certain inalienable rights; that among these are life, liberty and the pursuit of happiness. That, to secure these rights, governments are instituted among men, deriving their just powers from the consent of the governed'.
[23] See Bailyn, above n. 5, ch. 2; Morton White, *The Philosophy of the American Revolution* (New York: Oxford University Press, 1978).
[24] Jack N. Rakove, *Original Meanings: Politics and Ideas in the Making of the Constitution* (New York: Vintage Books, 1997), 290–292. See also Forrest McDonald, *Novus Ordo Seclorum: The Intellectual Origins of the Constitution* (Lawrence, Kansas: Kansas University Press, 1985).
[25] See, e.g., *Resolutions of the House of Representatives of Massachusetts*, 29 October 1765: '1. *Resolved*, That there are certain essential Rights of the *British* Constitution of government which are founded in the Law of God and Nature, and are the common Rights of Mankind—Therefore 2. *Resolved*, That the Inhabitants of this Province are *inalienably* entitled to those essential rights in common with all Men: and that no Law of Society can, consistent with the Law of God and Nature, divest them of those Rights.'; Virginia Declaration of Rights, 1776: '1. That all men are by nature equally free and independent, and have certain inherent rights, of which, when they enter into a state of society, they cannot by any compact deprive or divest their posterity.'; Pennsylvania Declaration of Rights, 1776: '1. That all men are born

The discourse of natural rights was often blended with historical arguments, both through appeals to traditional common law rights and to the principles of the British constitution. But the influence of these claims should not be taken too seriously.[26] The colonists invoked a highly rationalistic conception of the common law. This was the common law refracted through the prism of Coke, Locke, and Blackstone, that is, the common law permeated with the doctrine of natural rights.[27] Roger Sherman, one of the most influential of the American founders, summed up the way in which this historical argument was used: 'the colonies adopt the common law not as common law, but as the highest reason'.[28] Similarly, the precepts of the British constitution, the founders claimed, were rooted 'in the law of God and nature'.[29]

What the founders could not avoid, however, was the fact that traditional English liberties—the liberties expressed in the great charters of Magna Carta, the Petition of Right, and the Bill of Rights—were universally recognized to be concessions yielded by the sovereign. These liberties were 'civil privileges, provided by society, in lieu of the natural liberties given up by individuals'.[30] On this vital point, the Hobbesian approach had to be contrasted with American (that is, Lockean) ideas of individuals as the carriers of inalienable natural rights. Thus, the function of civil society and its government in the American conception, Wilson argued, was 'to secure and to enlarge the exercise of the natural rights of its members'.[31] This appeal to natural

---

equally free and independent, and have certain natural inherent and inalienable rights, amongst which are the enjoying and defending life and liberty, acquiring, possessing and protecting property, and pursuing and obtaining happiness and safety.' See Jack N. Rakove, *Declaring Rights: A Brief History with Documents* (Boston: Bedford Books, 1998), 48, 81, 85.

[26] Bailyn, above n. 5, 30–31: 'Just as the colonists cited with enthusiasm the theorists of universal reason, so too did they associate themselves, with offhand familiarity, with the tradition of the English common law . . . The common law was manifestly influential in shaping the awareness of the Revolutionary generation. But, again, it did not in itself determine the kinds of conclusions men would draw in the crisis of the time'.

[27] Cf. Michael Oakeshott, 'Contemporary British Politics' (1947–8) 1 *Cambridge Journal* 474–490, 490: 'The common law rights and duties of Englishmen were transplanted throughout the civilised world. . . . In this process some of their flexibility was lost; the rights and duties were exported; the genius that made them remained at home. Peoples, desirous of freedom, but dissatisfied with anything less than the imagination of an eternal and immutable law, gave to these rights the false title of Nature. Because they were not the fruit of their own experience, it was forgotten that they were the fruit of the experience of the British people. . . . What went abroad as the concrete rights of an Englishman have returned home as the abstract Rights of Man, and they have returned to confound our politics and corrupt our minds'.

[28] Cited in Becker, above n. 9, 116.

[29] Becker, ibid. 99. Cf. John Phillip Reid, 'The Irrelevance of the Declaration' in Hendrik Hartog (ed.), *Law in the American Revolution and the Revolution in the Law* (New York: New York University Press, 1981), 46–89.

[30] James Wilson, 'Lectures on Law' in his *Works*, J. De Witt Andrews ed. (Chicago: Callaghan & Co., 1898), i.296–309, 302; cited in Knud Haakonssen, 'From Natural Law to the Rights of Man: a European Perspective on American Debates' in Michael J. Lacey and Knud Haakonssen (eds), *A Culture of Rights: The Bill of Rights in Philosophy, Politics and Law—1791 and 1991* (Cambridge: Cambridge University Press, 1991), 19–61, 20.

[31] Wilson, ibid. 303. See also William S. Carpenter, *The Development of American Political Thought* (Princeton: Princeton University Press, 1930), 29: 'James Otis envisaged the transformation within the British constitution of the common-law rights of Englishmen into the natural rights of man, but he also saw these natural rights as limitations upon the authority of government'.

rights was nothing less than a call for deliverance from the shackles of history.[32] In American political discourse, natural rights provided the foundation for constructing a formal constitution of political society. And their consequent actions led to a revolution in constitutional understanding.

Although the term 'constitution' has been in use over many centuries, its meaning has changed in the modern period. In the fifteenth century, Sir John Fortescue, echoing Roman law usage, used the term as a synonym for formally enacted law. 'The customs and the judgements of the law of nature', Fortescue observed, 'after they have been reduced to writing, and promulgated by the sufficient authority of the prince, and commanded to be kept, are changed into a constitution or something in the nature of statutes'.[33] While the idea of limitations on government existed within the structure of medieval government, the terminology of constitutional government did not. Although a broader formulation gradually entered into common usage, constitution generally referred to the entire body of laws, institutions, and customs that comprised the commonwealth.[34] This sense of constitution is one which the British have retained within the technical vocabulary of the law.

The modern alteration in meaning of the term 'constitution' is directly traceable to the American act of founding. It is highlighted most clearly in the work of Thomas Paine. In *Rights of Man*, Paine argued that governments derive their authority from one of three sources: superstition (that is, priestcraft), force (especially of conquerors), and reason (especially concerning 'the common rights of man').[35] The general type to which particular regimes conform can be identified, he suggested, by asking whether governments have arisen *out* of the people or *over* the people. The answer lies in the constitution of a country. This requires a clear definition of that term. A constitution, Paine suggested, 'has not an ideal, but a real existence; and whenever it cannot be produced in a visible form, there is none'.[36] Elaborating, Paine declared that a constitution 'is a thing *antecedent* to a government, and a government is only the creature of a constitution. The constitution is not the act of its government, but of the people constituting a government'.[37]

---

[32] In this respect, the religious aspects of the revolutionary movement are vitally important: on which see Georg Jellinek, *The Declaration of the Rights of Man and of Citizens: A Contribution to Modern Constitutional History*, Max Farrand trans. (New York: Henry Holt & Co., 1901), ch. 7; Barry Alan Shain, *The Myth of American Individualism: The Protestant Origins of American Political Thought* (Princeton, NJ: Princeton University Press, 1994).

[33] Sir John Fortescue, *De Laudibus Legum Anglie*, S. B. Chrimes ed. and trans. (Cambridge: Cambridge University Press, 1942), 37. Cf. Justinian, *Institutes*, i.2.6: 'whatever the emperor has determined (*constituit*) by rescript or decided as a judge or directed by edict is established to be law: it is these that are called constitutions'. See also above, Ch. 3, 44.

[34] In 1738, for example, Viscount Bolingbroke defined the constitution as 'that Assemblage of Laws, Institutions and Customs derived from certain fix'd principles of Reason, that compose the general System, according to which the Community hath agreed to be governed'. Cited in Graham Maddox, 'Constitution' in Terence Ball, James Farr, and Russell L. Hanson (eds), *Political Innovation and Conceptual Change* (Cambridge: Cambridge University Press, 1989), 50–67, 59.

[35] Thomas Paine, *Rights of Man* in his *Rights of Man, Common Sense and other Political Writings*, Mark Philp ed. (Oxford: Oxford University Press, 1995), 83–331, 120.

[36] Ibid. 122.     [37] Ibid.

Using the analogy of the relation of court to legislature, Paine argued that a constitution 'is to a government, what the laws made afterwards by that government are to a court of judicature. The court of judicature does not make the laws, neither can it alter them; it only acts in conformity to the laws made: and the government is in like manner governed by the constitution'.[38] From Paine's perspective, English government, having arisen from conquest rather than society, arose over the people. Despite modifications, 'the country has never regenerated itself' and 'is therefore without a constitution'.[39]

Although the American revolution brought about a shift in the idea of the constitution, its new, modern sense carries a twofold meaning. For Paine the expression referred primarily to the constituting act—the constitution as antecedent to government—whereby a people constitutes itself as a state. But the term was also used to refer to the product of the constituting act, that is, to the formal document establishing the framework of government.[40]

The colonists were familiar with the idea of having the framework of government written in documentary form from the company charters that provided them with their institutions of government, so this latter sense of a constitution came readily to them.[41] But the use of a formal constitutional document was new in that it was intended to establish a body of fundamental law. The makers of the constitution wanted not only to establish the formal separation of governmental powers, in which 'ambition must be made to counteract ambition',[42] but also to ensure that the constitution took effect as higher-status law.[43] Alexander Hamilton recognized that it was for the judges to ascertain the meaning of the constitution just as they determined 'the meaning of any particular act proceeding from the legislative body' and that 'if there should happen to be an irreconcilable variance between the two, that which has the superior obligation and validity ought, of course, to be preferred; or, in other words, the Constitution ought to be preferred to the statute'.[44]

The American constitution thus instituted the idea of fundamental law embodied in a text, but also the sense that a constitution formed a hierarchy of laws. The integrity of this framework would be policed by the judiciary. This type of institutional protection must therefore rank as a further innovation flowing from the revolution.[45] The American constitution takes its place as the first modern constitution.

---

[38] Ibid. 123.     [39] Ibid.
[40] Cf. Arthur Young's comment on the French constitution in 1792, which he says 'is a new term they have adopted; and which they use as if a constitution was a pudding to be made by a receipt'. Cited in Charles Howard McIlwain, *Constitutionalism: Ancient and Modern* (Ithaca, NY: Cornell University Press, rev. edn. 1947), 1–2.
[41] See S. E. Finer, *The History of Government* (Oxford: Oxford University Press, 1997), iii. 1395–1405.
[42] James Madison, Alexander Hamilton, and John Jay, *The Federalist Papers* [1788], Isaac Kramnick ed. (Harmondsworth: Penguin, 1987), No. 51 (Madison).
[43] See Edward S. Corwin, 'The "Higher Law" Background to American Constitutional Law' (1928) 42 *Harvard Law Review* 149–185 (Pt. I), 365–409 (Pt. II).
[44] *The Federalist Papers*, above n. 42, No. 78 (Hamilton).
[45] See Gordon S. Wood, *The Creation of the American Republic, 1776–1787* (Chapel Hill: University of North Carolina Press, rev. edn. 1998), 273–282.

The American revolution was shortly followed by the French revolution, an action which Finer calls 'the most important single event in the entire history of government'.[46] While the American revolution imposed a new constitutional superstructure on an existing set of representative institutions, thereby formalizing a change in the governing regime, in France an entire system was destroyed and a new order recast. The French revolution 'razed and effaced all the ancient institutions of France, undermined the foundations of all other European states, and is still sending its shock-waves throughout the rest of the world'.[47]

The great significance of the American and French revolutions lies not so much in the fact that the established order had been overthrown in the name of the rights of the people, but that 'the people' had acted to vindicate their natural rights. On this point, the French were directly following the American revolutionaries.[48] In furtherance of their natural rights, the state was reconstituted and the functions of government delimited. By establishing a modern constitution that laid down this formal framework of government, the people no longer needed to rely on Locke's residual right of rebellion; citizens could now expect an independent judiciary to protect their basic rights.

NATURAL RIGHTS AND POSITIVE LAW

Utilizing a discourse of natural rights, the American and French revolutionaries reconstituted political order and formally adopted new model constitutions. The primary instrument through which these changes were instituted was the formal declaration of fundamental rights. These declarations set in train the positivization of natural rights.

The essence of positivization has been captured by Jürgen Habermas, who referred to the process as 'the autonomous creation, by contract, of legal compulsion springing solely from the compulsion of philosophical reason'.[49] But this shift, of supreme juristic significance, was not effected immediately, and was not without its ambiguities. It was not until 1803 that the Supreme Court asserted its power to refuse to enforce congressional legislation that conflicted with the court's interpretation of the constitution.[50] And notwithstanding Paine's commendation that 'in America the law is King',[51] it was only in the latter half of the twentieth century that the Supreme Court initiated a rights revolution.

---

[46] Finer, above n. 41, 1517. For Hegel, as Habermas notes, 'the French Revolution becomes the very key to the philosophic concept of World History': see Jürgen Habermas, 'Natural Law and Revolution' in his *Theory and Practice*, John Viertel trans. (Boston: Beacon Press, 1973), 82–120, 86.
[47] Finer, above n. 41.
[48] See Jellinek, above n. 32, 20: 'The French Declaration of Rights is for the most part copied from the American declarations or "bills of rights"'.
[49] Habermas, above n. 46, 86.   [50] *Marbury* v. *Madison* 5 US (1 Cranch) 137 (1803).
[51] Thomas Paine, 'Common Sense' in Paine, above n. 35, 5–59, 34.

These charters of rights were ambivalent. There is little evidence to suggest that they were ever intended to be of central importance. Significantly, they were presented either in the form of a preamble (in the case of the French and some earlier American state declarations) or as amendments (in the American case) to these new constitutions.[52] While these charters did reflect the spirit of the new arrangements, it was not obvious that they would give rise to justiciable rights. In part, this was because of the novelty of the exercise, which generated a degree of ambiguity concerning the role of the charters. But there is plenty of evidence to indicate that a distinction was maintained between a political discourse of rights and a legal discourse of rules.

While many constitutions and declarations of rights were drafted during the course of the American revolution,[53] it is instructive to compare the language adopted in the first, the Virginia Declaration of Rights in 1776, with that deployed in the Federal amendments of 1789. The Virginia Declaration uses normative language (e.g., 'That elections of members to serve as representatives of the people, in assembly, ought to be free'), suggesting that the declaration will merely provide a guide to the form government should take.[54] By contrast, the Federal Bill of Rights uses imperative language (e.g. 'Congress shall make no law respecting the establishment of religion . . .'), indicating that it was intended to have legal effect. Clearly, the revolutionary period was one in which the effects of rights institutionalization were actively being considered, and lessons were gradually being learned.

On this issue, the contrast between the American Bill of Rights and the French Declaration is interesting. Although the latter was intended to be modelled on the former, Arendt argues that the French Declaration laid down 'primary positive rights, inherent in man's nature, as distinguished from his political status, and as such [the rights] tried indeed to reduce politics to nature'.[55] Drawing directly on man's natural rights, the Declaration was meant to provide the source of all political power.

---

[52] That a bill of rights did not form part of the constitution approved by the Federal Convention in 1787 and then subsequently was added at the First Federal Congress in 1789 owes much, in both instances, to the influence of James Madison. See Lance Banning, *The Sacred Fire of Liberty: James Madison and the Founding of the American Republic* (Ithaca, NY: Cornell University Press, 1995), ch. 9. For a summary of Madison's position see Rakove, above n. 25, 100: 'Madison's ideas about the protection of human rights departed in significant ways from the beliefs that Americans held at the outset of the Revolution. Where traditional theory located the principal dangers to rights in the arbitrary acts of the executive, Madison realized that in a republic, the legislature could prove more oppressive. Where traditional theory held that the problem of rights was to protect the people *against* government, Madison realized that in a republic the pressing necessity was to find ways to protect one segment of the community—individuals and minorities—against the self-interested desires of popular majorities acting *through* government. And where traditional theory sought to protect the customary rights of local communities against the centralizing organs of the nation-state, Madison hoped to empower the national government to intervene *within* the states to defend rights against the threats that individuals faced within the very communities where they lived'.

[53] During the revolution, eleven of the thirteen states drafted new constitutions of government, and eight of the eleven attached some declaration of rights to these documents: see Rakove, above n. 25, 36.

[54] Rakove, above n. 25, 36–37, also notes that the Virginia Declaration was approved more than two weeks before the constitution was adopted. Neither document referred to the other and it remained unclear whether the Declaration was to form part of the constitution.

[55] Arendt, above n. 6, 108.

Functioning purely in the political realm, the Declaration therefore maintained a clear distinction between the political and the legal. Consider, for example, the terms of Article 4, which states:

Political liberty consists in the power of doing whatever does not injure another. The exercise of the natural rights of every man, has no other limits than those which are necessary to secure to every other man the free exercise of the same rights; and these limits are determinable only by the law.

Article 4 provides a good illustration of Rousseau's idea of the horizontalization of rights, of natural rights being restricted by what is necessary to secure the equality of such rights for all.[56] But in indicating that the limitations of such rights are to be determined by law, it reasserts law as a regime of sovereign commands.

The conception of law reflected in Article 4 thus maintains the Hobbesian distinction between law and right. And since this issue is central to the positivization of natural rights, it needs to be explicated. Hobbes argued that many people have become confused about the distinction between right and law. Right, he explained, 'consisteth in liberty to do, or to forbeare' whereas law 'determineth, and bindeth'. Law and Right, he continued, 'differ as much, as Obligation, and Liberty; which in one and the same matter are inconsistent'.[57] In *De Cive*, Hobbes elaborated on this position:

But since all the movements and actions of the citizens have never been brought within the scope of the law, and cannot be because of their infinite variety, the things that are neither commanded nor forbidden must be almost infinite; and each man can do them or not at his discretion. In these man is said to enjoy his own liberty, and liberty here is to be understood in this sense, viz. as that part of natural right which is allowed and left to the citizens by the civil laws. Water stagnates and corrupts when it is closed in by banks on all sides; when it is open on all sides it spreads, and the more outlets it finds the freer it is. So with the citizens: they would be without initiative if they did nothing except at the law's command; they would be dissipated if there were no legal restrictions, and the more things left unregulated by the laws, the more liberty they enjoy. Both extremes are faulty; for laws were invented not to extinguish human actions but to direct them; just as nature ordained banks not to stop the flow of the river but to direct it. The extent of this liberty is measured by the good of the citizens and of the commonwealth. Hence it is, in the first place, contrary to the duty of those who rule and have authority to make laws that there be more laws than the good of the citizens and the commonwealth do essentially require.[58]

Within the British tradition, this Hobbesian conception is relatively straightforward. Natural rights are essentially forms of political claim. Law, by contrast, presents itself as a body of rules authorized by the sovereign authority; legal rights are the consequence of positive law.[59] So the British have a political tradition of civil liberty to protect themselves from the restrictive effects of the law.

---

[56] See above, 117.   [57] Hobbes, above n. 12, 91.
[58] Hobbes, above n. 3, 150–151.
[59] See, e.g., William Blackstone, *Commentaries on the Laws of England* (Oxford: Clarendon Press, 1765), i.121: 'This natural liberty consists properly in a power of acting as one thinks fit, without any restraint or

This clear distinction between positive law (the body of rules) and politics (the discourse through which notions of the right and the good are deliberated and disputed) is complicated by the positivization of natural rights. In this respect, the American approach marked an advance over the French. Unlike the French Declaration, the American bills of rights were not intended to provide the foundation stone of the state. The American bills assumed both the existence of the state and the realities of political power and instituted a set of restraining controls on the exercise of that power. In doing so, however, the distinction between the political (the sphere of natural rights) and the legal (the sphere of command) became blurred.[60]

So long as a traditional understanding of the role of judges and courts in the system of government was maintained, the implications of this innovation were suppressed. As Jellinek has noted, 'the theory of natural rights for a long time had no hesitation in setting forth the contradiction between natural law and positive law without demanding the realization of the former through the latter'.[61] During the twentieth century, as the rights movement acquired momentum the extent of the juristic and political challenge was revealed. The rights revolution pioneered in the United States during the latter half of the twentieth century was the unfolding of Alexander Hamilton's claim that 'the majesty of the national authority must be manifested through the medium of the courts of justice'.[62] The rights revolution—the second great American revolution—is essentially the consequence of working through the institutional implications of the first.

THE RIGHTS REVOLUTION

The rights revolution, the juristic consequences of a political revolution, is a post-war phenomenon. American constitutional scholars have presented cogent arguments for treating both the period of reconstruction in the 1860s[63] and the New Deal in the 1930s[64] as critical moments in the constitutional transformation of rights discourse. Nevertheless, as Richard Primus has argued, the rights explosion stems from the

control, unless by the law of nature . . . Political . . . or civil liberty . . . is no other than natural liberty so far restrained by human laws (and no farther) as is necessary and expedient for the general advantage of the publick'.

[60] Furet (above n. 8, 74) expresses this point differently: 'In the American example, those rights were perceived as having preceded society and also being in harmony with its development; moreover, they had been inscribed in its past by the jurisprudential tradition of the English common law. In the France of 1789, however, emphasis was placed on a certain political voluntarism: the law, produced by the sovereign nation, was established as the supreme guarantee of rights. . . . So it was society's responsibility, through the intermediary of the law, to ensure the rights of individuals; that law which was constantly referred to in the articles of the declaration as the "expression of the general will" '.

[61] Jellinek, above n. 32, 56–57.
[62] Madison, Hamilton, and Jay, *The Federalist Papers*, above n. 42, No. 16 (Hamilton).
[63] See Akhil Amar, *The Bill of Rights: Creation and Reconstruction* (New Haven: Yale University Press, 1998).
[64] See Bruce Ackerman, *We the People: Foundations* (Cambridge, Mass.: Belknap Press, 1991).

post-war period.[65] Only in the latter half of the twentieth century do we see 'the resurgence of normative foundationalism in the form of "human rights" and other universal, non-positivist ideas, the thickening of rights against racial discrimination, against invasions in personal privacy, in favour of free expression'.[66] The rights phenomenon has recently become the subject of contentious debate in the United States.[67] But although rights talk has penetrated further and deeper in the United States, there is no doubt that its influence is rapidly extending.[68] Rights discourse now transcends the boundaries of nation-states, has entered the international arena and is even claimed by Hardt and Negri to form a central plank in the new global form of sovereignty that they call 'Empire'.[69]

In the course of being positivized, the language of natural rights has altered; most people now refer not to 'natural' rights but instead to 'human' rights. The phenomenon, nevertheless, remains the same:[70] it is essentially an appeal to some fundamental set of rights that inhere in the individual and demand recognition whether or not they have been enacted in the law of particular states. This rights explosion is a political response to twentieth century threats. This is explicit in Arendt's observation that anti-semitism, imperialism, and totalitarianism, 'one after the other, one more brutally than the other, have demonstrated that human dignity needs a new guarantee which can be found only in a new political principle, in a new law on earth, whose validity this time must comprehend the whole of humanity'.[71] The character of this modernized version of natural right has been identified by Michael Ignatieff:

---

[65] Richard A. Primus, *The American Language of Rights* (Cambridge: Cambridge University Press, 1999), esp. ch. 5. This thesis receives support from the work of Epp, above n. 2, who has shown that during the mid-1930s, fewer than 10 per cent of the cases of the Supreme Court's decisions involved individual rights (other than property rights) and that by the late 1960s almost 70 per cent of decisions concerned individual rights (ibid. 2). See further, Richard L. Pacelle Jr., *The Transformation of the Supreme Court's Agenda: From the New Deal to the Reagan Administration* (Boulder, Colorado: Westview Press, 1991).

[66] Primus, above n. 65, 179.

[67] See, e.g., Ronald Dworkin, *Taking Rights Seriously* (Cambridge, Mass: Harvard University Press, 1977); Robert H. Bork, *The Tempting of America: The Political Seduction of the Law* (London: Sinclair-Stevenson, 1990); Mary Ann Glendon, *Rights Talk: The Impoverishment of Political Discourse* (New York: Free Press, 1991).

[68] See, e.g., Epp, above n. 2, chs 5–10; David Beatty (ed.), *Human Rights and Judicial Review: A Comparative Perspective* (Dordrecht: Martinus Nijhoff, 1994); Philip Alston (ed.), *The EU and Human Rights* (Oxford: Oxford University Press, 1999); Tom Campbell, K. D. Ewing, and Adam Tomkins (eds), *Sceptical Essays on Human Rights* (Oxford: Oxford University Press, 2001), Pt. III.

[69] Michael Hardt and Antonio Negri, *Empire* (Cambridge, Mass.: Harvard University Press, 2000). Hardt and Negri argue that the emerging world order which they call Empire can be expressed as a juridical formation and that the concept of right—albeit understood as a transformative notion of 'imperial right' (62)—lies at the core of this global constitution. See above, Ch. 5, 96–98.

[70] See, e.g., Maurice Cranston, *Human Rights Today* (London: Ampersand, 1955), 20: human rights refers to 'what Locke and other theorists meant by "natural rights", but without any specific reference to a concept of nature'. See also John Finnis, *Natural Law and Natural Rights* (Oxford: Clarendon Press, 1980), 198: 'this book is about human rights ("human rights" being a contemporary idiom for "natural rights": I use the terms synonymously)'.

[71] Hannah Arendt, *The Origins of Totalitarianism* (San Diego, Calif.: Harcourt Brace Jovanovich, 2nd edn. 1968), ix.

Constitutions do not create our rights; they recognize and codify the ones we already have, and provide means for their protection. We already possess our rights in two senses: either because our ancestors secured them or because they are inherent in the very idea of being human. Such inherent rights would include the right not to be tortured, abused, beaten, or starved. These inherent rights we now call human rights, and they have force whether or not they are explicitly recognized in the laws of nation-states. Thus human rights may be violated even when no state law is being infringed.[72]

This emerging human rights discourse is a political response to pressing political issues, especially about the treatment of minorities in an era of democratization.[73] Our concern, however, is not with this political discourse, but with its juristic consequences. Through the modern process of constitutionalization, the doctrine of natural rights has insinuated itself into the fabric of positive law, engendering a radical shift in our understanding of the character of law.

Natural rights have generally taken the form of negative liberties, serving mainly to define a zone of individual autonomy which government must not invade. As a consequence of rights institutionalization, however, there has been a growing tendency to treat rights rather than rules as the basic items of legal order. Once this rights-based conception of law becomes fixed in juristic thought, rights that once operated to place statute law in bounds are conceived as forming the architectonic principles of legal order. Basic rights are thus transmuted from the sphere of subjective right into fundamental norms that penetrate and give shape to objective law.[74]

By assuming this architectonic status, rights revolutionize our understanding of positive law. Since rights acquire their weight from ethical considerations, the traditional attempt to separate law from matters of politics or morality no longer is convincing. This fuels a tremendous expansion in the creativity of legal argument, as basic values of dignity, autonomy, and equality are explicated into ever more ingenious forms of rights claims. With the appearance of the rights-bearing citizen,

[72] Ignatieff, above n. 2, 28. In response to de Maistre's famous quip that, while he had met many people in his life—Spanish, Portuguese, and English—he had never met Man, Ignatieff observes: 'We have met Man. He is us. Human rights derive their force in our conscience from this sense that we belong to one species, and that we recognize ourselves in every single human being we meet' (ibid. 39–40). Cf. Arendt, above n. 71, 299: 'The conception of human rights, based upon the assumed existence of a human being as such, broke down at the very moment when those who professed to believe in it were for the first time confronted with people who had lost all other qualities and specific relationships—except that they were still human. The world found nothing sacred in the abstract nakedness of being human'. For this reason Arendt asserts the critical importance of 'the right to have rights (and that means to live in a framework where one is judged by one's actions and opinions) and a right to belong to some kind of organized community' (ibid. 296–297). 'Our political life', she elaborates, 'rests on the assumption that we can produce equality through organization' (ibid. 301).

[73] See, e.g., Georg Jellinek, *The Rights of Minorities*, A. M. Baty and T. Baty trans. (London: P. S. King & Son, 1912). More recently, see: Will Kymlicka, *Multicultural Citizenship: A Liberal Theory of Minority Rights* (Oxford: Clarendon Press, 1995).

[74] See Jürgen Habermas, *Between Facts and Norms: Contributions to a Discourse Theory of Law and Democracy*, William Rehg trans. (Cambridge: Polity, 1996), 247–248. This seems also to be the implication of the thesis of Robert Alexy, arguing that constitutional rights are optimization requirements of a legal order: Robert Alexy, *A Theory of Constitutional Rights*, Julian Rivers trans. (Oxford: Oxford University Press, 2002).

individuals begin to present themselves as subjects of international law.[75] Rights discourse in effect elevates itself above the arena of state law and into the realm of universal right. Law, once a form of coercive order, now presents itself as a means of maintaining freedom. Once founded on sovereign authority and authorized by representative democracy, law is now based on rights and legitimated by an appeal to moral autonomy. Law, in short, is no longer fundamentally a matter of will, but an aspect of reason.

This expansion in law's empire has particularly important consequences for public law. Most obviously, public law—the prudential practices of political right—is susceptible to total institutionalization; once positive law presents itself as a universal phenomenon, such political precepts become liable to be given precise and authoritative meaning by a revitalized judiciary. Contrary to Hobbes's claim, 'all the movements and actions of the citizens' are now—potentially—'brought within the scope of the law'.[76] What is commanded or forbidden now more than ever depends on the circumstances in which the power of command is exercised, determined not by rules laid down by legislatures but through adjudicative processes concerned with resolving competing claims of rights. Liberty is no longer the sphere of individual autonomy beyond the constraints of the law; liberty must now be defined by the operations of the law. These shifts mark a boundary change between the political and the legal, with law being elevated to a transcendental realm that frames the conduct of politics. The consequence is that the political critique of law can no longer come mainly from the outside; the moralization of law means that political critique must also come from within.

CONCLUSION

In seeking to understand the impact of the contemporary rights revolution on the idea of public law, our starting point should be that although the rights revolution has been fuelled by the rhetoric of natural or human rights, the idea of nature no longer offers any fixed, objective point against which conduct can be evaluated. Although more sophisticated human rights advocates acknowledge this, the point is not always accepted. 'Human rights activism', Ignatieff notes, 'likes to portray itself as an anti-politics, in defense of universal moral claims designed to delegitimize "political" (i.e., ideological or sectarian) justifications for the abuse of human beings'.[77] But such activism, he concedes, 'is bound to be partial and political' and, in practice, 'impartiality and neutrality are just as impossible as universal equal

---

[75] See, e.g., Fernando Tesón, *A Philosophy of International Law* (Boulder, Colorado: Westview Press, 1998); Antonio Cassese, *Self-Determination of Peoples: A Legal Reappraisal* (Cambridge: Cambridge University Press, 1995); Henry Steiner and Philip Alston, *International Human Rights in Context: Law, Politics, Morals* (Oxford: Oxford University Press, 2nd edn. 2000).

[76] Hobbes, above 124.

[77] Michael Ignatieff, *Human Rights as Politics and Idolatry* (Princeton, NJ: Princeton University Press, 2001), 9.

concern for everyone's human rights'.[78] If the first American revolution was an emancipation from history, this second revolution is an emancipation from nature.[79]

Individuals may have good reasons for embracing a political discourse of human rights. From the perspective of institutionalization, however, this is beside the point. Recognizing the political character of rights discourse leads us directly to the challenge posed by the positivization of basic rights. Even if it is the case that 'human rights politics is disciplined or constrained by moral universals'[80] (whatever these may be[81]), handing over the responsibility for identifying, ranking, and enforcing basic rights to the processes of adjudication is a contentious and risky political manoeuvre. Every important social and political conflict can be reinterpreted in the form of a competing rights claim. Sometimes these involve rival conceptions of equality (e.g., equality of opportunity against equality of distribution), but more often they take the form of a conflict between right-as-freedom and right-as-security, between autonomy and the prevention of harm to others.[82] Despite the Herculean judge's claimed ability to reach the 'right answer',[83] the fact is that such disputes cannot be resolved through the deployment of the language of the law. Rights adjudication is intrinsically political; it requires judges to reach a determination on the relative importance of conflicting social, political, and cultural interests in circumstances in which there is no objective—or even consensual—answer.[84]

There may be sound practical reasons for vesting such political responsibilities in lawyers and judges. No one has articulated these reasons more eloquently than Tocqueville, who suggested that in the modern era lawyers provide 'the most powerful existing security against the excesses of democracy'.[85] Lawyers acquire 'certain habits of order, a taste for formalities, and a kind of instinctive regard for the regular connection of ideas, which naturally render them very hostile to the revolutionary spirit and the unreflecting passions of the multitude'.[86] In a democratic age, lawyers form the true aristocracy, and they 'secretly oppose their aristocratic propensities to the nation's democratic instincts, their superstitious attachment to what is old to its

---

[78] Ibid. See further, Antonio Cassesse, 'Are Human Rights Truly Universal?' in Obrad Savić, *The Politics of Human Rights* (London: Verso, 1999), 149–165.

[79] See Arendt, above n. 71, 298: 'Man of the twentieth century has become just as emancipated from nature as eighteenth-century man was from history. History and nature have become equally alien to us, namely, in the sense that the essence of man can no longer be comprehended in terms of either category'.

[80] Ignatieff, above n. 77, 9.

[81] For a discussion of this issue, see: Thomas L. Haskell, 'The Curious Persistence of Rights Talk in the "Age of Interpretation"' (1987) 74 *Journal of American History* 984–1012.

[82] See Martti Koskenniemi, 'The Effect of Rights on Political Culture' in Philip Alston (ed.), *The EU and Human Rights* (Oxford: Oxford University Press, 1999), 99–116, esp. 107–110.

[83] Ronald Dworkin, *Taking Rights Seriously* (Cambridge, Mass: Harvard University Press, 1977), 126: determining 'the right answer' involves 'identif[ying] a particular conception of community morality as decisive of legal issues; that conception holds that community morality is the political morality presupposed by the laws and institutions of the community'.

[84] This remains the case, notwithstanding the development of sophisticated theories, such as that of Alexy (above n. 74), that argue that balancing does not lead to radical openness.

[85] Alexis de Tocqueville, *Democracy in America* [1835], Henry Reeve trans. (New York: Vintage Books, 1990), vol. 1, 272.

[86] Ibid. 273.

love of novelty, their narrow views to its immense designs, and their habitual procrastination to its ardent impatience'.[87] In short, they provide the invaluable service of 'neutraliz[ing] the vices inherent in popular government'.[88] At a time when the executive dominates the legislature, the judiciary is able to offer a useful check on the exercise of governmental power.

As the institution which 'will always be the least dangerous to the political rights of the Constitution',[89] a judiciary which controls neither the purse nor the sword can still impose beneficial discipline and rationality over the processes of political reasoning. But such gains come at a price. Basing political order on individual rights, and therefore paradoxically basing the legitimacy of society on a thoroughly asocial principle, is in itself controversial.[90] But handing the task of explicating these rights to an institution whose entire *modus operandi* is rooted in a conviction that there are right answers to all disputes in law and that such answers are revealed through the deployment of some unique legal logic must be doubly contentious. For many, Tocqueville's bulwark—the secretive and aristocratic propensities of lawyers—has become what Koskenniemi labels 'a culture of bad faith', and this may be simply too high a price to pay.[91]

Ultimately, any stance on the positivization of natural rights involves an uncertain exercise in political judgment. This form of constitutional rights discourse appeals to canons of legal reason, but actually involves an exercise in prudential political reasoning. Our judgments turn on two basic questions. First, do we believe that this expanding culture of rights—which may soon extend to social and economic issues[92]—gives sound expression to our aspirations to autonomy, equality, dignity, and justice, or is its formalism and adversarialism more likely to generate a destructive stridency in political engagement?[93] Secondly, do we trust the judiciary to sustain a sound tradition of prudential reasoning through rights? Whatever judgment we reach, rights discourse will continue to exert a powerful influence over contemporary conceptions of public law.

---

[87] Ibid. 278.      [88] Ibid.

[89] *The Federalist Papers*, above n. 42, No. 78 (Hamilton).

[90] Pierre Manent, *Naissance de la politique moderne* (Paris: Payot, 1977), 11: 'To base the legitimacy of society (human relationships) on the autonomy of the individual is to base it on the most asocial principle' (cited in Ferry, above n. 11, 59).

[91] Koskenniemi, above n. 82, 100. For some, this issue is linked to the fact that today, as a consequence of rationalization and specialization, lawyers and judges no longer possess the deliberative and political skills to be able sensitively to handle these tasks: see Anthony T. Kronman, *The Lost Lawyer: Failing Ideals of the Legal Profession* (Cambridge, Mass: Belknap Press, 1993).

[92] For an analytical assessment see Cécile Fabre, *Social Rights under the Constitution: Government and the Decent Life* (Oxford: Oxford University Press, 1999).

[93] Cf. Louis Hartz, 'The Whig Tradition in America and Europe' (1952) 46 *American Political Science Review* 989–1002, 997 (n. 10): 'When half a nation believes in Locke and half in Filmer or Marx, the result is not law but philosophy. *Inter arma leges silent* . . . America's famous legalism is thus the reverse side of its philosophic poverty in politics'. See also John Gray, *Enlightenment's Wake: Politics and Culture at the Close of the Modern Age* (London: Routledge, 1995), 76: 'liberal legalism . . . is, perhaps, only an especially unambiguous example of an older liberal project, or illusion, of *abolishing politics*, or of so constraining it by legal and constitutional formulae that it no longer matters what are the outcomes of political deliberation'.

# 8

# *Method*

The argument of the book has been that public law must be recognized as a discrete field of legal knowledge. Some argue that there 'is no place in civil association for any but a conditional distinction between so-called "private" and "public" law'.[1] But lawyers are skilled at drawing differences in kind where others see only differences of degree.[2] And we should never underestimate the importance of classification as an instrument of world-building. In earlier chapters, I have identified the conceptual underpinnings of the subject. One question remains: if public law is a separate field of knowledge, what is special about its method? This chapter offers an answer. But I approach it indirectly, by first considering why this conception of public law has been neglected.

### CONTEMPORARY JURISPRUDENCE

One reason for the marginalization of public law has been the modern predilection for treating law as an autonomous, singular, and universal phenomenon. This is attributable mainly to the influence of legal positivism, the prevailing philosophy of the twentieth century. Legal positivism limits the idea of law 'properly so-called' to that of positive law, that is, to the edicts of the supreme authority in the state. Within a positivist frame, only the regulatory aspects of public law, those laws that have their source in the will of the sovereign authority, are afforded proper recognition, with the constitutive aspects of the subject being relegated to the sphere of 'positive morality'. Consequently, it has been difficult to see that public law is a singular entity; the fragmentation between its constitutive and regulative aspects has had a disfiguring effect.

The tendency to confine the idea of law to positive law has recently been questioned, yet reappraisal has done little to rejuvenate public law. The challenge has arisen because of the phenomenon of juridification, that is, the tendency to conceptualize extensive spheres of public life in legal terms.[3] Juridification highlights the limitations of legal positivism, not least because the meaning of formal rules regulating human conduct often depends on the social dimensions of normative authority.

---

[1] Michael Oakeshott, *On Human Conduct* (Oxford: Clarendon Press, 1975), 151.
[2] See F. W. Maitland, *Township and Borough* (Cambridge: Cambridge University Press, 1898), 22–23.
[3] See Jürgen Habermas, *The Theory of Communicative Action, vol. ii: Lifeworld and System: A Critique of Functionalist Reason*, Thomas MacCarthy trans. (Cambridge: Polity Press, 1987), 356–373.

The phenomenon of juridification has caused scholars to develop new approaches to the study of law, including methods drawn from the social sciences. These efforts have resulted in a number of projects for reconceptualizing modern law, most notably Jürgen Habermas's attempt to resolve the tension between system differentiation and social integration through the promotion of the idea of law as the democratic impetus in action.[4] The most influential of the Anglo-American challenges to positivism, however, has been one that treats law as a species of moral reasoning.[5] Whatever incidental benefits this may yield—offering a more incisive account of the logic of justification on display in modern adjudicative processes—the movement's universalizing tendencies have taken us further away from an understanding of public law. Reconstructing law as the institutionalization of moral rights has supplanted the rule-based reasoning of positivism with an inappropriate conception of legality. The conception of law lying at the core of the rights movement comes from a private law model that is unable to supply critical standards against which governmental action is to be measured.

Public law is a separate field of knowledge because of the singular character of its object, the activity of governing. With respect to this activity, law maintains the framework through which government is conducted. Whether presented as a model of rules or a regime of rights, modern accounts conceptualize law as an autonomous mode of action and as an enterprise to be differentiated from politics. Such claims eclipse the idea of public law, which, far from transcending politics, is an aspect of political practice.

We can advance our inquiry, then, only by displacing recent theories that skew this understanding. The way forward is to return to the early modern jurists who pursued their study of law into the political sphere and asked rudimentary questions about the authority of government. Only by analysing the work of scholars such as Bodin, Grotius, Hobbes, Pufendorf, and Rousseau, for example, can we understand sovereignty, the key concept of modern public law. Contemporary jurists reduce sovereignty to a legal doctrine that expresses the authority of institutions of government to enact law, but this is a shadow of its true meaning. As the early modern jurists established, sovereignty is a representation not only of public law but also the autonomy of the political sphere. Rediscovering the importance of their conception is a vital first step in understanding the nature and method of public law.

From the perspective of sovereignty, political power is absolute: the constituted authority of the state possesses complete autonomy of action. The state articulates this will only through those representative forms of law, and this recognition is significant. Sovereignty is understood to mean the sovereignty of law, an expression that is often transcribed as the rule of law. But 'the rule of law' is an ambiguous phrase. If it means that authority can only be wielded through recognized legal forms and that

---

[4] Jürgen Habermas, *Between Facts and Norms: Contributions to a Discourse Theory of Law and Democracy*, William Rehg trans. (Cambridge: Polity Press, 1996). Cf. Tim Murphy, *The Oldest Social Science? Configurations of Law and Modernity* (Oxford: Clarendon Press, 1997), ch. 7.

[5] See in particular, Ronald Dworkin, *Law's Empire* (London: Fontana, 1986).

the legal machinery of the state exists to ensure the compliance of office-holders with these forms, it is non-contentious. But when it is taken to mean that, depending on choice of metaphor, law either provides the foundation of political order or establishes a rule structure that transcends the political, things begin to go awry.

Contemporary lawyers have been particularly susceptible to such modes of thought. Having grown up under the influence of positivism, there is a danger of forgetting that the foundations of legal order are political. Having come to view law as an autonomous rule structure, thereby repressing the fact that the rule system expresses a political relationship, they assert that this rule structure must be constitutive of political order. Law, rather than being an expression of sovereignty, comes to be seen as a restriction on it. It is then but a short step to affirm that political practice must be subservient to legal logic. The silences and ambiguities within the authority structure are no longer treated as a necessary part of the accommodation between the legal and the political, but as dangerous lacunae which ought to be eliminated.

In the English system, jurists seeking to rationalize the common law method have been especially prone to this tendency. Dicey's rhetoric, which positioned law at the centre of British constitutional arrangements and presented the common law as the engine of constitutional development, is now taken literally. Armed with a technique that placed the common law at the centre of the constitution, lawyers reconceptualized the common law as a formal, rational, and architectonic structure. After dabbling with the notion that the common law provides the foundation of the constitution,[6] they have recently become more assertive. No one has pursued this matter with greater aplomb than Sir John Laws.

Working from orthodox postulates, Laws reaches controversial conclusions. He argues that sovereignty must rest 'not with those who wield governmental power, but in the conditions under which they are permitted to do so', maintaining that 'the constitution, not the Parliament, is in this sense sovereign'.[7] In Britain 'these conditions should now be recognised as consisting in a framework of fundamental principles'.[8] The most contentious shift is made at the last stage, when he contends that 'judicial power in the last resort rests in the guarantee that this framework will be vindicated'.[9] Laws here builds on the twin processes of common law rationalization and legal foundationalism to promote 'the imperative of higher-order law'.[10]

This type of legerdemain is revealed only by returning to the political conception of sovereignty. If sovereignty is to be expressed as a 'framework of fundamental principles' then we might note: that this framework is a political framework; that terms like 'fundamental' are being used rhetorically, amounting to an appeal to conventional

---

[6] See Sir Owen Dixon, 'The Common Law as an Ultimate Constitutional Foundation' (1957) 31 *Australian Law Journal* 240–245. Cf. Owen Dixon, 'The Law and the Constitution' (1935) 51 *Law Quarterly Review* 590–614. The Australian example offers a useful illustration; on which see George Williams, *Human Rights under the Australian Constitution* (Melbourne: Oxford University Press, 1999).
[7] Sir John Laws, 'Law and Democracy' 1995 *Public Law* 72–93, 92.    [8] Ibid.    [9] Ibid.
[10] Ibid. 84. In similar vein, see: T. R. S. Allan, *Law, Liberty, and Justice: The Legal Foundations of British Constitutionalism* (Oxford: Clarendon Press, 1993).

political practices; that any such 'principles' are fluid and must accommodate political necessities; that determination of the precise meaning of such principles involves an exercise in political judgment; and that the judiciary do not self-evidently possess either the institutional or knowledge-based competence to explicate this framework. Judgments of this nature can be assessed only in the context of public law as 'juristic civic consciousness'.[11] But because this conception has been submerged, its meaning can be conveyed only by expressing it in archaic or foreign languages: that is, as *jus publicum*, *droit politique*, or *Staatsrecht*.

To capture its spirit, we need to re-examine the relationship between law and government that once formed part of a general civil philosophy. This type of civil philosophy has today been buried beneath the modern philosophical tendencies of rationalism and empiricism, each of which has had a distortive effect. The idea of public law as political jurisprudence must now be restored.

PUBLIC LAW AS POLITICAL JURISPRUDENCE

Early modern jurists sought to adapt medieval legal thought in the light of social, economic, and technological change. Medieval scholars had been deeply influenced by Roman law, invoking Roman maxims that vested authority in the emperor to override the customary laws,[12] and arguing that the king possessed authority both to pronounce the law and be absolved from subjection to it. But the tensions between law and royal authority were there, as is illustrated by the work of the thirteenth century jurist generally known as Henry de Bracton.

In his celebrated text, *On the Laws and Customs of England*, Bracton claimed that although the king knows no equal, he is not a true king if he rules by arbitrary will rather than through law. Bracton acknowledged that if the king does wrong there can be no remedy through the king's courts. But although the king is not under any man, he remains under God and the law.[13] Bracton's text contains numerous statements that do not seem compatible. Thus, although the king occupies a position at the apex of legal order, he also appears to be subject to certain standards. Bracton's standards are obscure, as are the procedures by which they might be rendered explicit.

Modern writers have offered a range of explanations of Bracton's text. It has been suggested that Bracton distinguishes between two different spheres of government, *jurisdictio* and *gubernaculum*—between the sphere of adjudicative government (private

---

[11] Steven Lestition, 'The Teaching and Practice of Jurisprudence in Eighteenth Century East Prussia: Konigsberg's First Chancellor, R. F. von Sahme (1682–1753)' (1989) 16 *Ius Commune* 27–80, 30.

[12] See esp. Justinian, *Digest* [534], Alan Watson trans. (Philadelphia: University of Pennsylvania Press, 1998), i.4.1: 'What pleases the prince has the force of law, since by the *lex regia* which was enacted concerning his rule, the people confers on him all its authority and power'.

[13] Henry de Bracton, *De Legibus et Consuetudinibus Angliae (On the Laws and Customs of England)* [c.1258], George E. Woodbine ed., Samuel E. Thorne trans. (Cambridge, Mass.: Belknap Press, 1968), ii.33.

right) and executive government (public power).[14] It has also been contended that the reference to what pleased 'the king' here refers not to a personal will but only to an institutional will authorized by the king's council.[15] Other explanations have been offered: that the king's coronation oath provides the basis for self-restraint,[16] that constraint is supplied by *consuetudo* (custom),[17] or by the king's own dignity,[18] or that the relevant passages relate to the king as judge rather than as ruler.[19] But such analyses rely on legalistic and overly sophisticated arguments. Brian Tierney has suggested that Bracton was 'not sufficiently learned in [Roman and canon law], nor sufficiently imaginative nor, I am sure, sufficiently interested in this kind of problem, to achieve such a synthesis'.[20] Bracton's statements on the relationship between royal power and the law should not be subjected to such analytical rigour.

The main point is that Bracton expressed a general conviction that although governmental authority is limited, such limits were not imposed by positive law. These limits derive either from natural law or from an appeal to the prescriptive authority of the ancient customs of the land.

The problems implicit in Bracton's text came to the foreground during the early stages of modernization when the sovereign as an active force displaced the image of the sovereign as a dispenser of justice. Once the creative power of the sovereign authority was recognized, traditional limitations ceased to hold much authority. Once it was possible to present the essence of law as a form of command—that is, as an exercise of a will that carried binding force—the claims of customary or natural law subsided. Such claims no longer commended themselves as the product of

---

[14] Charles Howard McIlwain, *Constitutionalism: Ancient and Modern* (Ithaca, New York: Cornell University Press, 1947), ch. 4. See also S. J. T. Miller, 'The Position of the King in Bracton and Beaumanoir' (1956) 31 *Speculum* 263–296. Cf. Brian Tierney, 'Bracton on Government' (1963) 38 *Speculum* 295–317, 316–317: '[Bracton's] work was essentially an attempt to fit a massive structure of English private law into a rather flimsy framework of Romanesque public law and naturally there are signs of strain. The figure of a king, half feudal lord, half divine ruler, that he found in his plea rolls could not easily have been transformed into the first magistrate of a constitutional government even if Bracton had had any such conscious intention. It was indeed impossible to extract a theory of the constitutional state from the English materials because they simply lacked the idea of the state in the classical or modern sense'.

[15] Ernst H. Kantorowicz, *The King's Two Bodies: A Study in Mediaeval Political Theology* (Princeton, NJ: Princeton University Press, 1957), 151–152. Cf. Fritz Schulz, 'Bracton on Kingship' (1945) 60 *English Historical Review* 136–176, 173; Ewart Lewis, 'King above Law? *Quod principi placuit* in Bracton' (1964) 40 *Speculum* 240–269, 264–265.

[16] McIlwain, above n. 14, 71–72; Schulz, above n. 15, 155 (n. 2). Cf. Lewis, above n. 15, 242.

[17] McIlwain, above n. 14, 83; cf. Tierney, above n. 14, 309. But see C. J. Nederman, 'Bracton on Kingship Revisited' (1984) 5 *History of Political Thought* 66–73.

[18] Justinian, *Codex*, i.14.4: '*Digna vox maiestate . . .*' ('It is a saying worthy of the majesty of the ruler that the prince profess himself bound by the laws, since our authority depends on the authority of the law. And it is indeed a thing greater than empire that a prince submit his government to the laws'). See Tierney, above n. 14, 300–305. Cf. Lewis, above n. 15, 248.

[19] Lewis, ibid. 243, 258–259. Cf. Donald W. Hanson, *From Kingdom to Commonwealth: The Development of Civic Consciousness in English Political Thought* (Cambridge, Mass.: Harvard University Press, 1970), 111–114.

[20] Tierney, above n. 14, 317. See also, Kenneth Pennington, *The Prince and the Law, 1200–1600: Sovereignty and Rights in the Western Legal Tradition* (Berkeley, Calif.: University of California Press, 1993), 92–93.

ingenious and subtle argument; being forms of medieval scholasticism, they were treated as anachronisms.

This transition to modernity was captured with the greatest subtlety by Jean Bodin. Bodin is best known today as an early exponent of sovereignty, which he defined as 'the most high, absolute and perpetuall power over the citizens and subjects in a Commonweale'.[21] He conceived sovereignty, 'the greatest power to command',[22] as being exercisable only through law, and argued that 'the law is nothing else but the commandment of a sovereign, using of his sovereign power'.[23] But Bodin seems to equivocate on this central point. He readily acknowledged the existence of three types of limit to the exercise of sovereign power: natural law,[24] the fundamental laws of the realm (*leges imperii*) which establish the framework of rule,[25] and the inviolability of private property.[26] Bodin thus suggests that the sovereign is both absolute and limited in authority, both unbound and bound. Is Bodin, like Bracton, simply inconsistent, unconsciously shifting gears between positive law and natural law?

Nannerl Keohane argues that those who have interpreted Bodin in a legalistic manner—concluding that he struggled unsuccessfully to present a concept of sovereignty freed from medieval chains—have concentrated on the first of his *Six Books*.[27] Read as a whole, the *Six Books* is much less legalist than initially appears. Bodin recognized the vital importance to the sovereign of wise counsellors[28] and, despite insisting on the indivisibility of sovereignty, assumed the need to divide the functions of govern-

---

[21] Jean Bodin, *The Six Bookes of a Commonweale* [1576], Richard Knolles trans., Kenneth Douglas McRae ed. (Cambridge, Mass.: Harvard University Press, 1962), i.8 (84).

[22] Ibid. [23] Ibid. 108.

[24] Ibid. 92: 'But as for the lawes of God and nature, all princes and people of the world are unto them subject: neither is it in their power to impugne them, if will not be guiltie of high treason to the divine majestie . . . Wherefore in that we said the soveraigne power in a Commonweale to be free from all lawes, concerneth nothing the lawes of God and nature'.

[25] Ibid. 95: 'But touching the lawes which concerne the state of the realme, and the establishing thereof; forasmuch as they are annexed and united to the crowne, the prince cannot derogat from them, such as is the law Salique: and albeit that he so do, the successor may alwaies disanull that which hath bene done unto the prejudice of the laws royall, upon which the soveraigne maiestie is stayed and grounded'.

[26] Ibid. 110: '[T]he king cannot take nor give another mans goods, without the consent of the owner . . . For that which the common people commonly saith, *All to be the* princes, is to be understood concerning power and soveraintie, the proprietie and possession of everie mans things yet reserved to himselfe'.

[27] Nannerl O. Keohane, *Philosophy and the State in France: The Renaissance to the Enlightenment* (Princeton, NJ: Princeton University Press, 1980), 67–82.

[28] Bodin, above n. 21, iii.1 (255): 'For it is right certaine, that great learning in princes is often times a thing no lesse dangerous than a knife in a mad mans hand, except he be by nature well given, and the more vertuously instructed and brought up. Neither is there any thing more to be feared, than great learning accompanied with injustice, and armed with power. There was never yet prince less learned (except in deeds of armes) than *Trajan*, neither any of greater knowledge than *Nero*, and yet for all that, this man had never his peere for crueltie, nor the other for bountie: the one of them deadly hating the Senat, and the other in all things following the advice thereof. Seeing therefore that a Senat is a thing so profitable in a Monarchy, and so necessarie in all Popular and Aristocraticall estates, as is in man wit and reason, without which his body cannot long governe itselfe, or have at all any being: let us first speake of the qualities requisite in Senatours or Counsellors . . .'.

ment.[29] He even asserted that 'the less the power of the soveraigntie is (the true markes of majestie thereunto still reserved) the more it is assured'.[30] The limits on sovereignty that Bodin identified are 'most accurately understood as conditions for its exercise'.[31]

Bodin's acute observation that less means more—and that 'hard it is for high and stately buildings long to stand, except they be upholden and staid by most strong shores, and rest upon most sure foundations'[32]—has a resoundingly modern message to convey. This is the mark of Bodin's genius.[33] Using the analogy of grammar, Stephen Holmes has highlighted the importance of Bodin's claim that it is precisely because limits are disabling, that they are enabling. Rules governing the use of language are not barriers to, or restrictions on, speech. Grammatical rules are what Holmes calls 'possibility-creating rules', and they 'cannot be accurately described as manacles clamped upon a pre-existent freedom'.[34] Only by using the rules of grammar are we able to achieve precision in communication. Holmes draws out the implications for political jurisprudence:

Bodin's massive treatise is much too sprawling and loose-knit to be exhaustively summarized in any compact thesis. Nevertheless, this argument does stand out: laws of nature, laws of succession, nonalienability of domain lands, immemorial customs, a prohibition on taxation without consultation, and the informal prerogatives of parlements and Estates can substantially *increase* the power of a prince. Bodin treats restrictions on power, unconventionally, as a set of authority-reinforcing, will-empowering, and possibility-expanding rules.[35]

It is this paradox in Bodin's work that helps us understand public law as political jurisprudence.

Bodin's treatment of sovereignty builds on a distinction between public and private, between the state and the economy, between the sphere of power and that of domination.[36] It recognizes 'the brokenness of the political domain'[37] as the gulf existing between governors and governed that turns politics into conflict management[38] and

---

[29] Ibid. iv. 6 (518): 'But the best kind of Commonweale is that, wherein the soveraigne holdeth what concerneth his majestie, the Senat maintaineth the authoritie thereof, the magistrates execute their power, and justice hath her ordinarie course. Whereas otherwise if the prince or the people shall take upon themselves the authoritie of the Senat, or the commaunds, offices, or jurisdictions of the magistrates; it is much to be feared, least that they destitute of all helpe, shall at length be spoyled of their owne soveraigne majestie also'. (See further, ibid. v.4.)

[30] Ibid. iv.6 (517).  [31] Keohane, above n. 27, 74.  [32] Bodin, above n. 21, 517.

[33] Stephen Holmes, 'The Constitution of Sovereignty in Jean Bodin' in his *Passions and Constraint: On the Theory of Liberal Democracy* (Chicago: University of Chicago Press, 1995), 100–133, 108–109.

[34] Ibid. 109. See also Benedetto Croce, *Politics and Morals* [1925] (New York: Philosophical Library, 1945), 8–9.

[35] Holmes, above n. 33, 109–110.

[36] Bodin, above n. 21, i.2 ('Of a Familie, and what difference there is betweene a Familie and a Commonweale').

[37] See F. R. Ankersmit, *Aesthetic Politics: Political Philosophy Beyond Fact and Value* (Stanford, Calif.: Stanford University Press, 1996), 119.

[38] Bodin, above n. 21, vi.3 (705): 'To conclude, if we shall rip up all the Popular estates that ever were, we shall find, that either they have had warre always with the enemie, or within the state: or else that they have bene governed in shew by the people; but in effect by some of the citizens, or by the wisest among

which gives shape to the representative form of the public sphere.[39] But Bodin's primary concern was not with the formal right to rule but with the actual capacity of the ruler. By exercising authority only through customary forms, the sovereign strengthens the bonds of allegiance, and augments his power. Authority is enhanced when competence is limited. Bodin, in short, aimed to demonstrate how the sovereign 'becomes sovereign in fact as well as in law'.[40]

In Bodin's work the sovereign is an innovative power and this distinguishes his account from Bracton's. Of equal importance is the way that traditional limits on royal power which remain puzzling in Bracton's text are reworked by Bodin as conditions for the successful deployment of royal power. The tension between right conduct and the king's voluntary will of enactment is reconceptualized by Bodin as of strategic political significance. Natural law is still presented in the traditional manner as a bridle on the prince, but this masks the way in which the function of natural law has subtly changed.

The significance of this shift is exemplified, a century later, in the work of the German jurist, Samuel Pufendorf. Motivated by practical problems he encountered as a state counsellor in both Sweden and Prussia in the latter half of the seventeenth century, Pufendorf developed a doctrine of natural law which confined the scope of the discipline to that of 'the orbit of [man's] life'.[41] He argued that the precepts of natural law are 'laws which teach one how to conduct oneself to become a useful member of human society', thereby separating public or political conduct, which belonged to the sphere of natural law, and the pursuit of moral perfection, which took place in the private realm. For Pufendorf, the precepts of natural law yield one fundamental: 'every man ought to do as much as he can to cultivate and preserve sociality'.[42]

This foundational principle, Pufendorf argued, underpins the formation of states which exist 'to administer the means of their safety and security by common counsel and leadership'[43] and maintain civil peace and promote common security.[44] Contrary to such natural rights theorists as Hobbes and Locke, he contended that the political obligations of citizens 'had their own separate foundations in men's

---

them, who held the place of a prince and monarch. Whilest that the Commonweale of Athens did flourish, it was governed by the Senat of the Areopagits: and when as their power and authoritie was restrained, *Pericles* (saith *Thucidides*) was a very Monarch, although in shew it were Populax'.

[39] Ankersmit, above n. 37, 120: 'The prince is always a representation in the minds of the people . . . , whereas the people can only present themselves to the prince's mind as a representation—and there can be no medium, neutral, or common ground where these two representations meet or could be matched'. See further, F. R. Ankersmit, *Political Representation* (Stanford, Calif.: Stanford University Press, 2002).

[40] Holmes, above n. 33, 110.

[41] Samuel Pufendorf, *On the Duty of Man and Citizen According to Natural Law* [1673], Michael Silverthorne trans., James Tully ed. (Cambridge: Cambridge University Press, 1991), Preface.

[42] Ibid. i.2.8, i.2.9. On this point, Pufendorf's work follows Hugo Grotius, *The Rights of War and Peace* [1625], A. C. Campbell trans. (New York: Dunne, 1901), i.1.3: 'Now any thing is unjust, which is repugnant to the nature of society, established among rational creatures'.

[43] Pufendorf, above n. 41, ii.6.7.    [44] Ibid. ii.11.3.

sociability, rather than in state power founded upon contract'.[45] Pufendorf not only confined moral reasoning to the private sphere (the pursuit of salvation), but uncoupled sovereignty from moral truth, thereby permitting politics to emerge as an autonomous practice. 'By removing God and the eternal verities vested in Him from the compass of natural law', Hochstrasser suggests, 'Pufendorf had removed any point of external moral reference which transcended the legislative creations and obligations of human nature'.[46]

Pufendorf's great achievement was to have restricted natural law entirely to the preservation of man's sociability. Natural law was severed from any transcendental or metaphysical ideas of justice and goodness; rather than being derived from any appeal to some higher law, the norms of natural law must be drawn from the worldly nature of human beings. Natural law is not an expression of man's rational and moral being but of an unfolding civil relationship. Natural law provides the basic precepts of *Staatsrecht* and, as he makes plain, these are the product of a relational understanding of sovereignty.[47]

Ian Hunter has argued that the scale of Pufendorf's reconstruction of moral and political philosophy has been obscured by a modern rationalist interpretation of his work.[48] By making natural law and positive law subservient to the common end of civil peace, Hunter suggests that 'Pufendorf in effect makes natural laws norms immanent to the process of political governance through which citizens are formed'.[49] Such norms must be distinguished from transcendental moral norms; they are 'immanent to the historical circumstances in which the sovereign state emerged as a bulwark against man's limitless capacity for self-destruction and civil mayhem'.[50] Political coercion 'acquires its legitimacy not as a means of enforcing the self-governance that rational beings should be able to exercise by and on themselves (the rationalist model that continues to tie civil authority to transcendent truth)' but 'as a

---

[45] Istvan Hont, 'The Language of Sociability and Commerce: Samuel Pufendorf and the Theoretical Foundations of the "Four-Stages Theory"', in Anthony Pagden (ed.), *The Languages of Political Theory in Early-Modern Europe* (Cambridge: Cambridge University Press, 1987), 253–276, 265.

[46] T. J. Hochstrasser, *Natural Law Theories in the Early Enlightenment* (Cambridge: Cambridge University Press, 2000), 105.

[47] See Pufendorf, above n. 41, ii.6.10: 'A state so constituted is conceived as one person [*persona*], and is separated and distinguished from all particular men by a unique name; and it has its own special rights and property, which no one man, no multitude of men, nor even all men together, may appropriate apart from him who holds the sovereign power or to whom the government of the state has been committed. Hence a state is defined as a composite moral person, whose will blended and combined from the agreement of many is taken as the will of all so that it may employ the forces and capacities of every individual for the common peace and security'. The implications are drawn out by Tully (above n. 41, xxxiii), who notes that 'unlike doctrines of corporate popular sovereignty, the people, although it possesses unity, never possesses supreme authority and so cannot be said to "delegate" it to a ruler and repossess it if the ruler breaks the agreement'. Since sovereignty is the expression of a political relationship, it cannot reside in the people. Or as Hunter (below, n. 48, 190) puts it: 'If the sovereign power is an artefact of the political pact, and is not donated to government by its natural or metaphysical bearer—God, the king, the people, the general will—then neither monarchy, nor aristocracy nor democracy is its natural expression'.

[48] Ian Hunter, *Rival Enlightenments: Civil and Metaphysical Philosophy in Early Modern Germany* (Cambridge: Cambridge University Press, 2001).

[49] Ibid. 149.     [50] Ibid. 160.

means of enforcing the relations of dependency and guardianship that human beings have imposed on themselves, via the institution of civil sovereignty, as a means of achieving social peace'.[51]

This trajectory of thought from Bracton through Bodin to Pufendorf illuminates the idea of public law as political jurisprudence. Bracton's ambiguities of natural and positive law are reworked in the early modern period. In Bodin, natural law limitations assume political significance in the form of conditions for the successful deployment of sovereign power. Pufendorf later makes the decisive break by severing natural law from theology and ethics. Natural law is reconceptualized as a set of worldly precepts aimed at maintaining the state. Once politics is identified as an autonomous realm, natural law is transformed into the precepts of 'political right'. In modern thought, natural law is transmuted into *droit politique*.

This evolutionary development has been suppressed by the formalistic and rationalistic tendencies of modern jurisprudence. In order to recover this understanding, we must examine further the conception of law implicit in *droit politique* and re-assess the relationship between politics and morality. Only then will we be able to address the method of public law.

LAW AND *DROIT POLITIQUE*

Modern jurists regard Bodin as confused over the relationship between natural law and positive law. By contrast, Hobbes—the first theorist unambiguously to refer to law as the will of the sovereign power—is viewed as someone who eliminated natural law from civil society. Hobbes offered us a graphic image of natural law operating in a state of nature, 'where all men are equall, and judges of the justnesse of their own fears'[52] and life becomes a state of war of all against all. Civilization is achieved only through the formation of the office of the sovereign. For Hobbes, all law is positive law, a form of obligation that commands, prohibits, directs, and restrains. Does this mean that Hobbes, the arch-positivist, refused to admit of *droit politique*?

Hobbes was adamant that since positive law provided 'the measure of Good and Evil actions', there could be no such thing as an unjust law.[53] But he does accept that there can be such a thing as a 'good' law.[54] A good law is that which 'is *Needful*, for the *Good of the People*, and withall *Perspicuous*'.[55] Since the law-making power exists to promote the welfare of the people, a law that benefits rulers but not the people is not a good law.[56] Hobbes here recognizes the existence of certain prudential precepts influencing the exercise of sovereign authority. 'It is a weak Soveraign, that has weak Subjects', he wrote, 'and a weak People, whose Soveraign wanteth Power to rule them at his will'.[57]

---

[51] Ian Hunter, *Rival Enlightenments: Civil and Metaphysical Philosophy in Early Modern Germany* (Cambridge: Cambridge University Press, 2001), 160.

[52] Thomas Hobbes, *Leviathan* [1651], Richard Tuck ed. (Cambridge: Cambridge University Press, 1996), 96.

[53] Ibid. 223.   [54] Ibid. 239.   [55] Ibid.   [56] Ibid. 240.   [57] Ibid.

Sovereign authority is a form of public power exercised for the good of the people, and a well-governed state is one in which, without endangering the public good, civil liberty is maximized. This requires an acknowledgement of 'the art of making fit Lawes'.[58]

Hobbes recognized that the objective of statecraft is to create 'one firme and lasting edifice'.[59] Without the help of 'a very able Architect', however, what is likely to result is 'a crasie building' which the people will regard as unstable and which 'must assuredly fall upon the heads of their posterity'.[60] It is clear that although the sovereign/subject relationship is not regulated by law (*sc.*, positive law), the sovereign must be skilled in the arts of government.[61] These arts can be expressed as precepts of political right.

In developing his theory of sociability, Pufendorf was critical of Hobbes's portrayal of life in a state of nature;[62] after all (in Tuck's summary of Pufendorf), 'nations could and often did live in peace with one another without the necessity of a common power over them, and the same could be said about individuals in a state of nature'.[63] Pufendorf's benign anthropological image opened up the conceptual space that permitted *droit politique* to emerge. His analysis of the way in which a multitude constitute an association and establish a form of government with supreme authority also provides 'the most discriminating analysis' of the conceptual basis of state formation in early modern Europe.[64] For an elaboration of the broader conception of law implicit in this process, we must turn to Montesquieu.

Montesquieu's objective in *The Spirit of the Laws* had been to show how monarchical power could not be sustained unless it was regulated and bounded by 'fundamental laws'. Although 'the prince is the source of all political and civil power', the fundamental laws 'necessarily assume mediate channels through which power flows'.[65] If there is in the state 'only the momentary and capricious will of one alone, nothing can be fixed, and consequently there is no fundamental law'.[66] Incorporated within the expression 'fundamental law' are those forms and institutions that establish and regulate the exercise of governmental authority. Rather than being construed as limitations on state power, they should be viewed as conditions for maintaining state authority. Should adherence to these forms cease, 'fear would invade all spirits;

---

[58] Ibid. 221.      [59] Ibid.      [60] Ibid.
[61] Thomas Hobbes, *The Elements of Law Natural and Politic* [1640], Ferdinand Tönnies ed., M. M. Goldsmith intro. (London: Cass, 1969), ii.9.1: 'And as the art and duty of sovereigns consist in the same acts, so also doth their profit. For the end of art is profit; and governing to the profit of the subjects is governing to the profit of the sovereign . . . And these three: 1. the law over them that have sovereign power; 2. their duty; 3. their profit: are one and the same thing contained in this sentence, *Salus populi suprema lex*; by which must be understood, not the mere preservation of their lives, but generally their benefit and good. So that this is the general law for sovereigns: that they procure, to the uttermost of their endeavour, the good of the people'.
[62] Pufendorf, above n. 41, ii.1.
[63] Richard Tuck, *The Rights of War and Peace: Political Thought and the International Order from Grotius to Kant* (Oxford: Oxford University Press, 1999), 142.
[64] Tully, 'Introduction' to Pufendorf, above n. 41, xxxi.
[65] Montesquieu, *The Spirit of the Laws* [1748], Anne M. Cohler, Basia Carolyn Miller, and Harold Samuel Stone eds (Cambridge: Cambridge University Press, 1989), ii.4.
[66] Ibid.

one would see pallor on every face; there would be no more trust, honor, love, security, or monarchy'.[67] Montesquieu's 'fundamental laws' is synonymous with *droit politique*.

At the beginning of his great study Montesquieu defined laws 'as the necessary relations deriving from the nature of things'.[68] Arendt argues that Montesquieu here is using the word 'law' in its original Roman sense of *lex*, as the *rapport* or relation that exists between two different entities that have been brought together. For the Romans, no laws were necessary for a native people to exist as an organic unity; it was only after Aeneas arrived from Troy and war broke out between natives and invaders that laws were required to establish peace and forge a partnership of allies (*socii*) of Rome. Arendt also notes that 'the people of Rome itself, the *populus Romanus*, owed its existence to such war-born partnership, namely, to the alliance between patricians and plebeians, whose internal civil strife was concluded through the famous laws of the Twelve Tables'.[69] Using this relational idea of law, Montesquieu captures the 'spirit of the laws' without needing to identify an absolute source of authority. 'Neither religious nor natural laws', Arendt suggests, 'constitute for Montesquieu a "higher" law strictly speaking; they are no more than the relations which exist and preserve different realms of being'.[70]

Once the political sphere is recognized as a separate realm, public law can be understood not only as a formal system—a framework of positive law—but also more fundamentally as an intricate set of practices—*rapports* or relations—which condition and sustain the political as an autonomous realm. These practices—Hobbes's 'art of making fit Lawes', Pufendorf's natural law and Montesquieu's fundamental laws—are fundamental because they condition and maintain the political realm and thereby confer meaning on the framework of positive law regulating the system of government. Only by focusing on these practices are we able to understand the dynamic aspects of public law, to appreciate the open-textured nature of legal interpretation in this field, and to identify the 'constitutional' character of its positive laws.[71]

POLITICS AND MORALITY

In the medieval world-view, all Christians, and potentially all humans, formed a single corporate entity, the *Ecclesia*, which was not only a spiritual grouping but also

---

[67] Montesquieu, *The Spirit of the Laws* [1748], Anne M. Cohler, Basia Carolyn Miller, and Harold Samuel Stone eds (Cambridge: Cambridge University Press, 1989), vi.5.
[68] Ibid. i.1.   [69] Hannah Arendt, *On Revolution* (Harmondsworth: Penguin, 1963), 188.
[70] Ibid.
[71] Only by grasping this basic point, for example, is it possible to understand how, within a constitutional system such as Britain's that maintains no hierarchy of law, certain statutes (such as the European Communities Act 1972, the Human Rights Act 1998, and the Scotland Act 1998) can properly be designated to be 'constitutional statutes'—a designation that carries not only political but also juristic significance.

a universal body politic. This reflected a hierarchical principle of ordering and encompassed all aspects of social and political life.[72] The *Ecclesia* was an indivisible organic unity that expressed a universal mode of right living, with God acknowledged to be the *fons et origio* of all law. Within such a world-view, 'the juridical reality of the lawyer corresponds to the metaphysical reality of the philosopher and the divine reality of the theologian' and by this means 'the individual's relationship to society is transposed on to the higher plane of man's relationship to God'.[73] I do not intend to examine the various theological changes wrought by the Reformation, but one vital change was the degree of separation effected between the legal/political, the moral, and the theological.

In this respect, the writing of Hugo Grotius is exemplary. Working within a humanist and Calvinist context, Grotius argued that since only rational beings are subject to law, natural law should be understood to be an expression of human reason. This argument was expressed in *De Jure Belli ac Pacis* in 1625, a work which is generally accepted to have 'contained in an embryonic form most of the political theory of the following fifty years'.[74] But the Grotian position contained difficulties. In particular, it appeared that, without the authoritative support of revealed religion, natural law—and the positive law that constituted its expression—would dissipate into voluntarism. Hobbes had argued that within the state of nature there was one overriding duty derived from natural law, the duty of self-preservation. Since the exercise of this natural law involved a highly subjective judgment, however, it was difficult to see how, having rejected the hierarchical ordering of the *Ecclesia*, political order could be maintained. For Hobbes, this required a radical solution—the imposition, by will, of an all-powerful sovereign.

Pufendorf's response to this dilemma had been to argue that the Hobbesian concern for self-preservation was not incompatible with the maintenance of sociability.[75] By removing God from natural law, however, Pufendorf had eliminated any transcendental moral point of reference and, as Hochstrasser has pointed out, this made his position look distinctly Hobbesian.[76] By separating the political from the religious sphere, Pufendorf challenged the idea of a universal society rooted in divine justice, and paved the way for a liberal separation of church and state, morality and politics. But he had not done this for the purpose of protecting the individual from

---

[72] The *Ecclesia* corresponds to Oakeshott's usage of *universitas humana*: see above, Ch. 2, 18.

[73] Michael J. Wilks, *The Problem of Sovereignty in the Later Middle Ages* (Cambridge: Cambridge University Press, 1963), 25.

[74] Richard Tuck, *Natural Rights Theories: Their Origin and Development* (Cambridge: Cambridge University Press, 1979), 80.

[75] Pufendorf wrote: 'I judged that the first principle and source of all that can be known in this discipline was nothing else than the sociability of human nature. It is clear that it has been devised by the Creator himself . . . And I did not think that Hobbes, when he established the opposite of this view as his starting point, wanted it to be considered as a serious assertion, but rather as a pure hypothesis and one from which the laws of nature could be expounded as from an absurd and impossible basis'. Cited in Hochstrasser, above n. 46, 57.

[76] Ibid. 105.

the state; the separation was required to ensure the absolute rule of the state within the political domain. This was 'the "authoritarian" basis of Pufendorf's reconstruction of a zone of liberal religious freedoms'.[77] Uncoupling political rule from moral truth was an essential step in the establishment of an autonomous political sphere promoting security and welfare through prudential practice.[78]

Pufendorf's endeavours were subjected to vigorous criticism by G. W. Leibniz. Leibniz responded to the attempt to separate political reason and religious morality by seeking, through metaphysics, reconciliation at a higher level. In Hochstrasser's appraisal, Leibniz 'asserted that there are eternal verities, of which justice is one, which are not adjuncts of divine power, but ideas embedded (*inditus*) in God's mind, analogous to the truths of mathematics and logic'.[79] For Leibniz, 'neither the norm of conduct itself, nor the essence of the just, depends on [God's] free decision, but rather on eternal truths, objects of the divine intellect, which constitute, so to speak, the essence of divinity itself; and it is right that [Pufendorf] is reproached by theologians when he maintains to the contrary'.[80] Divine justice, Leibniz contended, is not simply the product of God's will since that would be a despotic power: rather *justitia est caritas sapientis* (justice is love governed by wisdom).[81]

The critical question was whether a fundamental distinction could be drawn between the sovereign's laws and God's rational natural law, between a civil realm governed by politics (the civil kingdom) and a religious sphere of morality (the kingdom of truth). The dispute between Pufendorf and Leibniz was subsequently overtaken by Kantian philosophy, which sought emancipation from a religious metaphysics by appealing to a formal transcendental philosophy. By invoking the categorical imperative as a transcendental law—'Act always in such a way as if you were through your maxims a law-making member of a universal kingdom of ends'[82]—Kant offered a way for moral philosophers to regain their authority within the realm of government. They re-entered the political world 'not as a clerical estate possessing its own share of civil authority, but as a clerisy of academic intellectuals, claiming powers from a source higher than the end of social peace—"critical reason"'.[83]

This debate over 'rival enlightenments' brings us to the core of the dispute in public law between politics and morality. The issue is not whether the political realm operates without reference to moral considerations or whether a moral sphere exists

---

[77] Hunter, above n. 48, 195.

[78] Pufendorf, above n. 41, ii.11.2: 'To know how to make a correct application of the general principles of prudent rule, the prince must have the most profound knowledge possible of the conditions of his own position and the character of the people subject to him'.

[79] Hochstrasser, above n. 46, 75.

[80] Gottfried Wilhelm Leibniz, *Political Writings*, Patrick Riley ed. (Cambridge: Cambridge University Press, 1972), 71.

[81] See Patrick Riley, *Leibniz' Universal Jurisprudence: Justice as the Charity of the Wise* (Cambridge, Mass: Harvard University Press, 1996).

[82] This is the third formulation of the categorical imperative: see Immanuel Kant, *Political Writings*, H. B. Nisbet trans., Hans Reiss ed. (Cambridge: Cambridge University Press, 1970), 18–19. See above, Ch. 7, 117.

[83] Hunter, above n. 48, 265.

which is on a higher plane than the political. Moral life cannot exist without economic and political life having first been established, and the ethical spirit is a vital aspect of political life. The critical issue is whether the public law that conditions this political domain is a form of political or moral discourse.

My argument has been that public law is an expression of the immanent precepts of an autonomous discourse of politics. This argument is directly contested by Kantian moral philosophers, who appeal to a rationalist political metaphysics in which 'political and legal rule appear as a debased mode of governance, required only until the moral community regains its capacity for reciprocal collective self-governance'.[84] Once this state is realized 'the need for law and state will wither away, displaced by the moral sovereignty of the community of rational beings, who, in accordance with a revivified political ecclesiology, will form an "ethico-civil society" or "kingdom of God on earth"'.[85]

Although my claim is that this Kantian argument must be rejected, its influence on public lawyers has been increasing. Most influential has been the work of Ronald Dworkin whose theory of law 'argues for a fusion of constitutional law and moral theory', a connection that, 'incredibly, has yet to take place'.[86] Recognizing that lawyers might feel some discomfort inside the intricacies of moral philosophy, he advises that 'better philosophy is now available than the lawyers may remember' and refers us to John Rawls's neo-Kantian theory of justice, a book 'which no constitutional lawyer will be able to ignore'.[87] Working within a Kantian frame, Dworkin develops the general thesis that citizens have moral rights against their governments and that 'the Constitution fuses legal and moral issues, by making the validity of a law depend on the answer to complex moral problems, like the problem of whether a particular statute respects the inherent equality of all men'.[88] Dworkin's work exemplifies the emergence of a new clerisy of legal intellectuals that claim special knowledge of the moral values on which the constitution of the state is founded.

Whatever the merits of Rawls's monumental treatise, *A Theory of Justice* has nothing to contribute to an understanding of the nature, tasks, or method of public law. Rawls himself seemed subsequently to recognize this, and modified his theory by arguing that his principles of justice are 'political not metaphysical'.[89] This enabled him to orientate his work towards the ordering of constitutional democracies, and therefore more directly to engage the concerns of public lawyers. The key technique Rawls uses is that of 'public reason'. The idea of public reason is hardly novel; after all, Hobbes had argued that 'we are not every one, to make our own private Reason, or Conscience, but the Publique Reason, that is the reason of Gods Supreme Lieutenant'.[90] But Hobbes's allusion is to the reason of the sovereign, and this is far

---

[84] Ibid. 366.     [85] Ibid.
[86] Ronald Dworkin, *Taking Rights Seriously* (Cambridge, Mass.: Harvard University Press, 1977), 149.
[87] Ibid. The reference is to John Rawls, *A Theory of Justice* (Oxford: Oxford University Press, 1972).
[88] Dworkin, above n. 86, 184, 185.
[89] John Rawls, 'Justice as Fairness: Political not Metaphysical' (1985) 14 *Philosophy & Public Affairs* 223–251.
[90] Hobbes, above n. 52, 306.

from Rawls's conception. For Rawls, the concept of public reason is the reason not of the sovereign but 'of its citizens, of those sharing the status of equal citizenship'.[91] Rawlsian public reason is intended to establish normative standards against which to measure the exercise of sovereign authority. He argues that the exercise of political power 'is proper only when we sincerely believe that the reasons we offer for our political actions . . . are sufficient, and we also reasonably think that other citizens might also reasonably accept those reasons'.[92] This is 'the liberal [sc. Kantian] principle of legitimacy'.[93]

When we focus on institutional considerations, things become clearer. Rawls argues that within a constitutional regime public reason applies 'in a special way to the judiciary and above all to a supreme court in a constitutional democracy with judicial review'.[94] Public reason, it transpires, is not the reason of the sovereign: 'Parliamentary supremacy is rejected'.[95] But neither is it an expression of the unmediated will of the people. In an illustration of the way in which constituent power becomes tied up in juristic categories, public reason is recognized as the reason of citizens only when translated into a rarefied form. Public reason is the 'higher law' that amounts to 'the expression of the people's constituent power'.[96] More precisely, public reason is 'the reason of its supreme court'.[97]

Rawls here aligns his task with Dworkin's. His argument that 'the court is the exemplar of public reason' means that judges 'try to develop and express in their reasoned opinions the best interpretation they can', and this means 'the one that best fits the relevant body of those constitutional materials'.[98] This mode of reasoning—equating public reason with legal reason, and legal reason with moral reason—has become highly influential. T. R. S. Allan argues for the 'necessary connection between law and justice, and between legal and moral obligation'.[99] Whilst suggesting that the 'task of reconciling competing principles of political morality is inevitably shared between courts and legislature',[100] Allan argues that common law adjudication, 'grounded in conventional morality' but proceeding 'by recourse to critical morality', unites 'law and justice' and hence 'is sometimes superior to legislation as a means of resolving questions of justice, even when the latter is proceeded by wide consultation to ascertain public opinion and stimulate public debate'.[101] This is precisely the type of reasoning that amounts to an elaboration of what Sir John Laws called 'the need for higher-order law [which] is dictated by the logic of the very notion of government under law'.[102]

---

[91] John Rawls, *Political Liberalism* (New York: Columbia University Press, rev. edn. 1996), 213.
[92] John Rawls, *The Law of Peoples* (Cambridge, Mass.: Harvard University Press, 1999), 137.
[93] Rawls, above n. 91, 137, 217.   [94] Ibid. 216.   [95] Ibid. 233.
[96] Ibid. 231. Cf. T. R. S. Allan, *Constitutional Justice: A Liberal Theory of the Rule of Law* (Oxford: Oxford University Press, 2001), 285–286.
[97] Rawls, above n. 91, 231.
[98] Ibid. 236. Cf. Ronald Dworkin, *Freedom's Law: The Moral Reading of the American Constitution* (Cambridge, Mass.: Harvard University Press, 1996), 2–3, 36–37.
[99] Allan, above n. 96, 283.   [100] Ibid. 294.   [101] Ibid. 290–292.
[102] Laws, above n. 7, 85.

The movement to invest a greater degree of rigour into the reasoning processes of courts may appear commendable. The great difficulty is that the mushrooming of highly sophisticated theories of constitutional adjudication presents us with conflicting and irreconcilable theories of interpretation. Thus, to refer solely to recent American literature, we find disputes between originalists maintaining that justice requires adherence to the precise terms of the settlement written down,[103] proceduralists arguing that the role of judicial review is to safeguard the political process by ensuring that the channels of democracy work fairly and equally,[104] Kantian moralists who promote a principled moral reasoning subject to the criterion of the 'best fit',[105] and substantive moralists who argue the necessity of giving due effect to the moral values expressed in the constitution.[106]

There is no need to engage in detailed analysis of the strengths and limitations of these theories. Each has been subjected to vigorous critique by the others to the effect that they misunderstand the nature of the interpretative method,[107] or that there is an inherent subjectivity involved in attempting to reconcile twin criteria of value and fit,[108] or that they are 'radically indeterminate and fundamentally incomplete',[109] or even that their position amounts to one of 'having no constitutional philosophy at all'.[110] One thing is clear: these sophisticated intellectual arguments have led neither to a broader consensus over the nature of constitutional adjudication nor to a bolstering of the authority of its processes.

The core difficulty with such theories is that they strive to present public law as a version of rationalist metaphysics, believing that the authority of the subject itself is to be founded on 'the moral sovereignty of the community of rational beings'.[111] They fail to heed Hegel's warning that the assumption that the claims of morality must succeed whenever there is a clash between politics and morality rests 'on superficial ideas about morality, the nature of the state, and the state's relation to the moral point of view'.[112] And this is not only a conceptual failing. As Weber put it,

---

[103] Robert H. Bork, *The Tempting of America: The Political Seduction of the Law* (London: Sinclair-Stevenson, 1990); Antonin Scalia, *A Matter of Interpretation: Federal Courts and the Law* (Princeton, NJ: Princeton University Press, 1997).

[104] John Hart Ely, *Democracy and Distrust: A Theory of Judicial Review* (Cambridge, Mass.: Harvard University Press, 1980).

[105] Dworkin, above nn. 86, 98.

[106] Michael J. Perry, *Morality, Politics, and Law: A Bicentennial Essay* (New York: Oxford University Press, 1988); Michael S. Moore, 'Moral Reality Revisited' (1992) 90 *Michigan Law Rev.* 2424–2533.

[107] See Stanley Fish, 'Working on the Chain Gang: Interpretation in Law and Literature' (1981–82) 60 *Texas Law Review* 551–567.

[108] Michael W. McConnell, 'The Importance of Humility in Judicial Review: A Comment on Ronald Dworkin's "Moral Reading of the Constitution"' (1997) 65 *Fordham Law Review* 1269–1293.

[109] Laurence Tribe, 'The Puzzling Persistence of Process-Based Constitutional Theories' (1979–80) 89 *Yale Law Journal* 1063–1080, 1064 (on Ely); see also Ronald Dworkin, *A Matter of Principle* (Cambridge, Mass.: Harvard University Press, 1985), ch. 2 (criticisms of originalism and proceduralism).

[110] Dworkin, above n. 98, 267 (of the originalists). See also, Dworkin, 'The Arduous Virtue of Fidelity: Originalism, Scalia, Tribe and Nerve' (1997) 65 *Fordham Law Review* 1249–1268.

[111] Hunter, above n. 48, 366.

[112] G. W. F. Hegel, *Philosophy of Right* [1821], T. M. Knox trans. (Oxford: Clarendon Press, 1952), § 337.

'increasing intellectualization and rationalization do *not*... indicate an increased and general knowledge of the conditions under which one lives'.[113] Rationalization may signal only an aesthetic preference, not an epistemological advance.

So what is needed to resolve these indeterminacies? What supplies the missing ingredient? What, in short, is the method of public law?

### THE METHOD OF PUBLIC LAW

Moral readings of the constitution are deficient because they refuse to accept the autonomy of the political domain. Specifically, they reject the fact that it is marked by brokenness,[114] an aspect of the political domain which dictates that rationalist exercises must remain unworkable. Public law must negotiate this gulf, but its intrinsic nature cannot be ignored. This is implicitly recognized in the Roman idea of *lex* as the relation between two different entities that are brought together in an accommodation in which the tensions can never entirely be overcome.[115] In public law, these tensions exist in the relationship between governors and governed—the singular object of public law—and arise from the irreconcilable nature of the conflicts between the interests of citizens.

Machiavelli was the first to highlight this critical aspect of political practice.[116] At the beginning of *The Prince*, in his dedicatory letter to Lorenzo de' Medici, he expressed concern that it 'will be considered impudent that a man of low and mean station presumes to discuss and arrange the governments of princes'. His justification is illuminating: 'just as those who draw maps place themselves low down on the plains to consider the nature of the mountains and high places, so in the same way it is necessary to be a prince in order to understand clearly the nature of the people and to be of the people to understand the nature of princes'.[117] The worlds of governors and governed are fundamentally different and cannot be collapsed into one another. This image is a metaphor of Machiavelli's entire philosophy, which is built on incommensurabilities and representation and rejects the claim that unity can be achieved through metaphysics. Politics is born of brokenness, of the need to manage conflicts and enmities because there is no authoritative morality through which these issues can be resolved.

Our starting point in understanding the method of public law must be to acknowledge this gulf and the creative agency required to traverse it. In seeking analogies, we

---

[113] Max Weber, 'Science as a Vocation' [1919] in H. H. Gerth and C. Wright Mills (eds), *From Max Weber: Essays in Sociology* (London: Routledge & Kegan Paul, 1948), 129–156, 139.

[114] See, e.g., Allan, above n. 96, 289: 'Legal reasoning and political argument, when properly conducted, seek fundamentally the same end: each seeks to identify principles of justice and conceptions of the common good that all can endorse without loss of personal integrity. In each case, necessarily, the relevant principles must be appropriate for a pluralistic society, in which divergent moral outlooks are an inevitable consequence of freedoms of speech and conscience'.

[115] Above, 142.   [116] See Ankersmit, above n. 37, 119.

[117] Machiavelli, *The Prince*, 'Letter of dedication'.

should return to the idea of public reason. Rather than assuming its Rawlsian form, however, we must begin by taking seriously Hobbes's suggestion that public reason is the reason of sovereigns. To reformulate, it might be said that public reason is reason of state.

The doctrine of *raison d'état* that emerged in the sixteenth century, however, might not take us very far, mainly because it was incapable of sustaining any settled meaning.[118] *Raison d'état* is often portrayed simply as the will to power, the pursuit of interest of state without proper regard to notions of equity and fairness. But this is a skewed interpretation. Although reason of state takes the well-being of the state and its people—the *salus populi*—as its ultimate value, the precept cannot be reduced to that of the power impulse *tout court*. Reason of state requires not only that the state act to promote the public good, but also with due regard to issues of morality and justice.[119] Once political power is recognized as a relational concept, limitations are necessary for its maintenance. 'Power which gushes out blindly', Meinecke observes, 'will end by destroying itself; it must follow certain purposive rules and standards, in order to preserve itself and to grow'.[120] Adherence to law is not only a constraint on state action, but also a condition of effective action.[121] Law observance is a prudential requirement.

The method of public law, then, is the method of prudence. This prudential method is a juristic interpretation of Machiavelli's thought.[122] Often regarded as the founder of reason of state (though he did not himself use the expression), for Machiavelli reason of state meant knowledge of the means by which a state is founded

---

[118] See Richard Tuck, *Philosophy and Government, 1572–1651* (Cambridge: Cambridge University Press, 1993), 31–64; Peter Burke, 'Tacitism, Scepticism and Reason of State' in J. H. Burns (ed.), *The Cambridge History of Political Thought, 1450–1700* (Cambridge: Cambridge University Press, 1991), 479–498; H. Höpfl, 'Orthodoxy and Reason of State' (2002) 23 *History of Political Thought* 211–237.

[119] See Gabriel Naudé, *Science des Princes, ou Considérations Politiques sur les Coups d'État* [1639] (Strasbourg: privately published, 1673). In this influential *raison d'état* text, Naudé argued that officers of state should possess three basic qualities: *force*, the disposition be firm, heroic, and determined; *justice*, the virtue of acting in accordance with the laws of God and Nature; and *prudence*, the ability to maintain secrets, act even-handedly, and suppress personal ambition (ibid. 784–805). These are the key ingredients of practice of statecraft, and are qualities that must all be accommodated in the constitutional framework of the state.

[120] Friedrich Meinecke, *Machiavellism: The Doctrine of Raison d'État and Its Place in Modern History*, Douglas Scott trans. (New Haven: Yale University Press, 1957), 10.

[121] See Machiavelli, *The Discourses* [1531], Leslie J. Walker trans., Bernard Crick ed. (Harmondsworth: Penguin, 1983), i.10: 'Let he who has become a prince in a republic consider, after Rome became an Empire, how much more praise is due to those emperors who acted, like good princes, in accordance with the laws, than those who acted otherwise. It will be found that Titus, Nerva, Trajan, Hadrian, Antoninus and Marcus, had no need of soldiers to form a praetorian guard, nor a multitude of legions to protect them, for their defence lay in their habits, the goodwill of the people, and the affection of the senate'.

[122] See Eugene Garver, *Machiavelli and the History of Prudence* (Madison, Wisconsin: Wisconsin University Press, 1987), 3–4: 'Machiavelli occupies a position in the history of prudence roughly analogous to that of Descartes in the history of theoretical reason and reflection on natural science . . . Machiavelli and Descartes occupy analogous positions in the history of practice and theory because each represents a turning to autonomy'.

and maintained.[123] And although sometimes treated as a theorist of the will to power, he recognized the necessity of governing in accordance with the law. Rulers 'lose their state', he maintained, 'the moment they begin to break the laws and to disregard the ancient traditions and customs under which men have long lived'.[124] Adherence to law is vital. But this is not because law is divinely prescribed, or that it reflects some natural equilibrium, or that it incorporates fundamental moral principles, and it is not because it is an expression of transcendent Reason. Governors adhere to law—to the extent that they do—as a prudential necessity.

So we can discount reason of state as an expression of some power-impulse and the claim that public reason is the reason of citizens conceived as an imaginary community of rational beings. When these are eliminated it becomes clear that the method of public law is reason of state. Pufendorf understood this in suggesting that 'the dictates of natural law and those of "reason of state" will generally coincide in the sovereign's duty to make civil law in accordance with natural law'.[125]

To modernize Pufendorf's claim, we might say that constitutional government flows from the growing authority of the state. Once the position of the state was consolidated during the modern period, the state no longer needed to rely on the religious unity of the people to secure their obedience; it was able to withdraw from this sphere and promote religious toleration. The formation of a zone of civil liberty, founded in religious liberty, strengthens the authority of the state by enabling it to avoid unnecessary conflicts with communal loyalties. Constitutional rules which ensure that officers of government do not confuse the state's interest with their own personal advantage similarly bolster the confidence of the people and thereby the power of the state. The growth of democracy, rendering government accountable to the people, further strengthens the state by extending the basis of legitimacy for its actions.[126] And formal constitutional frameworks are instruments of state-building which rather than reflecting consensus are just as likely to incorporate techniques for the avoidance of potentially dangerous conflicts.

Reason of state is a form of political reason driven by the need to ensure the survival and well-being of the state. Properly understood, it is a doctrine of civil prudence which, while remaining conscious of the fundamental interests of the state,

---

[123] Cf. Giovanni Botero, *The Reason of State* [1589], P. J. and D. P. Waley trans. (London: Routledge & Kegan Paul, 1956), 3: 'State is a stable rule over a people and Reason of State is the knowledge of the means by which such a dominion may be founded, preserved and extended'. Like many since, Botero follows Machiavelli while pretending to depart from his teaching: note, for example, the book's dedication which criticizes Machiavelli for founding his teaching on 'lack of conscience' and expresses amazement that 'so impious an author . . . should be held in such esteem' (ibid. xiii).

[124] Machiavelli, above n. 121, iii.5.

[125] Hunter, above n. 48, 192. Cf. Meinecke, above n. 120, ch. 9.

[126] See, e.g., Martin van Creveld, *The Rise and Decline of the State* (Cambridge: Cambridge University Press, 1999), 241: 'Regardless of whether their regimes were communist, fascist or liberal, all states [on the outbreak of WW2] hastened to assume control over the means of production . . . It might even be argued that a "democratic" country like Britain was able to go faster and further than "totalitarian" ones such as Germany, Italy, and Japan. None of the three had an elected government; hence, and for all the police apparatus at their disposal, initially at any rate, they proved more fearful of imposing sacrifice on their populations'.

recognizes that the state's authority is strengthened through the imposition of restraints on its action. Whilst orientating itself to the juridical, reason of state must always be conscious of the political. Aligning itself with the rights and duties of rule, it retains an awareness of the need to maintain the capacity to rule.[127] Reason of state is the reason of public law.

Some might argue that reason of state is a continental European doctrine with no relevance to the 'rule of law' tradition of the British state.[128] But this is based on a crude interpretation of the doctrine and a limited understanding of history. After all, the foundations of modern British government were laid by the Glorious Revolution of 1688, an event that in terms of motivation, justification, and outcome was entirely the product of reason of state thinking.[129] In Pufendorf's assessment, James II had preferred to subvert the religion and laws of his people rather than 'follow the character of his reasons of state' and the people were obliged to execute 'their rightful duty, under pressure of necessity, of guarding the safety of the state through which their religion, liberty, life and property are secured'.[130] Lord Halifax, one of the great statesmen of the period, recognized that 'there is a natural Reason of State, an undefinable thing grounded upon the common good of mankind, which is immortal, and in all changes and revolutions still preserveth its original right of saving a nation, when the letter of the law perhaps would destroy it'.[131] The British system of government has evolved in accordance with this logic, and it has been greatly assisted by the techniques of the common law operating in accordance with this prudential method.[132]

But what does the prudential method actually mean? Hobbes defined prudence as 'a *Praesumtion* of the *Future*, contracted from *Experience* of time *Past*'.[133] Because it is a virtue rooted in experience, it cannot be defined in determinate rules of universal application. The law relating to the activity of governing thus cannot be reduced to

---

[127] Cf. Hegel, above n. 112, § 336: 'welfare is the highest law governing the relation of one state to another. This is all the more the case since the Idea of the state is precisely the supersession of the clash between right (i.e. empty abstract freedom) and welfare (i.e. the particular content which fills that void)'.

[128] Note, e.g., the argument of the judges with respect to the prerogative claim in *Entick* v. *Carrington* (1765) 19 St.Tr.1030: 'If the king has no power to declare when the law ought to be violated for reason of State, I am sure we his judges have no such prerogative'.

[129] The Convention Parliament thus declared that James II 'having endeavoured to subvert the constitution of the kingdom by breaking the original contract between king and people, and by the advice of Jesuits and other wicked persons having violated the fundamental laws and having withdrawn himself out of his kingdom, has abdicated the government and that the throne is thereby become vacant'. See *Journals of the House of Lords*, xiv. 119.

[130] Samuel Pufendorf, *De rebus gestis Frederici III Electoris annos 1688–1690* [1784], 104, 107; cited in Leonard Krieger, *The Politics of Discretion: Pufendorf and the Acceptance of Natural Law* (Chicago: University of Chicago Press, 1965), 197–198.

[131] Marquess of Halifax, 'The Character of a Trimmer' [1684] in his *Complete Works*, J. P. Kenyon ed. (Harmondsworth: Penguin, 1969), 49–102, 60.

[132] See, e.g., Halifax, ibid. 56: 'If Princes consider laws as things imposed on them, they have the appearance of fetters of iron, but to such as would make them their choice as well as their practice they are chains of gold, and in that respect are ornaments, as in others they are a defence to them'.

[133] Hobbes, above n. 52, 23. See further Art Vanden Houten, 'Prudence in Hobbes's Political Philosophy' (2002) 23 *History of Political Thought* 266–287.

rules or principles. 'There is none more dangerous for the State', suggested Cardinal Richelieu, 'than those who wish to rule the kingdom according to the principles which they have got from their books'. This leads only to the ruin of the state 'because the past bears no relation to the present, and because the relative disposition of times, places and people, is quite different'.[134] Politics, we infer, is neither science nor metaphysics, but a practical activity guided by the light of experience. The role of its practitioner is that of the trimmer, one who recognizes 'the necessity of others facing in a different direction' but who 'disposes his weight so as to keep the ship upon an even keel'.[135] It is not just politicians but also the judiciary, acting as guardians of public law, who are obliged to adopt that disposition.

The prudential method is a form of practical reason in which rules serve as maxims whose meaning and application vary according to circumstance. This leads to a type of judgment that often revolves on analogical reasoning[136] and is a form of casuistry.[137] Although casuistry today has lost much of its respectability in certain circles, it remains an effective method of dealing with practical problems, especially those that involve conflicting obligations.[138] Casuistry operates by applying old illustrations to new problems—a dialectic between paradigm case and novel circumstance—and creates a type of knowledge that is not easily generalizable. In so doing, it replicates politics itself.

The prudential method is orientated both to an ethic of principle and an ethic of consequence, but fully embraces neither. Formal theories of rights and utility are easy to state but difficult to live by; prudence, by contrast, is easier to apply than to articulate. The method enables us to negotiate the brokenness of politics, to handle those tensions in legal discourse that arise from unresolved dispositions between the state as *societas* and *universitas*,[139] and supplies the ingredient that determines which of the various theories of constitutional reasoning will be put into practice.

[134] Richelieu, *Political Testament*, viii.2; cited in Meinecke, above n. 120, 167.

[135] Michael Oakeshott, *The Politics of Faith and the Politics of Scepticism*, Timothy Fuller ed. (New Haven: Yale University Press, 1996), 123. See further Halifax, above n. 131.

[136] See Cass R. Sunstein, *Legal Reasoning and Political Conflict* (New York: Oxford University Press, 1996), ch. 3.

[137] See Sunstein, ibid. ch. 5; Richard A. Posner, *The Problematics of Moral and Legal Theory* (Cambridge, Mass.: Belknap Press, 1999), 53–59, 121–129.

[138] See Albert R. Jonsen and Stephen Toulmin, *The Abuse of Casuistry: A History of Moral Reasoning* (Berkeley, Calif.: University of California Press, 1988).

[139] See above, Ch. 2, 13–19.

# 9

## *The Pure Theory of Public Law*

1. Public law is an autonomous subject. Many controversies surrounding the subject have arisen precisely because this claim has been neglected or even suppressed. Unless this autonomy is recognized, public law cannot properly be understood.

2. The pure theory is a theory of public law understood as an autonomous subject operating in accordance with its own distinctive method. Although the architecture of public law may vary according to context, the pure theory is a theory of public law in general.

3. The claim that public law is special rests on the singular character of its object—the activity of governing. This may sound trite: it is, after all, a commonplace that public law provides the framework of 'how a state is constituted and functions' or that public law is concerned with 'the rules regulating the system of government'. But this is only because the framework is taken as a given rather than treated as an issue of inquiry. We rarely pay sufficient attention to the special nature of the activity that the framework of rules is designed to regulate. The activity of governing is a feature of all associations of any degree of permanence. Within any such association an iron law of necessity holds: since any large-scale association is incapable of governing itself, the association is sustained only by drawing a distinction between members and officers. The nature of the relationship between members and officers offers a key to understanding public law.

4. Although the activity of governing is a feature of all human associations, there is a type of association that commands our special attention and over which the struggle to establish authority has been intense. This, in modern terminology, is generally referred to as 'the state'. The state claims the ultimate allegiance of its citizens and, in Max Weber's words, maintains 'the monopoly of the legitimate use of physical force within a given territory'. Because of its characteristic forms, distinctive ways and special tasks, the state should be regarded as an association *sui generis*. The idea of the modern state emerged from a two-stage process: first, from a distinction between private and public, between the concepts of ownership and rulership; secondly, from a distinction between the personality of the ruler and the impersonal character of the arrangements through which rulership could be exercised. Only in the modern era has the idea been articulated that the state is an entity distinct both from its members and its officers. Public law is the law relating to the activity of governing the state.

5. If public law is the law relating to the activity of governing the state, how are we to characterize the form of association that the modern state expresses? This question cannot be answered without having regard to the functions of the state. The basic responsibilities of the state are implicit in a single phrase, *salus populi suprema lex esto*. One difficulty with this phrase is that since the meaning of *salus* ranges from safety, through health and welfare, to salvation, it does not offer a determinate account of the role of the state. The statement retains its value largely by revealing the range of equivocation implicit in the idea of the modern state. But it also needs to be unpacked.

6. Within that range of equivocation, two dispositions have been especially influential in modern European political thought, generating diverging conceptions of the nature of the relationship between state and citizen. The idea of the state as a *universitas*, or of the governing relationship as pastorship, conceives of the state as a common undertaking. It also conveys some sense of superiority to those entrusted with governmental authority; they exercise a benign and paternal jurisdiction. By contrast, the idea of the state as *societas* presents the ruler as agent, the governors as servants of the people. The latter conception derives from ideas of individual right, consent, and obligation, while the former promotes the public interest, of striving to maximize community well-being. One disposition asserts the pre-eminence of autonomy, while the other accentuates the importance of identifying ourselves as partners in a common enterprise. Both have been powerful influences on modern thought and life. Their influence has been such that the modern state now embodies an unresolved tension between these two irreconcilable dispositions.

7. This characterization of the modern state is of particular importance for understanding public law. The tension permeates our understanding of the nature of the office of government, infusing and confounding explanations of the constitutional shape assumed by institutions of government. The tension also reveals the acute dilemma faced by those who offer a positive account of the role of law in regulating the activity of governing. The dilemma is that although the image of the state as *societas* predominates in legal thought, it is the role of the state as *universitas* that has prevailed in practice. The result is that many of the most coherent juristic schemes seem false, while those that are more sociologically informed displace law from a pivotal position in the ordering of the state. The solution is not obvious. Claims to autonomy are often challenged by the claims of community, rights by the need to promote collective well-being, liberty by security, freedom from constraint by freedom to realize potential, equality of opportunity by equality of outcome, difference by normality, deviation by sanity, privacy by authenticity, self-government by the need for treatment, and so on. What is clear is that normative theories of public law that promote one mode to the exclusion of the other will fail to address a central aspect of the situation and should be rejected. A positive theory of public law must seek to account for the tension inherent in the modern idea of the state.

8. The claim is not simply that public law is special because of the singularity of its object; the distinctive nature of public law also arises from the singularity of the tasks that law carries out with respect to the activity of governing. A positive theory of public law must not only accommodate the Janus-faced character of the modern state but also the special range of tasks that law is obliged to perform. Besides establishing a framework for enacting the rules that order social life, law also plays a role in identifying and maintaining the authority structure of the state. Law cannot therefore be understood simply to be an expression of sovereign authority. Nor can the boundaries be marked by laws which establish and regulate the principal institutions of the state. The subject must include those conditions of conduct through which governmental authority is established and sustained. Public law must express both the constitutive as well as the regulative aspects of the governing relationship.

9. A positive theory of public law cannot therefore be a theory of positive law. Public law extends beyond a concern with the edicts of the sovereign authority and embraces precepts of right conduct. Public law is neither a code of rules nor a set of principles, but a practice. Understood as the law relating to the activity of governing, public law can be defined as that assemblage of rules, principles, canons, maxims, customs, usages, and manners that condition, sustain, and regulate the activity of governing. These practices comprise conventions and rules of speech—a vocabulary and a syntax—which are being continuously developed.

10. The standards of judgment of the practice of public law are not laid down from above, but are generated internally. Such standards evolve from traditions of conduct; they are expressions of those conditions of effective performance that relate to the activity of governing. Being internal to the practice, such standards have nothing to do with morality in the sense of 'strong evaluation', that is, of making discriminations between right and wrong independent of the ways of the practice. This immanent conception of public law as practice has the advantage of accommodating those irreconcilable dispositions that mark the character of the modern state. It also brings us closer to the idea of public law as a pure theory.

11. The activity of governing has given birth to a special practice—politics—that is now bound up with the activity itself. If government were a divinely authorized office and its objects fixed by higher decree—if, that is, the issue of authority remained entirely uncontested—then although there would exist a regime of rule, there would be no politics. Politics emerges as a product of contests for authority in government; it arises only when the composition and conduct of governmental authority is debated, criticized, and determined. Politics is a consequence of the recognition that the arrangements of government are the result of human choice.

12. If politics is bound up with the idea of public law as practice, we need to be clear about what is meant by politics. Carl Schmitt argues that if 'the political' is to

be identified as an autonomous activity, it must rest on its own distinctions. Just as morality rests on good and evil and aesthetics on beautiful and ugly, Schmitt argues that the concept of the political rests on the distinction between friend and enemy. It is the ever-present possibility of conflict that gives rise to specifically political behaviour. Although Schmitt's thesis has generated much controversy, his argument is relevant here for two main reasons. First, although humans are norm-loving animals, they live in a world comprising a multiplicity of moral maps, and it is the inevitability of clashes between these that lies at the root of the political. The second is that the concept of the state presupposes the concept of the political. These insights help us focus on state formation as a process through which these inevitable conflicts can be managed. Only within the frame of a viable system of government are the practices of politics—a mode operating on a different plane to that of 'the political'—able to flourish.

13. Politics as a set of practices concerning the art of the state constitutes an autonomous domain operating in accordance with its own rules and principles. Politics evolves from the necessity of having to make choices between rival goods in circumstances where there can be no authoritative yardstick for resolving differences. In this sense, politics is a significant human achievement. It incorporates those practices through which humans, without resorting to violence, struggle with a range of possible answers to the most basic question: how am I to live? Consequently, although politics is concerned with the contest for authority—and therefore is bound up with the struggle for domination—it is an error to reduce our understanding of politics to that of a struggle for domination. The practices of politics are just as closely—and just as ambiguously—associated with the virtues of civility and freedom.

14. Although conflict remains an inevitable aspect of politics, the cultivation of a sense of even-handedness also constitutes a vital aspect of the project of state-building. For conflict to be managed and cooperative arrangements established a less partisan framework of rule needs to be devised. This is the function of positive constitutional law. The formation of robust institutional forms of government which promote deliberation over, and review of, decisions not only promotes efficacy of action but also strengthens confidence and allegiance. The establishment of a law-governed state is a means of generating political power. In this sphere, formal constraints are often enabling.

15. Does this body of constitutional law transcend the political? The formation of a durable legal framework of government and the evolution of institutions of government that aspire to work at one remove from power-wielders are both considerable achievements. Because of them, governors have to act within the precepts of 'fundamental law'. But despite grandiose claims about the 'rule of law', these precepts have no transcendental validity. The framework must be conceived as a set of formal

practices rooted within, and acquiring identity from, a wider body of political practices. The expression 'fundamental law' is a reference to these wider political practices. Once this is understood, we are able to appreciate the distinctive method of public law. In public law, we make use of a variety of devices—rhetorical tricks, silences, accommodations, self-imposed jurisdictional limitations and the like—that enable us to pay lip-service to universal ideals of justice while according due recognition to the interests of the state. When touching on core issues relating to the activity of governing, law speaks in a different register. This conception of public law as a form of political discourse demands elaboration.

16. Since politics has emerged to handle basic conflicts which have no objective answers, there can be no fixed foundations to the practices of politics. And if this is so with respect to politics, it must also be the case with public law. In this domain, truth is the product of opinion and belief. There can be no room for a 'reality' beyond the surface of appearances. With this realization, it is possible to address the aesthetic dimension of politics: the recognition that representationalism lies at the base of all political interaction. Political reality exists only through representation, and this reality is therefore something that is made, not found. The concept of representation is the nearest we get to identifying the foundation of public law.

17. Within the political sphere, most discussion about the concept of representation focuses on the role of political (i.e. governmental) actors who mediate between society and the state. But the roots of representation lie much deeper than the arrangements for political representation. In order to appreciate the importance of this concept, it is essential to consider the role of representation in the constitution of authority. That is, we should be conscious not only of the way in which the king or the crown assumed a role as representative of 'the community of the realm', or parliament as representative of 'the people', or the third estate as representative of 'the nation', or the state as representative of the totality of 'citizens', but also of the way in which all the nouns in such formulations are representations. Politics functions through the art of representation.

18. The basic elements of the modern form of representation are revealed in the work of Thomas Hobbes. In *Leviathan*, a work that seeks to show how 'by Art' a system of government is established, Hobbes builds a system of public law entirely on the foundation of artificial—or representative—personality. In doing so, he highlights the critical importance to public law of the concept of office. This concept distinguishes between the duties which attach to the post and the personality of the post-holder. It is on such a basis that the public can be differentiated from the private.

19. Hobbes also provides a powerful account of how the modern state is established. Within this account, based on the creation of the 'office of the sovereign representative' which acts as the unlimited representative of 'the people', the representational

aspects are central. Through the use of representation, Hobbes is able to clarify both the meaning of and the relationships between three critical concepts: the state as the artificial person created by the authorization of a multitude; the sovereign as the representative of the person of the state; and sovereignty as the relation between the state/sovereign and subjects. This provides us with a basic framework for conceptualizing public law.

20. The Hobbesian account can be embellished. Samuel Pufendorf, for example, argued that state formation required three discrete stages: the unanimous agreement by a multitude of male heads of household to form an association; a majority agreement of members of the association as to the form that the system of government would take; and a reciprocal agreement of rights and responsibilities between sovereign and subject. Nevertheless, however it is elaborated, there is an ambiguity lying dormant at the core of such early modern accounts. This relates to the concept of sovereignty, and it came to the fore during the modern era, when the established order of the state was overthrown by revolutionary action taken in the name of the people. Is sovereignty an expression of the relationship between sovereign and subject, or between the state and the people? This question had been compressed in Hobbes's formulation, and it was not possible to identify the issue until a distinction was drawn between 'the people' or 'the nation' on one hand and 'the government' on the other. This distinction—powerfully made by the Abbé Sieyes during the French revolutionary debates—was interpreted to mean that 'the people' may, in the name of sovereignty, overthrow their governments. In order to take further this aspect of representation, we should pay particular attention to two critical concepts. One is that of 'constituent power', the power of the people or the nation to renew its governing arrangements. The other, and the first we must consider, is the concept of sovereignty.

21. If representation provides us with the foundation of public law, then sovereignty is the most basic concept of modern public law. Sovereignty, however, has been given such a variety of meanings that discussions invoking the concept invariably dissipate into ambiguity and confusion. It is essential to offer a precise explanation of its meaning. Our starting point is that sovereignty emerges from the formation of the modern state as both a claim to the supremacy of law and a symbol of the autonomy of the political. The nature of sovereignty is disclosed by close analysis of the nexus between state, law, and politics.

22. The key is to recognize political power as 'power to'. This is a form of power generated from the living together of an identifiable group of people that expresses the ability of humans to undertake concerted action. Thus, political power is differentiated from 'power over', epitomized by the power conferred by control over material resources. The latter, often referred to as domination, is not irrelevant to the activity of governing. After all, our starting point (above, para. 4) was to define the state as an

institution of domination, one that claimed 'the monopoly of the legitimate use of physical force'. This now needs to be qualified on two counts. First, political power must be distinguished from violence or coercion, a point that Hannah Arendt expresses in aphoristic form: 'the extreme form of power is All against One, the extreme form of violence is One against All'. Secondly, the reference to the 'legitimate' use of force alludes to the exercise of authority, and authority is a peculiar type of domination. Since authority commands obedience, it is sometimes equated with domination, coercive force, or even violence. But it is more accurate to treat authority as the augmentation (and application or distribution) of political power, a relational understanding that Cicero articulated in his famous formulation, *cum potestas in populo auctoritas in senatu sit* (while power resides in the people, authority rests in the Senate).

23. The distinction between political power generated through collective action and material power acquired through the ownership of resources is central to the claim that politics is an autonomous sphere of activity. It provides the basis for another distinction, that between public and private modes of being (para. 18). This public/private distinction lies at the root of the modern state, an institution vested through the agency of law with an absolute power (*sc.* authority). Here we can identify the legal conception of sovereignty. In essence, the legal conception of sovereignty expresses the claim of governing institutions to possess the last word, or ultimate legal authority.

24. Legal sovereignty expresses an absolute authority of rule exercised through the deployment of public power. But lawyers sometimes forget that this institutional authority is built on a political relationship. This oversight can lead to sterile debate, such as the question of whether sovereignty means that the United Kingdom Parliament can pass laws prohibiting smoking in the streets of Paris. It can, however, also become more serious, as is the case when lawyers are incapable of adequately explaining why the British state is unable to reassert sovereign authority over a former colony. In general, however, the nature of the legal doctrine of sovereignty is not difficult to grasp.

25. Those who focus on capacity rather than competence, and are concerned with power rather than authority, promote a more overtly political conception of sovereignty. This orientation has led to such doctrines as popular sovereignty. Although popular sovereignty will be considered further in the discussion of constituent power, what needs to be emphasized is that, contrary to Rousseau's radical claim that the people's will does not permit of representation, popular sovereignty makes sense only as a form of representation. And while lawyers overlook the link between authority and power, theorists of popular sovereignty err in the other direction, and assume that the link is between principal and agent. Mimetic theories of representation, which argue that the identity and policies of governors should reflect the composition and

beliefs of citizens, amount to a denial of politics. Politics is rooted in aesthetic not mimetic representation. Popular sovereignty is a symbolic representation of political reality.

26. The concept of sovereignty is clarified only once the political (as the generative) and the legal (as the distributive) conceptions of sovereignty are accepted as dual aspects of a single process. Once power and authority are drawn into an appropriate relationship, it is evident that sovereignty does not reside in any specific locus, whether that be the monarch, the people, or an institutional form such as the crown in parliament. Sovereignty is relational; sovereignty inheres in the authority/power relationship. In this respect, sovereignty is the representative form of power itself, in that political power is not a thing and cannot be owned, but exists only through the public capacity of collective action.

27. Relational sovereignty provides the key to the pure theory of public law. The pure theory is a positive theory that encompasses both the constitutive as well as the regulative aspects of the governing relationship (para. 8), converges on the precepts of 'right conduct' that condition and sustain the authority/power nexus (para. 10), and gives more precise meaning to general formulations such as 'fundamental law' (para. 15). The pure theory of public law is an expression of the autonomy of the political.

28. Because political power can be constrained without being diminished (para. 14), recent developments affecting the role of the nation-state, whether in the form of newly emerging supra- or sub-national institutional configurations of government, do not directly challenge sovereignty. By strengthening bonds of allegiance or enhancing government effectiveness, institutional constraints, far from reducing political power, have the potential to generate more power. Constitutional restraints are not limitations on sovereignty, but are expressions of the sovereign authority of the state. This has not been widely recognized because of a tendency to conflate the concept of the sovereign with that of sovereignty. Although complex institutional arrangements can make it more difficult to identify the 'representative of the person of the state' who possesses the last word (para. 19), this does not amount to an erosion of sovereignty. So long as the relationship between citizens and state is effectively managed, developments such as the emerging governing framework of the European Union do not impinge on sovereignty.

29. One reason why lawyers treat sovereignty as an issue of competence rather than capacity is that, especially under the influence of legal positivism, they tend to conceptualize law as a static phenomenon. Relational sovereignty brings the dynamic aspects of public law to the foreground. In modern times, the dynamic principle of public law, the most powerful motor of constitutional development, is that of democracy. But incorporating the idea of democracy within legal thought has turned out to be extremely difficult. Democracy has invariably been treated as an ideology, often

treated with apprehension, sometimes with hostility, and occasionally by way of counterblast elevated to a hallowed status. Although the democratic impetus cannot be eliminated from modern public law, it must be treated as a positive, i.e. an actually functioning, phenomenon. The juristic aspects of democracy can only be explored through an explication of the concept of constituent power.

30. Constituent power is the juristic expression of the democratic impetus. Democracy and positive law exist in a relation of tension. Democracy, encoding a principle of openness, is orientated to the future, whereas law, being focused on the past, actively seeks the closure of that which democracy tries to keep open. By a process of selection, law seeks to reduce complexity by converting the possible into the probable. Constituent power is the concept through which these tensions between change and stability are mediated. It is the generative principle of modern constitutions.

31. The origins of the constituent power lie in the recognition by early modern scholars that government is instituted by and for 'the people'. In such writing, however, 'the people' is portrayed as an ideal entity, one that has nothing in common with the unruly force of the mob. This benign image soon needed reassessment when, as a result of revolutionary action, the belief that political power resided in the people was converted into actuality. Whilst embracing this dynamic impetus, jurists also felt the need to contain its potentially destructive aspects. This was realized through the formation of modern constitutional frameworks that assume the status of 'higher law'. Modern constitutions invariably acknowledge the principle that government is an expression of the 'will of the people' whilst containing the concept within restrictive juristic categories or in such vague political abstractions as 'the nation'.

32. Democracy and constitutionalism are often treated as antagonistic concepts; after all, constitutionalism offers a series of devices explicitly to curb the power of majorities. From the perspective of the pure theory, however, this is a distortion, one that constituent power enables us to overcome. Understood as an expression of the generative aspect of political power, constituent power can be identified as a concept of representation. It could not be otherwise. Since politics is the product of ineradicable conflict, it is evident that ideas like the 'will of the multitude' lead us nowhere. Similarly, as a political concept, constituent power must be recognized as a representational dynamic distinguishable from the material strength that socio-economic power confers. Through representation, constituent power performs the vital task of converting the articulated desires of the multitude into a form of political agency.

33. The concept of constituent power helps us identify more clearly the nature and purpose of modern constitutions. Two features are particularly important. First, modern constitutions are not simply devices that impose restraints on the exercise of

authority; they are ways of organizing and generating power and thereby conferring authority. But—the second point—the concept of constituent power also enables us to acknowledge the fact that the institutional framework of authority is conditional. Constituted power always remains subject to political pressures for change. In this sense, the norm rests on the exception.

34. One especially powerful form of constitutional constraint is expressed in the language of rights. Rights discourse is such a prevalent theme in contemporary thought that it has the potential to effect a revolution in public law thought. From a traditional concern with the rights of sovereigns and duties of subjects, the focus of the discipline is shifting to that of the rights of citizens and the obligations of government. Contrary to some of the rhetorical claims made on its behalf, however, the modern phenomenon of individual rights is not an expression of some universal order that transcends the political. Individual rights discourse is a creation of the modern state: rights and sovereignty go hand in hand.

35. In the pure theory, the most important aspect of the modern rights movement has been its impact on the structure of public law thought. The positivization of rights is closely associated with two related political developments. The first is the growing importance of modern constitutional texts, first produced as products of the late eighteenth century American and French revolutions, in regulating the activities of government. The second has been the recent extension, under the influence of the political theory of constitutionalism, to the constitutional responsibilities of the judiciary. The impact of positivization is evident in the distinction traditionally drawn between law, the command of the sovereign authority, and right, the liberty to act without constraint. In accordance with this Hobbesian scheme, rights were treated as a species of political claim, to be contrasted with the duties, and their correlative rights, created by positive law. In effect, the scheme laid down the boundary between the legal and the political, or between positive law and natural law. By contrast, the movement for the 'constitutionalization' of basic rights has led to the transformation of such rights into fundamental norms that give shape to objective law. When rights achieve such architectonic status, they have the potential to effect a revolutionary shift in our understanding of positive law. The constitutionalization of rights not only perforates the boundary between the legal and the political but also elevates law into a framework for reviewing all governmental action.

36. One consequence of the constitutionalization of basic rights is that the political critique of law no longer comes solely from the outside. Under the influence of this movement, the sphere of constitutional adjudication extends to cover greater swathes of governmental activity, and this means that the judiciary increasingly adopts an explicitly political jurisdiction. In the guise of adjudicating rights claims, judges are required to resolve disputes in circumstances where there can be no objective, or even consensual, answer. Whether or not this development is a sound constitutional

strategy can be resolved only by assessing whether this judicial power is exercised prudently and is perceived to be an initiative that strengthens the state.

37. As an immanent practice that conditions and sustains the activity of governing, public law is best conceived as political jurisprudence (*droit politique*). Public law is a form of political jurisprudence that incorporates no transcendental or metaphysical ideas of justice and goodness; it is concerned solely with those precepts of conduct that have evolved through political practice to ensure the maintenance of the public realm as an autonomous entity. By adopting this idea of public law as political jurisprudence, we acquire a more precise understanding of Bodin's analysis of sovereignty, of Hobbes's notion of a 'good' law, of Pufendorf's conception of natural law, and of Montesquieu's sense of the 'spirit of the laws'. Since public law is an intricate set of practices (para. 9) expressing a relational conception of sovereignty (para. 27), public law itself must be recognized as being relational.

38. Public law is a form of political reason that is best expressed as reason of state. This does not equate law with the 'will to power', however, since its relational character ensures that adherence to the forms and rules of law remains a vital aspect of power maintenance. Governors are obliged to adhere to law as a prudential necessity. This reveals the method of public law as that of prudence, a form of practical reason that, although orientated both to an ethic of principle and an ethic of consequence, fully embraces neither.

39. Although public law discourse revolves around a common core of general principles—such as necessity, rationality, propriety, reasonableness, and proportionality—the application of these principles to specific cases remains indeterminate. This is because public law is not an exercise in moral reasoning built on philosophical premisses, but a form of political reasoning driven by prudential considerations. The prudential method makes use of analogical reasoning and the techniques of casuistry to yield decisions rooted in particular circumstances. Although such decisions may subsequently be justified in the generalized forms of constitutional adjudication, these rational forms do not yield the substance of public law decision.

40. Two significant features of the prudential method should be highlighted. The first is that the method acknowledges the gulf that exists between governors and governed (para. 3), the brokenness of politics (paras 11–13). It thus recognizes the creative agency needed to traverse this. Secondly, we might note that the method enables us to accommodate the tensions between *societas* and *universitas* that permeate the modern state (paras 6, 7). Whatever the prudential method lacks in economy and universality of formulation is made up for by practicality of application.

# Bibliography

ACKERMAN, B., *We the People: Foundations* (Cambridge, Mass.: Belknap Press, 1991).
AGAMBEN, G., *Homo Sacer: Sovereign Power and Bare Life*, D. Heller-Roazen trans. (Stanford, Calif.: Stanford University Press, 1998).
ALEXY, R., *A Theory of Constitutional Rights*, J. Rivers trans. (Oxford: Oxford University Press, 2002).
ALLAN, T. R. S., *Law, Liberty, and Justice: The Legal Foundations of British Constitutionalism* (Oxford: Clarendon Press, 1993).
—— *Constitutional Justice: A Liberal Theory of the Rule of Law* (Oxford: Oxford University Press, 2001).
ALLISON, J. W. F., *A Continental Distinction in the Common Law: A Historical and Comparative Perspective on English Public Law* (Oxford: Clarendon Press, 1996).
ALSTON, P. (ed.), *The EU and Human Rights* (Oxford: Oxford University Press, 1999).
AMAR, A., *The Bill of Rights: Creation and Reconstruction* (New Haven: Yale University Press, 1998).
ANDERSON, B., *Imagined Communities: Reflections on the Origin and Spread of Nationalism* (London: Verso, rev. edn. 1991).
ANKERSMIT, F. R., *Aesthetic Politics: Political Philosophy Beyond Fact and Value* (Stanford, Calif.: Stanford University Press, 1996).
—— *Political Representation* (Stanford, Calif.: Stanford University Press, 2002).
ARENDT, H., *The Human Condition* (Chicago: University of Chicago Press, 1958).
—— *The Origins of Totalitarianism* (San Diego, Calif.: Harcourt Brace Jovanovich, 2nd edn. 1968).
—— *On Violence* (San Diego, Calif.: Harcourt, Brace & Co., 1970).
—— *On Revolution* (Harmondsworth: Penguin, 1973).
—— *Between Past and Future: Eight Exercises in Political Thought* (Harmondsworth: Penguin, 1977).
ARISTOTLE, *The Politics* [c.335–323 BC], T. A. Sinclair trans., T. J. Saunders ed. (Harmondsworth: Penguin, 1981).
AUSTIN, J., *The Province of Jurisprudence Determined* [1832], W. E. Rumble ed. (Cambridge: Cambridge University Press, 1995).
BACOT, G., *Carré de Malberg et L'Origine de la Distinction entre Souveraineté du Peuple et Souveraineté Nationale* (Paris: CNRS Éditions, 1985).
BAGEHOT, W., *The English Constitution* [1867], M. Taylor ed. (Oxford: Oxford University Press, 2001).
BAILYN, B., *The Ideological Origins of the American Revolution* (Cambridge, Mass: Belknap Press, 1967).
BALAKRISHNAN, G., *The Enemy: An Intellectual Portrait of Carl Schmitt* (London: Verso, 2000).
BALFOUR, EARL OF, 'Introduction' to Walter Bagehot, *The English Constitution* (Oxford: Oxford University Press, 1928), v–xxvi.
BALSDON, J. P. V. D., 'Auctoritas, Dignitas, Otium' (1960) 54 *The Classical Quarterly* 43–50.
BANNING, L., *The Sacred Fire of Liberty: James Madison and the Founding of the American Republic* (Ithaca, NY: Cornell University Press, 1995).

BARBER, B., *Strong Democracy: Participatory Politics for a New Age* (Berkeley, Calif.: University of California Press, 1984).
BARKER, E., 'The Rule of Law' (1914) 1 (o.s.) *Political Quarterly* 117–140.
—— 'The Discredited State: Thoughts on Politics before the War' (1915) 2 (o.s.) *Political Quarterly* 101–121.
BARKER, R., *Political Legitimacy and the State* (Oxford: Clarendon Press, 1990).
—— *Legitimating Identities: The Self-Preservation of Rulers and Subjects* (Cambridge: Cambridge University Press, 2001).
BARTELSON, J., *The Critique of the State* (Cambridge: Cambridge University Press, 2001).
BEARD, C. A., *An Economic Interpretation of the Constitution of the United States* [1913] (New York: Macmillan, 1954).
BEATTY, D. (ed.), *Human Rights and Judicial Review: A Comparative Perspective* (Dordrecht: Martinus Nijhoff, 1994).
BECKER, C., *The Declaration of Independence: A Study in the History of Political Ideas* (New York: Harcourt, Brace & Co., 1922).
BEETHAM, D., *The Legitimation of Power* (London: Macmillan, 1991).
BENN, S. I., 'The Uses of "Sovereignty"' (1955) 3 *Political Studies* 109–122.
BENTHAM, J., *A Fragment on Government* [1776], W. Harrison ed. (Oxford: Blackwell, 1948).
BERLIN, I., 'The Originality of Machiavelli' in his *Against the Current: Essays in the History of Ideas* (Oxford: Clarendon Press, 1989), 25–79.
BIERSTEKER, T. J. & WEBER, C. (eds), *State Sovereignty as Social Construction* (Cambridge: Cambridge University Press, 1996).
BLACKSTONE, W., *Commentaries on the Laws of England* (Oxford: Clarendon Press, 1765), 4 vols. (Facsimile of first edition published: Chicago: University of Chicago Press, 1969).
BLYTHE, J. M., *Ideal Government and the Mixed Constitution in the Middle Ages* (Princeton, NJ: Princeton University Press, 1992).
BOBBIO, N., *The Age of Rights*, A. Cameron trans. (Cambridge: Polity Press, 1996).
BÖCKENFÖRDE, E.-W., 'The Concept of the Political: A Key to Understanding Carl Schmitt's Constitutional Theory' in Dyzenhaus (ed.), 37–55.
BODIN, J., *The Six Bookes of a Commonweale* [1576], R. Knolles trans., K. D. McRae ed. (Cambridge, Mass.: Harvard University Press, 1962).
BORK, R. H., *The Tempting of America: The Political Seduction of the Law* (London: Sinclair-Stevenson, 1990).
BOTERO, G., *The Reason of State* [1589], P. J. & D. P. Waley trans. (London: Routledge & Kegan Paul, 1956).
BOURDIEU, P., *Distinction: A Social Critique of the Judgement of Taste*, R. Nice trans. (London: Routledge, 1984).
—— *The Logic of Practice*, R. Nice trans. (Stanford, Calif.: Stanford University Press, 1990).
—— 'The Force of Law: Toward a Sociology of the Juridical Field' (1986–87) 38 *Hastings Law Journal* 814–853.
BOUTMY, É., *The English Constitution*, I. M. Eaden trans. (London: Macmillan, 1891).
—— *Studies in Constitutional Law: France, England, United States*, E. M. Picey trans. (London: Macmillan, 1891).
BRACTON, H. DE, *De Legibus et Consuetudinibus Angliae (On the Laws and Customs of England)* [c.1258], G. E. Woodbine ed., S. E. Thorne trans. (Cambridge, Mass.: Belknap Press, 1968), 2 vols.

BRAND, P., 'The Formation of the English Legal System, 1150–1400' in A. Padoa-Schioppa (ed.), *Legislation and Justice* (Oxford: Clarendon Press, 1997), 103–121.
BREUILLY, J., *Nationalism and the State* (Manchester: Manchester University Press, 2nd edn. 1993).
BREWER, J., *The Sinews of Power: War, Money and the English State, 1688–1783* (London: Unwin Hyman, 1989).
BROWNLIE, I., *Principles of Public International Law* (Oxford: Clarendon Press, 5th edn. 1998).
BURCKHARDT, J., *The Civilization of the Renaissance in Italy* (Oxford: Phaidon Press, 1945).
BURDEAU, G., *Traité des sciences politique* (Paris: Librairie générale de droit et de jurisprudence, 1983), vol. 4.
BURKE, E., 'Speech to the Electors of Bristol, 1774' in his *Speeches and Lectures on American Affairs*, H. Law ed. (London: Dent, 1908), 68–75.
—— *Reflections on the Revolution in France* [1790], C. Cruise O'Brien ed. (London: Penguin, 1986).
BURKE, P., 'Tacitism, scepticism and reason of state' in J. H. Burns (ed.), *The Cambridge History of Political Thought, 1450–1700* (Cambridge: Cambridge University Press, 1991), 479–498.
BURLAMAQUI, J.-J., *The Principles of Natural and Politic Law* [1754], T. Nugent trans. (London: Nourse, 2nd edn. 1763), 2 vols.
BURNS, J. H., 'Majorities: An Exploration' (2003) 24 *History of Political Thought* 66–85.
BURROW, J. W., *A Liberal Descent: Victorian Historians and the English Past* (Cambridge: Cambridge University Press, 1981).
CAENEGEM, R. C. van, *The Birth of the English Common Law* (Cambridge: Cambridge University Press, 2nd edn. 1988).
—— *An Historical Introduction to Western Constitutional Law* (Cambridge: Cambridge University Press, 1995).
CALDWELL, P. C., *Popular Sovereignty and the Crisis of German Constitutional Law: The Theory and Practice of Weimar Constitutionalism* (Durham, NC: Duke University Press, 1997).
CAMPBELL, J., 'The Significance of the Anglo-Norman State in the Administrative History of Western Europe' in his *Essays in Anglo-Saxon History* (London: Hambledon Press, 1986), ch. 11.
CAMPBELL, T., EWING, K. D. & TOMKINS, A. (eds), *Sceptical Essays on Human Rights* (Oxford: Oxford University Press, 2001).
CANETTI, E., *Crowds and Power*, C. Stewart trans. (Harmondsworth: Penguin, 1973).
CARNOY, M., *The State and Political Theory* (Princeton, NJ: Princeton University Press, 1984).
CARPENTER, W. S., *The Development of American Political Thought* (Princeton: Princeton University Press, 1930).
CASSESSE, A., *Self-Determination of Peoples: A Legal Reappraisal* (Cambridge: Cambridge University Press, 1995).
—— 'Are Human Rights Truly Universal?' in O. Savić, *The Politics of Human Rights* (London: Verso, 1999), 149–165.
CHAPMAN, R. A. & GREENAWAY, J. R., *The Dynamics of Administrative Reform* (London: Croom Helm, 1980).
CHESTER, SIR N., *The English Administrative System, 1780–1870* (Oxford: Clarendon Press, 1981).

CHRIMES, S. B., *English Constitutional Ideas in the Fifteenth Century* (Cambridge: Cambridge University Press, 1936).
CHRISTODOULIDIS, E., *Law and Reflexive Politics* (Dordrecht: Kluwer, 1998).
CICERO, M. T., *De Legibus* [c.51 BC], C. Walker Keyes trans. (London: Heinemann, 1928).
—— *De Officiis* [c.43 BC], C. R. Edmonds trans. (London: Bell & Daldy, 1865).
—— *De Respublica* [c.52 BC], C. Walker Keyes trans. (London: Heinemann, 1928).
CLINTON, R. L., *Marbury v. Madison and Judicial Review* (Lawrence, Kansas: University Press of Kansas, 1989).
COHEN, J. & SABEL, C., 'Directly Deliberative Polyarchy' (1997) 3 *European Law Journal* 313–342.
COICAUD, J.-M., *Legitimacy and Politics: A Contribution to the Study of Political Right and Political Responsibility* (Cambridge: Cambridge University Press, 2002).
COKER, F. W., 'The Technique of the Pluralist State' (1921) 15 *American Political Science Review* 186–213.
COLEMAN, C. & STARKEY, D. (eds), *Revolution Reassessed: Revisions in the History of Tudor Government and Administration* (Oxford: Clarendon Press, 1986).
CONDREN, C., *George Lawson's Politica and the English Revolution* (Cambridge: Cambridge University Press, 1989).
CONNOLLY, W. E., *Identity/Difference: Democratic Negotiations of Political Paradox* (Ithaca, NY: Cornell University Press, 1991).
CORWIN, E. S., 'The "Higher Law" Background to American Constitutional Law' (1928) 42 *Harvard Law Review* 149–185 (Pt. I), 365–409 (Pt. II).
CRAIG, P., 'Britain in the European Union' in J. Jowell & D. Oliver (eds), *The Changing Constitution* (Oxford: Oxford University Press, 4th edn. 2000).
CRANSTON, M., *Human Rights Today* (London: Ampersand, 1955).
—— 'The Sovereignty of the Nation' in C. Lucas (ed.), *The French Revolution and the Creation of Modern Political Culture. Vol. 2: The Political Culture of the French Revolution* (Oxford: Pergamon Press, 1988), 97–104.
CREVELD, M. VAN, *The Rise and Decline of the State* (Cambridge: Cambridge University Press, 1999).
CROCE, B., *Politics and Morals* [1925], S. J. Castiglione trans. (New York: Philosophical Library, 1945).
DAVIES, G., *A History of Money: From Ancient Times to the Present Day* (Cardiff: University of Wales Press, 1994).
DERRIDA, J., 'Declarations of Independence' (1986) 15 *New Political Science* 7–15.
DEUTSCH, K. W., *Nationalism and Social Communication: An Inquiry into the Foundations of Nationality* (Cambridge, Mass.: MIT Press, 2nd edn. 1966).
DEWEY, J., *Outlines of a Critical Theory of Ethics* [1891] (New York: Hilary House, 1957).
DICEY, A. V., *Introduction to the Study of the Law of the Constitution* (London: Macmillan, 8th edn. 1915).
—— *Lectures on the Relation between Law and Public Opinion in England during the Nineteenth Century* (London: Macmillan, 1905).
—— & RAIT, R. S., *Thoughts on the Union between England and Scotland* (London: Macmillan, 1920).
DIXON, O., 'The Law and the Constitution' (1935) 51 *Law Quarterly Review* 590–614.

—— 'The Common Law as an Ultimate Constitutional Foundation' (1957) 31 *Australian Law Journal* 240–245.
DRYZEK, J. S., *Deliberative Democracy and Beyond: Liberals, Critics, Contestations* (Oxford: Oxford University Press, 2000).
DUNN, J., *The Cunning of Unreason: Making Sense of Politics* (London: Harper Collins, 2000).
—— '"Trust" in the politics of John Locke' in his *Rethinking Modern Political Theory* (Cambridge: Cambridge University Press, 1985), 34–54.
—— 'What is Living and What is Dead in the Political Theory of John Locke?' in his *Interpreting Political Responsibility* (Cambridge: Polity Press, 1990), 9–25.
—— 'Contractualism' in his *The History of Political Theory and Other Essays* (Cambridge: Cambridge University Press, 1996), 39–65.
—— 'Specifying and Understanding Racism' in his *History of Political Theory*, 148–159.
—— (ed.), *The Economic Limits to Modern Politics* (Cambridge: Cambridge University Press, 1990).
DURAND, B., 'Royal Power and its Legal Instruments in France, 1500–1800' in A. Padoa-Schioppa (ed.), *Legislation and Justice* (Oxford: Clarendon Press, 1997), 291–312.
DWORKIN, R., *Taking Rights Seriously* (Cambridge, Mass.: Harvard University Press, 1977).
—— *Law's Empire* (London: Fontana, 1986).
—— *A Matter of Principle* (Cambridge, Mass.: Harvard University Press, 1985).
—— *Freedom's Law: The Moral Reading of the American Constitution* (Cambridge, Mass.: Harvard University Press, 1996).
—— 'The Arduous Virtue of Fidelity: Originalism, Scalia, Tribe and Nerve' (1997) 65 *Fordham Law Review* 1249–1268.
DYZENHAUS, D., *Legality and Legitimacy: Carl Schmitt, Hans Kelsen and Herman Heller in Weimar* (Oxford: Oxford University Press, 1997).
—— (ed.), *Law as Politics: Carl Schmitt's Critique of Liberalism* (Durham: Duke University Press, 1998).
EASTON, D., *The Political System: An Inquiry into the State of Political Science* (New York: Knopf, 1953).
ELSTER, J., *Ulysses Unbound: Studies in Rationality, Precommitment, and Constraints* (Cambridge: Cambridge University Press, 2000).
ELTON, G. R., *The Tudor Revolution in Government: Administrative Changes in the Reign of Henry VIII* (Cambridge: Cambridge University Press, 1953).
—— *The Tudor Constitution: Documents and Commentary* (Cambridge: Cambridge University Press, 1960).
ELY, J. H., *Democracy and Distrust: A Theory of Judicial Review* (Cambridge, Mass.: Harvard University Press, 1980).
EMDEN, C. S., *The People and the Constitution* (Oxford: Clarendon Press, 1933).
EPP, C. R., *The Rights Revolution: Lawyers, Activists, and Supreme Courts in Comparative Perspective* (Chicago: University of Chicago Press, 1998).
ERTMAN, T., *Birth of the Leviathan: Building States and Regimes in Medieval and Early Modern Europe* (Cambridge: Cambridge University Press, 1997).
—— '*The Sinews of Power* and European State-building Theory' in L. Stone (ed.), *An Imperial State at War* (London: Routledge, 1993), 33–51.
EWALD, F., 'Norms, Discipline and the Law' in R. Post (ed.), *Law and the Order of Culture* (Berkeley: University of California Press, 1991), 138–161.

FABRE, C., *Social Rights under the Constitution: Government and the Decent Life* (Oxford: Oxford University Press, 1999).

FALK, R., 'Evasions of Sovereignty' in R. B. J. Walker & S. H. Mendlovitz (eds), *Contending Sovereignties: Redefining Political Community* (Boulder, Colorado: Lynne Rienner, 1990), 61–78.

FERRY, L., *Rights—The New Quarrel between the Ancients and the Moderns. Political Philosophy, vol. 1*. F. Philip trans. (Chicago: University of Chicago Press, 1990).

FINER, S. E., *The Life and Times of Sir Edwin Chadwick* (London: Methuen, 1952).

—— *The History of Government from the Earliest Times* (Oxford: Oxford University Press, 1997), 3 vols.

FINNIS, J., *Natural Law and Natural Rights* (Oxford: Clarendon Press, 1980).

FISH, S., 'Working on the Chain Gang: Interpretation in Law and Literature' (1981–82) 60 *Texas Law Review* 551–567.

FLIEGELMAN, J., *Declaring Independence: Jefferson, Natural Language, and the Culture of Performance* (Stanford, Calif.: Stanford University Press, 1993).

FLEISHER, M., 'A Passion for Politics: The Vital Core of the World of Machiavelli' in Fleisher (ed.), *Machiavelli and the Nature of Political Thought* (New York: Atheneum, 1972), 114–147.

FOLEY, M., *The Silence of Constitutions: Gaps, 'Abeyances' and Political Temperament in the Maintenance of Government* (London: Routledge, 1989).

FONTANA, B., 'Democracy and the French Revolution' in J. Dunn (ed.), *Democracy: The Unfinished Journey 508 BC to AD 1993* (Oxford: Oxford University Press, 1992), 107–124.

FORSYTH, M., *Reason and Revolution: The Political Thought of the Abbé Sieyes* (Leicester: Leicester University Press, 1987).

—— 'Thomas Hobbes and the Constituent Power of the People' (1981) 29 *Political Studies* 191–203.

FORTESCUE, SIR J., *De Laudibus Legum Anglie* [1468–71], S. B. Chrimes trans. (Cambridge: Cambridge University Press, 1942).

FOUCAULT, M., *Discipline and Punish: The Birth of the Prison*, A. Sheridan trans. (Harmondsworth: Penguin, 1977).

—— *The History of Sexuality*, R. Hurley trans. (Harmondsworth: Penguin, 1981), vol. 1.

—— *Power/Knowledge*, C. Gordon trans. (Brighton: Harvester, 1980).

—— '*Omnes et singulatim*: towards a criticism of "political reason"' in S. M. McMurrin (ed.), *The Tanner Lectures on Human Values II* (Salt Lake City: University of Utah Press, 1981), 225–254.

—— 'What is Enlightenment?' in P. Rabinow (ed.), *The Foucault Reader* (Harmondsworth: Penguin, 1986), 32–50.

—— 'Governmentality' in G. Burchell, C. Gordon, & P. Miller (eds), *The Foucault Effect: Studies in Governmentality* (Hemel Hempstead: Harvester Wheatsheaf, 1991), 87–104.

FRANCIS, M. with MORROW, J., 'After the Ancient Constitution: Political Theory and English Constitutional Writings, 1765–1832' (1988) 9 *History of Political Thought* 232–302.

FRANKLIN, W., 'The US Constitution and the Textuality of American Culture' in V. Hart & S. C. Stimson (eds), *Writing a National Identity: Political, Economic, and Cultural Perspectives on the Written Constitution* (Manchester: Manchester University Press, 1993), 9–20.

FREUND, J., *L'Essence du Politique* (Paris: Sirey, 1965).

## Bibliography

FULLER, L. L., *The Law in Quest of Itself* (Boston: Beacon Press, 1940).
FURET, F., *The French Revolution, 1770–1814*, A. Neill trans. (Oxford: Blackwell, 1996).
GARNETT, G., 'The Origins of the Crown' in J. Hudson (ed.), *The History of English Law: Centenary Essays on 'Pollock and Maitland'* (Oxford: Oxford University Press, 1996), 171–214.
GARVER, E., *Machiavelli and the History of Prudence* (Madison, Wisconsin: Wisconsin University Press, 1987).
GAUTHIER, D., *The Logic of Leviathan: The Moral and Political Theory of Thomas Hobbes* (Oxford: Clarendon Press, 1969).
GAY, P., *The Enlightenment: An Interpretation* (New York: Knopf, 1966).
GELLNER, E., *Nations and Nationalism* (Oxford: Blackwell, 1983).
—— *Plough, Sword and Book: The Structure of Human History* (London: Paladin, 1991).
—— *Reason and Culture: The Historic Role of Rationality and Rationalism* (Oxford: Blackwell, 1992).
GERSTENBERG, O., 'Law's Polyarchy: A Comment on Cohen and Sabel' (1997) 3 *European Law Journal* 343–358.
GEUSS, R., *History and Illusion in Politics* (Cambridge: Cambridge University Press, 2001).
GILBERT, F., *Machiavelli and Gucciardini: Politics and History in Sixteenth Century Florence* (Princeton: Princeton University Press, 1965).
GILMORE, M. P., *Argument from Roman Law in Political Thought, 1200–1600* (Cambridge, Mass: Harvard University Press, 1941).
GLASS, D. V., *Numbering the People: The Eighteenth-Century Population Controversy and the Development of Census and Vital Statistics in Britain* (Farnborough, Hants: D. C. Heath, 1973).
GLENDON, M. A., *Rights Talk: The Impoverishment of Political Discourse* (New York: Free Press, 1991).
GOLDSWORTHY, J., *The Sovereignty of Parliament: History and Philosophy* (Oxford: Clarendon Press, 1999).
GORDON, C., 'The Soul of the Citizen: Max Weber and Michel Foucault on Rationality and Government' in S. Whimster & S. Lash (eds), *Max Weber, Rationality and Modernity* (London: Allen & Unwin, 1987), 293–316.
GRAY, J., *Enlightenment's Wake: Politics and Culture at the Close of the Modern Age* (London: Routledge, 1995).
GREENBERG, J., 'Our Grand Maxim of State, "The King Can Do No Wrong"' (1991) *History of Political Thought* 209–228.
GREENLEAF, W. H., *The British Political Tradition*, iii: *A Much Governed Nation* (London: Methuen, 1987).
GRIMM, D., 'Does Europe Need a Constitution?' (1995) 1 *European Law Journal* 282–302.
GROTIUS, H., *The Rights of War and Peace* [1625], A. C. Campbell trans. (New York: Dunne, 1901).
HAAKONSSEN, K., 'From Natural Law to the Rights of Man: a European Perspective on American Debates' in M. J. Lacey and K. Haakonssen (eds), *A Culture of Rights: The Bill of Rights in Philosophy, Politics and Law—1791 and 1991* (Cambridge: Cambridge University Press, 1991), 19–61.
HABERMAS, J., *The Theory of Communicative Action, vol. ii: Lifeworld and System: A Critique of Functionalist Reason*, T. MacCarthy trans. (Cambridge: Polity Press, 1987).

HABERMAS, J., *The Structural Transformation of the Public Sphere: An Inquiry into a Category of Bourgeois Society*, T. Burger trans. (Cambridge, Mass: MIT Press, 1989).
—— *Between Facts and Norms: Contributions to a Discourse Theory of Law and Democracy*, W. Rehg trans. (Cambridge: Polity Press, 1996).
—— 'Natural Law and Revolution' in his *Theory and Practice*, J. Viertel trans. (Boston: Beacon Press, 1973), 82–120.
—— 'Remarks on Dieter Grimm's "Does Europe Need a Constitution?"' (1995) 1 *European Law Journal* 303–307.
HALIFAX, MARQUESS OF, 'The Character of a Trimmer' [1684] in his *Complete Works*, J. P. Kenyon ed. (Harmondsworth: Penguin, 1969), 49–102.
HAMPTON, J., *Hobbes and the Social Contract Tradition* (Cambridge: Cambridge University Press, 1986).
HANSEN, M. H., *The Athenian Democracy in the Age of Demosthenes* (Oxford: Blackwell, 1991).
HANSON, D. W., *From Kingdom to Commonwealth: The Development of Civic Consciousness in English Political Thought* (Cambridge, Mass.: Harvard University Press, 1970).
HARDIN, R., *Liberalism, Constitutionalism, and Democracy* (Oxford: Oxford University Press, 1999).
HARDT, M. & NEGRI, A., *Empire* (Cambridge, Mass: Harvard University Press, 2000).
HARRINGTON, J., *The Commonwealth of Oceana* [1656], J. G. A. Pocock ed. (Cambridge: Cambridge University Press, 1992).
HARRIS, J., *Unemployment and Politics: A Study of English Social Policy, 1886–1914* (Oxford: Clarendon Press, 1972).
HART, H. L. A., *The Concept of Law* (Oxford: Clarendon Press, 1961).
HARTZ, L., 'The Whig Tradition in America and Europe' (1952) 46 *American Political Science Review* 989–1002.
HASKELL, T. L., 'The Curious Persistence of Rights Talk in the "Age of Interpretation"' (1987) 74 *Journal of American History* 984–1012.
HAWTHORN, G., *Enlightenment and Despair: A History of Social Theory* (Cambridge: Cambridge University Press, 2nd edn. 1987).
HAY, D., 'Property, Authority and the Criminal Law' in Hay *et al* (eds), *Albion's Fatal Tree* (Harmondsworth: Penguin, 1975), 17–63.
HECHTER, M., *Containing Nationalism* (Oxford: Oxford University Press, 2000).
HEGEL, G. W. F., *Natural Law* [1802–3], T. M. Knox trans. (Philadelphia: University of Pennsylvania Press, 1975).
—— *Philosophy of Right* [1821], T. M. Knox trans. (Oxford: Clarendon Press, 1952).
HELD, D., MCGREW, A., GOLDBLATT, D., & PERRATON, J., *Global Transformations: Politics, Economics and Culture* (Cambridge: Polity Press, 1999).
HELLER, A., 'The Concept of the Political Revisited' in D. Held (ed.), *Political Theory Today* (Cambridge: Polity Press, 1991), 330–343.
HENKIN, L., *The Age of Rights* (New York: Columbia University Press, 1990).
HIGONNET, P., *Sister Republics: The Origins of French and American Republicanism* (Cambridge, Mass.: Harvard University Press, 1988).
HINTZE, O., *The Historical Essays of Otto Hintze*, F. Gilbert ed. (New York: Oxford University Press, 1975).
HIRST, P. Q., *The Pluralist Theory of the State: Selected Writings* (London: Routledge, 1989).

HOBBES, T., *The Elements of Law Natural and Politic* [1640], F. Tönnies ed., M. M. Goldsmith intro. (London: Cass, 1969).
—— *On the Citizen* [1647], R. Tuck & M. Silverthorne eds (Cambridge: Cambridge University Press, 1998).
—— *Leviathan* [1651], R. Tuck ed. (Cambridge: Cambridge University Press, 1996).
—— *Behemoth, or the Long Parliament* [1682], F. Tönnies ed. (London: Cass, 1969).
HOCHSTRASSER, T. J., *Natural Law Theories in the Early Enlightenment* (Cambridge: Cambridge University Press, 2000).
HOHFELD, W. N., *Fundamental Legal Conceptions as Applied in Judicial Reasoning* (New Haven: Yale University Press, 1923).
HOLMES, S., *Passions and Constraint: On the Theory of Liberal Democracy* (Chicago: University of Chicago Press, 1995).
HOLT, J. C., *Magna Carta* (Cambridge: Cambridge University Press, 2nd edn. 1992).
HONT, I., 'The Language of Sociability and Commerce: Samuel Pufendorf and the Theoretical Foundations of the "Four-Stages Theory"' in A. Pagden (ed.), *The Languages of Political Theory in Early-Modern Europe* (Cambridge: Cambridge University Press, 1987), 253–276.
—— 'The Permanent Crisis of a Divided Mankind: "Contemporary Crisis of the Nation State" in Historical Perspective' in J. Dunn (ed.), *Contemporary Crisis of the Nation State?* (Oxford: Blackwell, 1995), 166–231.
HÖPFL, H., 'Orthodoxy and Reason of State' (2002) 23 *History of Political Thought* 211–237.
HOUTEN, A. V., 'Prudence in Hobbes's Political Philosophy' (2002) 23 *History of Political Thought* 266–287.
HOWARD, M., *War in European History* (Oxford: Oxford University Press, 1976).
—— 'Empires, Nations and Wars' in his *The Lessons of History* (Oxford: Clarendon Press, 1991), 21–48.
HOWSE, R., 'From Legitimacy to Dictatorship—and Back Again: Leo Strauss's Critique of the Anti-Liberalism of Carl Schmitt' in D. Dyzenhaus (ed.), 56–91.
HOYT, R. S., 'The Coronation Oath of 1308' (1955) 11 *Traditio* 235–257.
HUNTER, I., *Rival Enlightenments: Civil and Metaphysical Philosophy in Early Modern Germany* (Cambridge: Cambridge University Press, 2001).
IGNATIEFF, M., *A Just Measure of Pain: The Penitentiary in the Industrial Revolution 1750–1850* (London: Macmillan, 1978).
—— *The Rights Revolution* (Toronto: Anansi, 2000).
—— *Human Rights as Politics and Idolatry* (Princeton, NJ: Princeton University Press, 2001).
JELLINEK, G., *Allgemeine Staatslehre* (Berlin: Springer, 1900).
—— *The Declaration of the Rights of Man and of Citizens: A Contribution to Modern Constitutional History*, M. Farrand trans. (New York: Henry Holt & Co., 1901).
—— *The Rights of Minorities*, A. M. Baty & T. Baty trans. (London: P. S. King & Son, 1912).
JOHANNISSON, K., 'Society in Numbers: The Debate over Quantification in Eighteenth-Century Political Economy' in T. Frängsmyr, J. L. Heilbron, & R. E. Rider (eds), *The Quantifying Spirit in the Eighteenth Century* (Berkeley, Calif.: University of California Press, 1990), 343–361.
JOHN OF SALISBURY, *Policraticus* [c.1154–1156], C. J. Nederman trans. (Cambridge: Cambridge University Press, 1990).
JOHNSON, N., *In Search of the Constitution: Reflections of State and Society in Britain* (Oxford: Pergamon Press, 1977).

JONSEN, A. R. & TOULMIN, S., *The Abuse of Casuistry: A History of Moral Reasoning* (Berkeley, Calif.: University of California Press, 1988).

JOUVENEL, B. DE, *Sovereignty: An Inquiry into the Political Good*, J. F. Huntington trans. (Cambridge: Cambridge University Press, 1957).

JUSTINIAN, *Digest* [534], A. Watson trans. (Philadelphia: University of Pennsylvania Press, 1998).

—— *Institutes* [534], P. Birks & G. McLeod trans. (London: Duckworth, 1987).

KANT, I., *Political Writings*, H. Reiss ed. (Cambridge: Cambridge University Press, 2nd edn. 1991).

KANTOROWICZ, E. H., *The King's Two Bodies: A Study in Mediaeval Political Theology* (Princeton, NJ: Princeton University Press, 1957).

KATEB, G., 'The Moral Distinctiveness of Representative Democracy' (1981) 91 *Ethics* 357–374.

KEATING, M., *Plurinational Democracy: Stateless Nations of the United Kingdom, Spain, Canada and Belgium in a Post-Sovereign World* (Oxford: Oxford University Press, 2001).

KELLY, D., 'Rethinking Franz Neumann's Route to *Behemoth*' (2002) 23 *History of Political Thought* 458–496.

KELSEN, H., *Das Problem der Souveränität und die Theorie des Völkerrechts* (Tübingen: Mohr, 1920).

—— *Introduction to the Problems of Legal Theory*, B. L. Paulson & S. L. Paulson trans. of first edn. [1934] of *Reine Rechtslehre* (Oxford: Clarendon Press, 1992).

—— 'God and the State' [1922] in his *Essays in Legal and Moral Philosophy*, O. Weinberger intro. (Dordrecht: Reidel, 1973), ch. 3.

KEOHANE, N. O., *Philosophy and the State in France: The Renaissance to the Enlightenment* (Princeton, NJ: Princeton University Press, 1980).

KIRK, G. S., RAVEN, J. E., & SCHOFIELD, M., *The Presocratic Philosophers: A Critical History with a Selection of Texts* (Cambridge: Cambridge University Press, 2nd edn. 1983).

KOSKENNIEMI, M., *The Gentle Civilizer of Nations: The Rise and Fall of International Law 1870–1960* (Cambridge: Cambridge University Press, 2002).

—— 'The Effect of Rights on Political Culture' in P. Alston (ed.), *The EU and Human Rights* (Oxford: Oxford University Press, 1999), 99–116.

KRASNER, S. D., *Sovereignty: Organized Hypocrisy* (Princeton, NJ: Princeton University Press, 1999).

KRAUS, J. S., *The Limits of Hobbesian Contractarianism* (Cambridge: Cambridge University Press, 1993).

KRIEGEL, B., *The State and the Rule of Law*, M. A. LePain & J. C. Cohen trans. (Princeton: Princeton University Press, 1995).

KRIEGER, L., *The Politics of Discretion: Pufendorf and the Acceptance of Natural Law* (Chicago: University of Chicago Press, 1965).

KRONMAN, A. T., *The Lost Lawyer: Failing Ideals of the Legal Profession* (Cambridge, Mass.: Belknap Press, 1993).

KYMLICKA, W., *Multicultural Citizenship: A Liberal Theory of Minority Rights* (Oxford: Clarendon Press, 1995).

LABAND, P., *Das Staatsrecht des Deutschen Reiches* (Tübingen: Mohr, 1901).

LASKI, H. J., 'The Pluralistic State' in his *The Foundations of Sovereignty and Other Essays* (London: Allen & Unwin, 1921), 232–249.

LAWS, SIR J., 'Law and Democracy' 1995 *Public Law* 72–93.
LAWSON, G., *An Examination of the Political Part of Mr Hobbs, his Leviathan* (London: privately published, 1657).
—— *Politica Sacra et Civilis or, A Modell of Civil and Ecclesiasticall Government* [1660], C. Condren ed. (Cambridge: Cambridge University Press, 1992).
LE MAY, G. H. L., *The Victorian Constitution* (London: Duckworth, 1979).
LEIBNIZ, G. W., *Political Writings*, P. Riley ed. (Cambridge: Cambridge University Press, 1972).
LESTITION, S., 'The Teaching and Practice of Jurisprudence in Eighteenth Century East Prussia: Konigsberg's First Chancellor, R. F. von Sahme (1682–1753)' (1989) 16 *Ius Commune* 27–80.
LEWIS, E., 'King above Law? *Quod principi placuit* in Bracton' (1964) 40 *Speculum* 240–269.
LINDAHL, H., 'The Purposiveness of Law: Two Concepts of Representation in the European Union' (1998) 17 *Law and Philosophy* 481–505.
LLOYD, H. A., 'Constitutionalism' in J. H. Burns (ed.), *The Cambridge History of Political Thought* (Cambridge: Cambridge University Press, 1991), 254–297.
LOBEL, J., 'Emergency Power and the Decline of Liberalism' (1989) 98 *Yale Law Journal* 1385–1433.
LOCKE, J., *Two Treatises of Government* [1680], P. Laslett ed. (Cambridge: Cambridge University Press, 1988).
LOUGHLIN, M., *Public Law and Political Theory* (Oxford: Clarendon Press, 1992).
—— *Sword and Scales: An Examination of the Relationship between Law and Politics* (Oxford: Hart, 2000).
—— 'Courts and Governance' in P. B. H. Birks (ed.), *Frontiers of Liability* (Oxford: Oxford University Press, 1994), i.91–112.
—— 'Pathways of Public Law Scholarship' in G. P. Wilson (ed.), *Frontiers of Legal Scholarship* (Chichester: Wiley, 1995), 163–188.
—— 'The State, the Crown, and the Law' in M. Sunkin & S. Payne (eds), *The Nature of the Crown: A Legal and Political Analysis* (Oxford: Oxford University Press, 1999), 33–76.
LOYSEAU, C., *A Treatise of Orders and Plain Dignities* [1610], H. A. Lloyd trans. (Cambridge: Cambridge University Press, 1994).
—— *Traicté des Seigneuries* (Paris: Abel l'Angelier, 1614).
LUHMANN, N., *Political Theory in the Welfare State*, J. Bednarz trans. (Berlin: de Gruyter, 1990).
—— *Social Systems*, J. Bednarz Jr. trans. (Stanford, Calif.: Stanford University Press, 1995).
LUSTGARTEN, L. & LEIGH, I., *In From the Cold: National Security and Parliamentary Democracy* (Oxford: Clarendon Press, 1994).
MACCORMICK, N., *Questioning Sovereignty: Law, State, and Nation in the European Commonwealth* (Oxford: Oxford University Press, 1999).
—— 'Beyond the Sovereign State' (1993) 56 *Modern Law Review* 1–18.
—— 'Sovereignty: Myth and Reality' in N. Jareborg (ed.), *Towards Universal Law: Trends in National, European and International Law-making* (Uppsala: Iustus Förlag, 1995), 227–248.
MACDONAGH, O., *Early Victorian Government, 1830–1870* (London: Weidenfeld and Nicolson, 1977).
MACHIAVELLI, N., *The Prince* [1513] (London: Dent, 1995).
—— *The Discourses* [1531], L. J. Walker trans., B. Crick ed. (Harmondsworth: Penguin, 1983).

MacIntyre, A., *After Virtue: A Study in Moral Theory* (London: Duckworth, 2nd edn. 1985).
Macpherson, C. B., *The Political Theory of Possessive Individualism: Hobbes to Locke* (Oxford: Clarendon Press, 1962).
Maddox, G., 'Constitution' in T. Ball, J. Farr, & R. L. Hanson (eds), *Political Innovation and Conceptual Change* (Cambridge: Cambridge University Press, 1989), 50–67.
—— 'The Limits of Neo-Roman Liberty' (2002) 23 *History of Political Thought* 418–431.
Madison, J., Hamilton, A., & Jay, J., *The Federalist Papers* [1788], I. Kramnick ed. (Harmondsworth: Penguin, 1987).
Maine, Sir H. S., *Popular Government* [1885] (Indianapolis: Liberty Classics, 1976).
Maistre, J. de, *The Works of Joseph de Maistre*, J. Lively ed. (London: Allen & Unwin, 1965).
Maitland, F. W., *Justice and Police* (London: Macmillan, 1885).
—— *Township and Borough* (Cambridge: Cambridge University Press, 1898).
—— *The Constitutional History of England* (Cambridge: Cambridge University Press, 1908).
—— *Selected Essays*, H. D. Hazeltine, G. Lapsley, & P. H. Winfield eds (Cambridge: Cambridge University Press, 1936).
—— 'Introduction' to O. Gierke, *Political Theories of the Middle Age* (Cambridge: Cambridge University Press, 1900).
Manent, P., *Naissance de la politique moderne* (Paris: Payot, 1977).
Manin, B., *The Principles of Representative Democracy* (Cambridge: Cambridge University Press, 1997).
—— 'The Metamorphoses of Representative Government' (1994) 23 *Economy and Society* 133–171.
Mann, M., *The Sources of Social Power. Vol. 1: A History of Power from the Beginning to AD 1760* (Cambridge: Cambridge University Press, 1986), *Vol. 2: The Rise of Classes and Nation-States, 1760–1914* (Cambridge: Cambridge University Press, 1994).
Mansfield, H. C., *Taming the Prince: The Ambivalence of Modern Executive Power* (Baltimore: Johns Hopkins University Press, 1993).
—— *Machiavelli's Virtue* (Chicago: University of Chicago Press, 1996).
—— *Machiavelli's New Modes and Orders: A Study of the* Discourses on Livy (Chicago: University of Chicago Press, 2001).
—— 'Hobbes and the Science of Indirect Government' (1971) 65 *American Political Science Review* 97–110.
Marquand, D., *The Unprincipled Society: New Demands and Old Politics* (London: Fontana, 1988).
Marshall, G., *Police and Government* (London: Methuen, 1965).
Marx, K., 'The German Ideology' in K. Marx & F. Engels, *Selected Works* (Moscow: Progress Publishers, 1969), i.16–80.
McConnell, M. W., 'The Importance of Humility in Judicial Review: A Comment on Ronald Dworkin's "Moral Reading of the Constitution"' (1997) 65 *Fordham Law Rev.* 1269–1293.
McCormick, J. P., *Carl Schmitt's Critique of Liberalism: Against Politics as Technology* (Cambridge: Cambridge University Press, 1997).
McDonald, F., *Novus Ordo Seclorum: The Intellectual Origins of the Constitution* (Lawrence, Kansas: Kansas University Press, 1985).
McIlwain, C. H., *Constitutionalism: Ancient and Modern* (Ithaca, NY: Cornell University Press, rev. edn. 1947).

McKenna, J. W., 'The Myth of Parliamentary Sovereignty in Late-Medieval England' (1979) 94 *English Historical Review* 481–506.

Meier, H., *Carl Schmitt and Leo Strauss: The Hidden Dialogue*, J. H. Lomax trans. (Chicago: University of Chicago Press, 1995).

—— *The Lesson of Carl Schmitt: Four Chapters on the Distinction between Political Theology and Political Philosophy* (Chicago: University of Chicago Press, 1998).

Meinecke, F., *Machiavellism: The Doctrine of Raison d'État and Its Place in Modern History*, D. Scott trans. (New Haven: Yale University Press, 1957).

Mill, J., *An Essay on Government* [1820], E. Barker intro. (Cambridge: Cambridge University Press, 1937).

Mill, J. S., *Considerations on Representative Government* [1861] in his *Three Essays* (Oxford: Oxford University Press, 1975), 145–423.

Millar, J., *Historical View of the English Government* [1787] (London: J. Marmon, 3rd edn. 1803), 4 vols.

Miller, S. J. T., 'The Position of the King in Bracton and Beaumanoir' (1956) 31 *Speculum* 263–296.

Milward, A. S., *The European Rescue of the Nation-State* (London: Routledge, rev. edn. 1994).

Mitchell, J. D. B., 'The Anatomy and Pathology of the Constitution' (1955) 67 *Juridical Review* 1–22.

Montesquieu, C. L., Baron de, *The Spirit of the Laws* [1748], A. M. Cohler, B. C. Miller, & H. S. Stone eds (Cambridge: Cambridge University Press, 1989).

Moore, M. S., 'Moral Reality Revisited' (1992) 90 *Michigan Law Review* 2424–2533.

Mouffe, C. (ed.), *The Challenge of Carl Schmitt* (London: Verso, 1999).

Mount, F., *The British Constitution Now* (London: Heinemann, 1992).

Murphy, T., *The Oldest Social Science? Configurations of Law and Modernity* (Oxford: Clarendon Press, 1997).

Naudé, G., *Science des Princes, ou Considérations Politiques sur les Coups d'État* [1639] (Strasbourg: privately published, 1673).

Nederman, C. J., 'Bracton on Kingship Revisited' (1984) 5 *History of Political Thought* 66–73.

Negri, A., *Insurgencies: Constituent Power and the Modern State*, M. Boscagli trans. (Minneapolis: University of Minnesota Press, 1999).

Neumann, F. L., *The Rule of Law: Political Theory and the Legal System in Modern Society* [1936], M. Ruete intro. (Leamington Spa: Berg, 1986).

Nicholls, D., *The Pluralist State: The Social and Political Ideas of J. N. Figgis and his Contemporaries* (London: Macmillan, 2nd edn. 1994).

Oakeshott, M., *The Politics of Faith and the Politics of Scepticism* [c.1952], T. Fuller ed. (New Haven: Yale University Press, 1996).

—— *Morality and Politics in Modern Europe: The Harvard Lectures* [1958], S. R. Letwin ed. (New Haven: Yale University Press, 1993).

—— *Rationalism in Politics and Other Essays* (London: Methuen, 1962).

—— *On Human Conduct* (Oxford: Clarendon Press, 1975).

—— 'Introduction' in T. Hobbes, *Leviathan* (Oxford: Blackwell, 1946).

—— 'Contemporary British Politics' (1947–8) 1 *Cambridge Journal* 474–490.

—— 'The Vocabulary of a Modern European State' (1975) 23 *Political Studies* 319–341; 409–414.

OAKLEY, F., 'Jacobean Political Theology: The Absolute and Ordinary Powers of the King' (1968) *J. of the History of Ideas* 323–346.

PACELLE, R. L. JR., *The Transformation of the Supreme Court's Agenda: From the New Deal to the Reagan Administration* (Boulder, Colorado: Westview Press, 1991).

PAINE, T., *Rights of Man, Common Sense and other Political Writings*, M. Philp ed. (Oxford: Oxford University Press, 1995).

PASQUINO, P., 'Emmanuel Sieyes, Benjamin Constant et le "Gouvernement des Modernes"' (1987) 37 *Revue Française de Science Politique* 214–228.

—— 'The Constitutional Republicanism of Emmanuel Sieyès' in B. Fontana (ed.), *The Invention of the Modern Republic* (Cambridge: Cambridge University Press, 1994), ch. 5.

—— 'Locke on King's Prerogative' (1998) 26 *Political Theory* 198–208.

PAULSON, S., 'The Neo-Kantian Dimension of Kelsen's Legal Theory' (1992) 12 *Oxford Journal of Legal Studies* 311–332.

PENNINGTON, K., *The Prince and the Law, 1200–1600: Sovereignty and Rights in the Western Legal Tradition* (Berkeley, Calif.: University of California Press, 1993).

PERRY, M., *Morality, Politics, and Law: A Bicentennial Essay* (New York: Oxford University Press, 1988).

PETTIT, P., *Republicanism: A Theory of Freedom and Government* (Oxford: Oxford University Press, 1997).

PHILLIPS, A., *The Politics of Presence: The Political Representation of Gender, Ethnicity, and Race* (Oxford: Clarendon Press, 1995).

PITKIN, H. F., *The Concept of Representation* (Berkeley, Calif.: University of California Press, 1967).

PIOUS, R. M., *The American Presidency* (New York: Basic Books, 1979).

PLATO, *The Laws* [c.335–323 BC], R. G. Bury trans. (London: Heinemann, 1926).

—— 'Euthypro' in *The Dialogues of Plato* [c.399–387 BC], R. E. Allen trans. (New Haven: Yale University Press, 1984).

PLOTKE, D., 'Representation is Democracy' (1997) 4 *Constellations* 19–34.

POCOCK, J. G. A., *The Machiavellian Moment: Florentine Political Thought and the Atlantic Republican Tradition* (Princeton, NJ: Princeton University Press, 1975).

—— 'Historical Introduction' in *The Political Works of James Harrington* (Cambridge: Cambridge University Press, 1977).

POLE, J. R., *Political Representation in England and the Origins of the American Republic* (Berkeley, Calif.: University of California Press, 1971).

POLLARD, A. F., *The Evolution of Parliament* (London: Longmans, 1920).

POLLOCK, SIR F., 'The King's Peace' in his *Oxford Lectures and Other Discourses* (London: Macmillan, 1890).

PORTER, B., *The Origins of the Vigilant State: The London Metropolitan Special Branch Before the First World War* (London: Weidenfeld and Nicolson, 1987).

POSNER, R. A., *The Problematics of Moral and Legal Theory* (Cambridge, Mass.: Belknap Press, 1999).

POST, G., *Studies in Medieval Legal Thought: Public Law and the State, 1100–1322* (Princeton, NJ: Princeton University Press, 1964).

POWICKE, F. M., 'Reflections on the Medieval State' in his *Ways of Medieval Life and Thought: Essays and Addresses* (London: Odhams Press, 1949), 130–148.

PREUSS, U. K., 'Political Order and Democracy: Carl Schmitt and His Influence' in C. Mouffe (ed.), 155–179.
PRIMUS, R. A., *The American Language of Rights* (Cambridge: Cambridge University Press, 1999).
PROKHOVNIK, R., 'The State of Liberal Sovereignty' (1999) 1 *Brit. J. of Politics & International Relations* 63–83.
PRZEWORSKI, A., STOKES, S. C., & MANIN, B. (eds), *Democracy, Accountability and Representation* (Cambridge: Cambridge University Press, 1999).
PTOLEMY OF LUCCA, *On the Government of Rulers. De Regimine Principum* [c.1300], J. M. Blythe trans. (Philadelphia: University of Pennsylvania Press, 1997).
PUFENDORF, S., *On the Duty of Man and Citizen According to Natural Law* [1673], M. Silverthorne trans., J. Tully ed. (Cambridge: Cambridge University Press, 1991).
—— *De Jure Naturae et Gentium Libri Octo (On the Law of Nature and Nations)* [1688], C. H. & W. A. Oldfather trans. (Oxford: Clarendon Press, 1934).
RADIN, M., 'Natural Law and Natural Rights' (1950) 59 *Yale Law Journal* 214–237.
RAKOVE, J. N., *Original Meanings: Politics and Ideas in the Making of the Constitution* (New York: Vintage Books, 1997).
—— *Declaring Rights: A Brief History with Documents* (Boston: Bedford Books, 1998).
RAWLS, J., *A Theory of Justice* (Oxford: Oxford University Press, 1972).
—— *Political Liberalism* (New York: Columbia University Press, rev. edn. 1996).
—— *The Law of Peoples* (Cambridge, Mass.: Harvard University Press, 1999).
—— 'Justice as Fairness: Political not Metaphysical' (1985) 14 *Philosophy & Public Affairs* 223–251.
REES, W. J., 'The Theory of Sovereignty Restated' (1950) 59 *Mind* 495–521.
REID, J. P., 'The Irrelevance of the Declaration' in H. Hartog (ed.), *Law in the American Revolution and the Revolution in the Law* (New York: New York University Press, 1981), 46–89.
REINHARD, W. (ed.), *Power Elites and State Building* (Oxford: Clarendon Press, 1996).
RICHARDSON, H. G., 'The Coronation Oath in Medieval England: The Evolution of the Office and the Oath' (1960) 16 *Traditio* 111–202.
RIESENBERG, P. N., *Inalienability of Sovereignty in Medieval Political Thought* (New York: Columbia University Press, 1956).
RILEY, P., *Leibniz' Universal Jurisprudence: Justice as the Charity of the Wise* (Cambridge, Mass.: Harvard University Press, 1996).
ROBERTS, D., *Victorian Origins of the British Welfare State* (New Haven: Yale University Press, 1960).
ROSSITER, C. L., *Constitutional Dictatorship: Crisis Government in the Modern Democracies* (Princeton, NJ: Princeton University Press, 1948).
ROUSSEAU, J.-J., *The Social Contract* [1762], M. Cranston trans. (Harmondsworth: Penguin, 1968).
RUDÉ, G., *The Crowd in the French Revolution* (Oxford: Clarendon Press, 1959).
RUIZ, L. E. J., 'Sovereignty as a Transformative Practice' in R. B. J. Walker & S. H. Mendlovitz (eds), *Contending Sovereignties: Redefining Political Community* (Boulder, Colorado: Lynne Rienner, 1990), 79–96.
RUNCIMAN, D., *Pluralism and the Personality of the State* (Cambridge: Cambridge University Press, 1997).

RUNCIMAN, D., 'What Kind of a Person is Hobbes's State? A Reply to Skinner' (2000) 8 *J. of Political Philosophy* 268–278.
—— 'Is the State a Corporation?' (2000) 35 *Government & Opposition* 90–104.
SALMOND, J. W., *Jurisprudence*, P. J. Fitzgerald ed. (London: Stevens, 12th edn. 1966).
SARTORI, G., 'Constitutionalism: A Preliminary Discussion' (1962) 56 *American Political Science Review* 853–864.
SCALIA, A., *A Matter of Interpretation: Federal Courts and the Law* (Princeton, NJ: Princeton University Press, 1997).
SCHEUERMAN, W. E., *Carl Schmitt: The End of Law* (Lanham: Rowan & Littlefield, 1999).
SCHMITT, C., *Die Diktatur* (Leipzig: Duncker & Humblot, 1921).
—— *Political Theology: Four Chapters on the Concept of Sovereignty* [1922], G. Schwab trans. (Cambridge, Mass.: MIT Press, 1988).
—— *The Crisis of Parliamentary Democracy* [1923], E. Kennedy trans. (Cambridge, Mass.: MIT Press, 1985).
—— *Verfassungslehre* (Munich: Duncker & Humblot, 1928).
—— *Théorie de la Constitution* [*Verfassungslehre*, 1928], L. Deroche trans. (Paris: Presses Universitaires de France, 1993).
—— *The Concept of the Political* [1932], G. Schwab trans. (Chicago: University of Chicago Press, 1996).
—— *Der Begriff des Politischen. Text von 1932 mit einem Vorwort und drei Corollarien* (Berlin: Duncker & Humblot, 1963).
SCHULZ, F., 'Bracton on Kingship' (1945) 60 *English Historical Review* 136–176.
SELDEN, J., *Table Talk* [1689] (London: Dent, 1898).
SHAIN, B. A., *The Myth of American Individualism: The Protestant Origins of American Political Thought* (Princeton, NJ: Princeton University Press, 1994).
SHKLAR, J. N., 'Political Theory and the Rule of Law' in A. C. Hutchinson & P. Monahan (eds), *The Rule of Law: Ideal or Ideology?* (Toronto: Carswell, 1987), 1–16.
SHUE, H., 'Eroding Sovereignty: The Advance of Principle' in R. McKim & J. McMahon (eds), *The Morality of Nationalism* (New York: Oxford University Press, 1997), 340–359.
SIEYÈS, E. J., *What is the Third Estate?* [1789], M. Blondel trans. (London: Pall Mall Press, 1963).
SKINNER, Q., *The Foundations of Modern Political Thought* (Cambridge: Cambridge University Press, 1978), 2 vols.
—— *Machiavelli* (Oxford: Oxford University Press, 1981).
—— 'The State' in T. Ball, J. Farr, & R. L. Hanson (eds), *Political Innovation and Conceptual Change* (Cambridge: Cambridge University Press, 1989), 90–131.
—— 'Hobbes and the Purely Artificial Person of the State' (1999) 7 *J. of Political Philosophy* 1–29.
SMALL, A. W., *The Cameralists: The Pioneers of German Social Polity* (Chicago: University of Chicago Press, 1909).
SMITH, A., *Lectures on Jurisprudence* [1766], R. L. Meek, D. D. Raphael, & P. G. Stein eds (Oxford: Clarendon Press, 1978).
SMITH, R., *Liberalism and American Constitutional Law* (Cambridge, Mass.: Harvard University Press, 1985).
SMITH, S. D., *The Constitution and the Pride of Reason* (New York: Oxford University Press, 1998).

SOMMERVILLE, J. P., *Politics and Ideology in England, 1603–1642* (London: Longman, 1986).
STAPLETON, J., *Englishness and the Study of Politics: The Social and Political Thought of Ernest Barker* (Cambridge: Cambridge University Press, 1994).
STEINER, H. & ALSTON, P., *International Human Rights in Context: Law, Politics, Morals* (Oxford: Oxford University Press, 2nd edn. 2000).
STEPHENS, P., *Politics and the Pound: The Tories, the Economy and Europe* (London: Macmillan, 1996).
STEWART, A., *Theories of Power and Domination* (London: Sage, 2001).
STRANGE, S., *The Retreat of the State: The Diffusion of Power in the World Economy* (Cambridge: Cambridge University Press, 1996).
STRAUSS, L., *What is Political Philosophy? and other Studies* (New York: Free Press, 1959).
—— 'Notes on Carl Schmitt, *The Concept of the Political*' in Schmitt, *The Concept of the Political*, 81–107.
STUBBS, W., *The Constitutional History of England in its Origins and Development* (Oxford: Clarendon Press, 1880), 3 vols.
SUNSTEIN, C. R., *Legal Reasoning and Political Conflict* (New York: Oxford University Press, 1996).
TACITUS, C., *The Histories* [c.109], W. H. Fyfe trans., D. S. Levene ed. (Oxford: Oxford University Press, 1977).
TALMON, J. L., *The Social Origins of Totalitarian Democracy* (London: Mercury, 1961).
TAYLOR, C., 'Foucault on Freedom and Truth' in his *Philosophy and the Human Sciences: Philosophical Papers, vol. 2* (Cambridge: Cambridge University Press, 1985), 152–184.
—— 'The Diversity of Goods' in his *Philosophical Papers, vol. 2*, 230–247.
TESÓN, F., *A Philosophy of International Law* (Boulder, Colorado: Westview Press, 1998).
TEUBNER, G., *Law as an Autopoietic System* (Oxford: Blackwell, 1993).
—— (ed.), *Global Law without a State* (Aldershot: Dartmouth, 1997).
THOMPSON, D. F., *Political Ethics and Public Office* (Cambridge, Mass.: Harvard University Press, 1987).
THOMPSON, E. P., *Whigs and Hunters: The Origin of the Black Act* (Harmondsworth: Penguin, 1975).
TIERNEY, B., *The Idea of Natural Rights: Studies on Natural Rights, Natural Law and Church Law, 1150–1625* (Atlanta, Ga.: Scholars Press, 1997).
—— 'Bracton on Government' (1963) 38 *Speculum* 295–317.
—— 'Tuck on Rights: Some Medieval Problems' (1983) 4 *History of Political Thought* 429–441.
—— 'Origins of Natural Rights Language: Texts and Contexts, 1150–1250' (1989) 10 *History of Political Thought* 615–646.
TILLY, C. (ed.), *The Formation of National States in Western Europe* (Princeton, NJ: Princeton University Press, 1975).
TOCQUEVILLE, A. DE, *Democracy in America* [1835], H. Reeve trans., D. J. Boorstin intro. (New York: Vintage Books, 1990), 2 vols.
TRIBE, L., 'The Puzzling Persistence of Process-Based Constitutional Theories' (1979–80) 89 *Yale Law Journal* 1063–1080.
TUCK, R., *Natural Rights Theories: Their Origins and Development* (Cambridge: Cambridge University Press, 1979).
—— *Philosophy and Government, 1572–1651* (Cambridge: Cambridge University Press, 1993).

Tuck, R., *The Rights of War and Peace: Political Thought and the International Order from Grotius to Kant* (Oxford: Oxford University Press, 1999).
Ullmann, W., 'The Development of the Medieval Idea of Sovereignty' (1949) 64 *English Historical Review* 1–33.
—— 'This Realm of England is an Empire' (1979) 30 *J. of Ecclesiastical History* 175–203.
Vile, M. J. C., *Constitutionalism and the Separation of Powers* (Indianapolis: Liberty Fund, 2nd edn. 1998).
Villey, M., 'L'idée du droit subjectif et les systèmes juridiques romains' (1946) 24–25 *Revue historique de droit* 201–228.
Viroli, M., 'Machiavelli and the Republican Idea of Politics' in G. Bock, Q. Skinner, & M. Viroli (eds), *Machiavelli and Republicanism* (Cambridge: Cambridge University Press, 1990), 143–171.
Wade, H. W. R., 'The Basis of Legal Sovereignty' [1955] *Cambridge Law Journal* 172–197.
Wagner, P., *A Sociology of Modernity: Liberty and Discipline* (London: Routledge, 1994).
—— *A History and Theory of the Social Sciences* (London: Sage, 2001).
Waldron, J., 'A Rights-Based Critique of Constitutional Rights' (1993) 13 *Oxford J. of Legal Studies* 18–51.
Walker, N., 'Sovereignty and Differentiated Integration in the European Union' (1998) 4 *European Law Journal* 355–388.
—— 'Late Sovereignty in the European Union', European Forum Discussion Paper, Robert Schuman Centre, EUI (2001).
—— 'The Idea of Constitutional Pluralism' (2002) 65 *Modern Law Review* 317–359.
Walker, R. B. J., *Inside/Outside: International Relations as Political Theory* (Cambridge: Cambridge University Press, 1993).
Walters, M. D., 'Nationalism and the Pathology of Legal Systems: Considering the *Quebec Secession Reference* and its Lessons for the United Kingdom' (1999) 62 *Modern Law Review* 371–396.
Walzer, M., 'The Lonely Politics of Michel Foucault' in his *The Company of Critics: Social Criticism and Political Commitment in the Twentieth Century* (New York: Basic Books, 1988), 191–209.
Ward, A. J., 'Devolution: Labour's Strange Constitutional "Design"' in J. Jowell & D. Oliver (eds), *The Changing Constitution* (Oxford: Oxford University Press, 4th edn. 2000), ch. 5.
Warren, W. L., *The Governance of Norman and Angevin England, 1086–1272* (London: Edward Arnold, 1987).
Weber, M., *Economy and Society: An Outline of Interpretive Sociology*, G. Roth & C. Wittich eds (Berkeley: University of California Press, 1978).
—— 'Politics as a Vocation' [1919] in H. H. Gerth & C. Wright Mills (eds), *From Max Weber: Essays in Sociology* (London: Routledge & Kegan Paul, 1948), 77–128.
—— 'Science as a Vocation' [1919] in H. H. Gerth & C. Wright Mills (eds), 129–156.
Weiler, J. H. H., *The Constitution of Europe: 'Do the New Clothes have an Emperor?'* (Cambridge: Cambridge University Press, 1999).
Weinrib, E. J., *The Idea of Private Law* (Cambridge, Mass.: Harvard University Press, 1995).
—— 'The Intelligibility of the Rule of Law' in A. C. Hutchinson & P. Monahan (eds), *The Rule of Law: Ideal or Ideology?* (Toronto: Carswell, 1987), 59–84.
—— 'Legal Formalism: On the Immanent Rationality of Law' (1988) 97 *Yale Law Journal* 949–1016.

WHITE, H., *Tropics of Discourse: Essays in Cultural Criticism* (Baltimore: Johns Hopkins University Press, 1978).

WHITE, M., *The Philosophy of the American Revolution* (New York: Oxford University Press, 1978).

WILKS, M. J., *The Problem of Sovereignty in the Later Middle Ages* (Cambridge: Cambridge University Press, 1963).

WILLIAMS, G., *Human Rights under the Australian Constitution* (Melbourne: Oxford University Press, 1999).

WILSON, J., 'Lectures on Law' in his *Works*, J. De Witt Andrews ed. (Chicago: Callaghan & Co., 1898), i.296–309.

WITTE, B. DE, 'Direct Effect, Supremacy, and the Nature of the Legal Order' in P. Craig & G. de Búrca (eds), *The Evolution of EU Law* (Oxford: Oxford University Press, 1999), 177–213.

WOLIN, S. S., *Tocqueville between Two Worlds: The Making of a Political and Theoretical Life* (Princeton, NJ: Princeton University Press, 2001).

—— 'Collective Identity and Constitutional Power' in his *The Presence of the Past: Essays on the State and the Citizen* (Baltimore: Johns Hopkins University Press, 1989), 8–31.

WOLTER, U., 'The *officium* in Medieval Ecclesiastical Law as a Prototype of Modern Administration' in A. Padoa-Schioppa (ed.), *Legislation and Justice* (Oxford: Clarendon Press, 1997), 17–36.

WOOD, G. S., *The Creation of the American Republic, 1776–1787* (Chapel Hill: University of North Carolina Press, rev. edn. 1998).

WORMUTH, F. D., *The Royal Prerogative 1603–1649: A Study in English Political and Constitutional Ideas* (Ithaca, NY: Cornell University Press, 1939).

—— *The Origins of Modern Constitutionalism* (New York: Harper & Brothers, 1949).

# Index

Act of Settlement, 1700  24n
administrative law,
    growth of  25–7
Allan, T. R. S.  28n, 67n, 68n, 133n, 146, 148n
American,
    bills of rights  123–4
    constitution  108, 120, 121–2
    constitutional law  108, 147
    Declaration of Independence  108
    revolution  67n, 108, 114–15, 122, 162
Ankersmit, F. R.  38, 63n, 64n, 70, 110n, 137n, 138n, 148n
Aquinas, T.  93
Arendt, H.  32n, 39, 77, 78, 81, 86, 86n, 92n, 93, 110, 115n, 123n, 126, 129n, 142, 159
Aristotle  6n, 13, 41, 83
Austin, J.  88n, 89, 90
authority
    and liberty  82
    and power  22, 81, 160

Bagehot, W.  24, 41n
Balakrishnan, G.  35–6
Balfour, Lord  41
Bank of England  9
Barker, E.  6n, 26, 41n, 72n
*Bate's case* (1606)  45n
Becker, C.  118
Bill of Rights, 1689  45n, 119
Blackstone, W.  9n, 14n, 22, 24, 119, 124n
Bodin, J.  13, 14, 23, 76, 80, 82, 87n, 132, 136–8, 140, 163
body politic  23, 44, 79
Bourdieu, P.  30n, 65n
Bracton, H. de  54, 134–5, 138, 140
*British Coal Corp.* v. *The King* (1935)  85n
British constitution  2–4, 26–7, 99–100, 107, 119, 133, 151
*Brunner* v. *TEU* (1994)  95
Burckhardt, J.  36
Burdeau, G.  100
Burke, E.  44n, 64n, 106n, 110–11

Cabinet  24, 26
canon law  79, 135
Charles I  106
Cicero, M. T.  6n, 7, 93, 159
civil liberty  150
    British tradition of  124
Coke, E.  119

common law  119n, 133, 146, 151
constituent power  4, 61–4, 67, 84, 99–113, 161–2
constitution
    balanced  23
    as fundamental law  47, 145
    idea of  44–7, 120, 161–2
    as instrument of state-building  50, 69, 162
    as process of becoming  113
constitutional law
    as third order of political  42–4, 52
constitutional legalism  47–52
constitutionalism  46, 69, 104, 112–13, 162
*Costa* v. *ENEL* (1964)  94n
Creveld, M. van  6n, 9, 10n, 81n, 150n
Croce, B.  82, 83, 137n
crown  20–1, 24, 25, 157
    coronation oath  20
    crown-in-council  21
    crown-in-parliament  21, 25, 46, 80, 84
    king and  79
    prerogative powers of  45
currency (coinage)  9–10, 23

democracy  31, 53, 56, 104–5, 106, 110–11, 114, 160–1
    and constitutionalism  112–13
    direct  63, 70
    and law  100
    representative  63, 112–13
        (*see also* representation)
Dicey, A. V.  27, 43n, 66n, 67n, 84n, 88n, 107n, 133
*droit politique*  3, 43n, 66, 69, 71, 134, 140–2, 163
*Duchy of Lancaster, case of* (1561)  20n
Dunn, J.  13n, 33, 37n, 52n
Durand, B.  75
Dworkin, R.  28n, 50n, 51, 68, 126n, 129n, 132n, 145, 146
Dyzenhaus, D.  35n, 99

Easton, D.  31
*ecclesia*  142–3
English
    constitution  45
    *see also* British constitution, Montesquieu
    government  121
    revolution  107
Enlightenment  109, 114, 144–5
European Union  66, 94–5, 160
executive, idea of  47

Federalist papers 62n, 78n, 108, 130n
*Ferrer's case* (1543) 22
Fleisher, M. 39
Finer, S. E. 21
Foley, M. 50
Fortescue, J. 44n, 79n, 120
Foucault, M. 14–15, 96, 98
French
  Declaration of Rights (1789) 109, 123–4
  revolution 10, 61, 109–10, 114–15, 122, 162

Gellner, E. 12n, 36n, 69n
Glorious Revolution, 1688 10, 24, 106–7, 151
government
  European tradition of 31
  *gubernaculum* and *jurisdictio* 45, 134–5
  mixed 23, 107
  modes of 13–19, 27, 154
  office of 20–5
  tasks of 7–12, 154
Greece, ancient 5, 76
Grotius, H. 132, 138n, 143

Habermas, J. 97n, 107n, 122, 127n, 131n, 132
Halifax, Lord 151
Hamilton, A. 61n, 108, 121, 125
  *see also* Federalist papers
Hardt, M. 96, 98, 126
Harrington, J. 107
Hart, H. L. A. 1n, 28n, 88n
Hegel, G. W. F. 30n, 63n, 147, 151
Henry II 26
Henry VIII 21–2
Hobbes, T. 5, 7, 14, 34, 35n, 36n, 63, 66n, 76, 84, 114n, 132
  forms of government 47–8
  good law 128, 140–1, 142, 163
  law and right 124
  legal positivism 116
  *meum* and *tuum* 76
  marks of sovereignty 23
  natural rights 86, 116, 119, 138
  office of sovereign 20, 55, 61, 80, 83
  the people 102–3
  political power 64, 78, 103
  public reason 145–6, 149
  representation 55–9, 69–70, 92n, 157–8
  the state 13, 58–61, 83, 102, 157–8
  state of nature 54–5, 116, 140, 143
  tasks of government 8
Hochstrasser, T. J. 139, 143, 144n
Holmes, S. 49n, 69n, 86n, 113n, 137
Holy Roman Emperor 74
human rights 126–7, 128–9
Hunter, I. 139, 140n, 144n, 147n, 150n

Instrument of Government, 1653 23
Ignatieff, M. 126–7, 128–9

Jackson, R. 91
James II 151
Jefferson, T. 118
Jellinek, G. 82n, 88, 120n, 125, 127n
Jouvenel, B. de 73
juridification 131–2
Justinian 43n, 44n, 75n, 82n

Kant, I. 90, 105, 117, 144, 145, 147
Kantorowicz, E. H. 57n, 135n
Kelsen, H. 1, 2, 90–1
Keohane, N. 136, 137n
*Kompetenz-Kompetenz* 82
Koskenniemi, M. 2n, 91n, 129n, 130

law
  as command 43, 71, 75, 88, 107, 140, 162
  as political right 43
  (*see also droit politique*)
  *see also* administrative law, canon law, constitutional law, common law, juridification, natural law, Roman law, rights and law, rule of law
Laws, J. 133–4, 146
Lawson, G. 66–8, 85
legal positivism 1, 2, 66, 73, 88–9, 116, 131, 160
Leibniz, G. W. 144
*lex regia* 3
liberty 128, 162
  *see also* authority, civil liberty, Machiavelli, Montesquieu
Locke, J. 13n, 14, 46, 138
  executive power 48
  federative power 48
  function of government 77, 117
  natural rights 116–17, 119
  influence 118
  rebellion 49, 103–4, 117, 122
  state of nature 116
  separation of powers 23
Loyseau, C. 73n, 76, 77

MacCormick, N. 89–91
*MacCormick* v.
  *Lord Advocate* (1953) 80n
Machiavelli, N. 43, 48, 62, 104, 105, 107, 108, 148
  liberty 42, 64, 101
  natural law 38
  politics 38–42, 101, 148
  prudence 39–40, 102, 149–50
  reason of state 149–50
  statecraft 37–42

# Index

tyranny 38
*virtù* and *fortuna* 37, 101
MacIntyre, A. 29
Madison, J. 62n, 108, 109, 123n
  *see also* Federalist papers
*Madzimbamuto* v.
  *Lardner-Burke* (1969) 25n, 85n
Magna Carta, 1215 21, 119
Maine, H. 28
Maistre, J. de 40n, 62n, 78n, 127n
Maitland, F. W. 16, 26, 60, 65, 131n
Manin, B. 53n, 63, 83n
Mansfield, H. 42n, 49, 53, 101n, 102n
*Marbury* v. *Madison* (1803) 47n, 122
Marx, K. 77
Medici, L. de 148
Meier, H. 35n, 36n, 40
Mill, J. S. 21n, 64n
monarchy 28, 55–6
  distinguished from aristocracy and democracy 83
  distinguished from tyranny 87n
  English 76, 106
Montesquieu, Baron de
  despotism 92
  English constitution 23–4
  English revolution 106
  fundamental laws 141–2
  liberty 87
  rule of law 43
  separation of powers 23–4, 48–9
  spirit of the laws 163

nation, idea of 61–2, 65, 66, 68n, 84, 112, 158
nationalism 41, 114
natural law 1, 38, 66, 67, 116, 136, 138–9, 143, 144, 162, 163
natural rights 13, 54, 86, 114, 115–25
  positivization of 125, 127–8
Negri, A. 96–8, 102, 105, 109, 113, 126
Northern Ireland 37n, 50n

Oakeshott, M. vii, 5n, 24n, 28, 59n, 131n, 135n, 143n
  character of modern state 15–19, 75, 78
  civil condition 79
  Hobbes 60n
  order 49–50
  politics 41–2
  practice 29–30
  rights 119n
*officium* (office) 79–80

Paine, T. 46, 120–1
papacy 18, 74
parliament 21, 25, 67
  *see also* crown in parliament

Pasquino, P. 48, 62n, 67n
people
  bearers of sovereignty 111, 161
  and constituent power 100–1, 102, 161
  contrast with multitude 56, 65, 83, 102–3
  idea of 56, 84, 158
Petition of right, 1628 119
Pitkin, H. 57
Plato 34
*plenitudo potestatis* 18, 74
*polis* 5, 13
  contrasted with *oikos* 6, 39, 76
political
  autonomy of 39, 43, 52, 155–6
  concept of 32n, 33–5
  primacy of 51
political pluralism 6, 72
political power
  nature of 50–1, 64, 77, 158–9, 161
  not based on property 76–7
  not empirical phenomenon 89–90
  relational character 81–2, 132
political theology 40–1
politics 4, 31
  agonal conception of 40
  and the state 35–7
  as statecraft 37–42
  contrasted with tyranny 48
  definitions of 32, 52, 155–7
  dynamic quality of 51
Pollard, A. F. 21, 80
practice, idea of 29–31, 155–6
Preuss, U. 41
Primus, R. 125–6
prudence 30, 39–40, 48, 49, 52, 93, 149–52, 163
public-private distinction 6, 13, 21, 57, 77–80, 153, 159
Pufendorf, S. 132, 138–40, 141, 142, 144, 150, 151, 158, 163
pure theory of public law 4, 153–63

Rawls, J. 51n, 105n, 145–6, 149
reason of state (*raison d'état*) 149–52, 163
Reformation 61, 143
representation 4, 31, 53, 158
  aesthetic and mimetic 70, 159–60
  of sovereign authority 54–61, 80, 157–8
  political 61–9
representative government 53, 62–3
  *see also* democracy
*res publica* 5, 6
  *see also* public-private distinction
Richelieu, Cardinal 152
rights 4, 28, 31
  constitutional 118–24, 162
  expression of sovereignty 86–7

rights (*cont.*):
  and law 86, 124–5, 162
  political order 115–17
  revolution 114, 122, 125–8
  subjective 86, 116
  *see also* human rights, natural rights
Robespierre, M. 115
Roman 5, 42, 79, 109
  ancient maxims 54, 56, 78, 82, 134
  empire 149n
  law 3, 75, 120, 135, 142, 148
  republic 42
  *see also* Holy Roman Emperor
Roman church 21
Rousseau, J.-J. 64n, 104–5, 109, 115, 117, 124, 132, 159
Royal Commission
  on the Constitution 11–12
Royal will 75, 80, 135
Ruiz, L. 81
rule of law 42–3, 49, 52, 68, 75, 132–3, 156–7
Runciman, D. 6n, 59–60

Saint-Just, L. A. de 110
*Salus populi suprema lex esto* 7–8, 17, 45, 55, 57, 78, 149, 154
Sartori, G. 3
Schmitt, C.
  agonal conception of politics 40
  concept of the political 32n, 33–5, 37, 43, 155–6
  constitutions 51n
  constituent power 69
  Kelsen 90–1
  sovereignty 46, 68, 92n
  state 35–7
self-government 46, 47, 53
Shklar, J. 43
Sieyes, E. J. 61–3, 65, 67, 70, 85, 109, 158
Skinner, Q. 5n, 54n, 59, 101, 103n

social contract 13–14, 58, 61, 86, 102, 103, 104–5
*societas* 16–17, 19, 20, 28, 30n, 98, 154, 163
sovereign 58–9, 75, 80, 83, 86, 87, 89, 93, 95, 158
sovereignty 4, 31, 58, 69, 114, 136–7, 158
  imperial 96–8
  legal/legislative 22, 25, 70, 80, 82, 86, 87–8, 91, 136, 159, 160
  marks of 23
  political 70, 83, 91, 92, 93, 160
  popular 54, 63, 111, 159, 160
  real and personal 66–7
  relational 65, 66, 70, 83–6, 88–9, 93, 139, 160, 163
  state 75, 80, 83
*Staatsrecht* 134, 139
state 5–6, 8, 13, 15–16, 20, 22, 153–4, 158–9
  form of 26, 55, 157–8
  Hobbes's concept of 58–61, 65
  *persona ficta* 17, 59–60
  and sovereignty 73–5, 80
state of nature (*see* Hobbes, Locke)
statistics 8
Strauss, L. 33n, 36n, 117
Stubbs, W. 21

Tacitus, C. 9n
taxation 8–9
Taylor, C. 3, 30n, 98n
*Terminello* v. *City of Chicago* (1949) 91n
Tierney, B. 86n, 115n, 135
*Tinoco Concessions* arbitration (1923) 65n
Tocqueville, A. de 111, 129–30
Tuck, R. 86n, 115n, 117–18, 141, 143n, 149n

*universitas* 17–19, 20, 28, 30n, 98, 154

*Van Gend en Loos* (1963) 94n
Vile, M. 48n, 107n